P9-BJU-536

WITHDRAWN
UTSA LIBRARIES

PHILOSOPHY, LITERATURE AND THE HUMAN GOOD

'Weston's book is admirable at a number of levels. It includes readings of Bataille, Blanchot and Derrida that are as lucid as I have seen. It also offers one of the first serious engagements with the influential work of Murdoch, Nussbaum, Cavell and Rorty. On top of this, Weston advances a bold thesis of his own about the ethical significance of philosophy and literature. Written in a clear and rigorous style, Weston's book is strongly recommended for anyone with an interest in the relations between philosophy, literature and ethics.'

Nicholas Smith, *Macquarie University*

Philosophy, Literature and the Human Good is an exciting and challenging new interpretation of the elements of literature which concern our reflections on, and choices about, what constitutes the good life. Philosophy has grappled with the significance of literature since Plato, particularly as literature seems to show us life in terms of values it cannot itself justify.

Michael Weston examines these relationships and the role of literature as it has been addressed by both the analytic and continental traditions. He initiates a dialogue between them and explores the growing importance of these issues for major contemporary thinkers. Each chapter explores a philosopher or literary figure who has written on the relationship between literature and the good life such as Bataille, Derrida and Kierkegaard, contemporary philosophers including Rorty and Nussbaum, and literary writers such as Murdoch and Blanchot. *Philosophy, Literature and the Human Good* is ideal for all students of philosophy and literature. It is an insightful and provocative examination of the philosophical, moral and religious significance of literature.

Michael Weston is Lecturer in Philosophy at the University of Essex.

PHILOSOPHY, LITERATURE AND THE HUMAN GOOD

Michael Weston

London and New York

First published 2001
by Routledge
11 New Fetter Lane, London EC4P 4EE

Simultaneously published in the USA and Canada
by Routledge
29 West 35th Street, New York, NY 10001

Routledge is an imprint of the Taylor & Francis Group

© 2001 Michael Weston

Typeset in Times by RefineCatch Limited, Bungay, Suffolk
Printed and bound in Great Britain by
TJ International, Padstow, Cornwall

All rights reserved. No part of this book may be reprinted or
reproduced or utilised in any form or by any electronic,
mechanical, or other means, now known or hereafter
invented, including photocopying and recording, or in any
information storage or retrieval system, without permission in
writing from the publishers.

British Library Cataloguing in Publication Data
A catalogue record for this book is available from the British Library

Library of Congress Cataloging in Publication Data
Weston, Michael, 1946–
Philosophy, literature, and the human good / Michael Weston.
p.   cm.
Includes bibliographical references and index.
1. Literature and morals.   2. Literature, Modern–History and
criticism.   I. Title.
PN49 .W44   2001
174′.98–dc21   00–051721

ISBN 0–415–24337–8 (hbk)
ISBN 0–415–24338–6 (pbk)

Library
University of Texas
at San Antonio

Untuk keluargaku, Margaret, Will dan James –
dan Tuan Jim, permulaannya masih.

CONTENTS

PREFACE

This book aims to provide an introduction to the thought of some recent and contemporary thinkers, European, American and British, who have given to literature a central role in philosophical reflection. Some, indeed, have argued that a distinction between philosophy and literature is no longer viable. While, of course, I wish to argue for a certain position in relation to the issues raised, one deriving from the thought of Kierkegaard and Wittgenstein, I would nevertheless like the expositions of the thinkers concerned to be useful whether one is convinced by it or not. I have, therefore, tried to provide sufficient detail of their thought and reference to their writings to constitute in each case a brief introduction to their work.

I would like to thank the students on my 'Philosophy and Literature' course at Essex University for their interest and questions, and the members of my family who are a constant reminder that in respect of what matters in life philosophy has no authority.

Michael Weston

INTRODUCTION

It began, of course, with Plato, who announced[1] that there had long been a quarrel between philosophy and poetry. Plato refers to a traditional view of the importance of poetry in the *Phaedrus* when he says that poetry 'by adorning countless deeds of the ancients educated later generations',[2] a defence echoed by Aeschylus in Aristophanes' *Frogs* who, comparing himself to Homer, says that he too 'bodied forth many patterns of greatness' hoping that his fellow Athenians might 'take on the stamp of heroical types at the sound of the trumpeter calling'.[3] Literature on this account plays an essential cultural role in the transmission of values, showing us patterns of excellence in such a way that we are drawn towards their imitation, a process which Socrates in the *Ion* likens to the activity of a magnet: 'You – the rhapsode or the actor – are the middle link, and the poet himself is the first. Through all these, the god draws the human mind in any direction he wishes, hanging a chain of force from one to the other.'[4] But what if a sophist such as Thrasymachus in the *Republic* asks whether these patterns are really patterns of excellence, whether it can be shown why we should follow them? Having acquired adherence to these patterns through upbringing and the influence of literature, we can nevertheless surely stand back and ask whether their claim to be patterns of excellence is justified, otherwise we cannot answer the sophist. But we can't justify them by referring to some other aspect of our culture, or anyone else's, since the same kind of question could be asked about them. We need, apparently, to refer to something beyond human cultures which can judge them, a timeless measure for the patterns of excellence cultures and their literatures present. Plato found these, of course, in the Forms. Literature, far from presenting us with the standard, is itself to be judged. And, of course, this kind of questioning can be developed generally. Just as, apparently, I can ask how I know that what I take to be excellent and good really is so, so I can ask how I can know that what I take to be true really is so. In order to answer such questions we would have to appeal to something which transcends the actual procedures of any given community for justifying one's life, actions and beliefs, since what is at issue is whether those procedures can produce good lives and actions or true beliefs. As

Richard Rorty has argued,[5] we need then to refer to a 'common ground' for all communities since their actual procedures are to be judged by it, a ground which in that sense is transcendent to them. Such a ground may be found, as with Plato, in the realm of timeless Being as opposed to the world of coming to be and passing away, or, as in the seventeenth century, in the nature of the human mind itself. By reference to this ground we can determine the intrinsic 'nature' of what we are interested in and determine procedures of justification which are in contact with 'the truth' rather than just being a contingent community's way of doing what they call 'justifying'.

Access to the transcendent position may be variously conceived, by intellectual vision, by faith, by reason, for example. The human significance of literature will be determined by its relation to life guided by these modes of access. It may be regarded as positively harmful, as Plato saw it, obstructing the development of those faculties required for access to the Forms, or as providing philosophical wisdom in a form appropriate for those incapable of the real thing, as the neo-Platonist Proclus thought. Or, as with Dante, it may be able to picture for us what is beyond our world but in which we must believe through faith. But, in any event, literature has no distinctive philosophical role to play, for philosophy attempts to answer sceptical questioning by giving us knowledge in terms of which our lives are to be guided, and literature is unable, as fiction, to contribute to this.

This philosophical position begins to be dismantled by Kant, but only to a degree. He argued that we can only know what we can experience and the conditions of that experience. Nevertheless, when we reflect upon our lives as knowers and agents, we see we must believe in the transcendent position, that there is the truth already written, as it were, into the world and ourselves. We have to believe that we are free immortal souls embodied in a world made by a benevolent deity to fit our capacities for knowledge and moral action, and who will reward us according to our moral desert in the life to come. Now, Kant develops an account of beauty and the arts in connection with reflection on the possibility of judgement, the subsumption of the particular under a general idea. Judgement is usually determinate, involving concepts we already possess, as when we say that Jemima is a cat. But such judgement presupposes what Kant called reflective judgement, the formation of concepts. Kant sees concept formation as involving the principle that there are concepts to be formed, that is, that the world is, as it were, already conceptualized so that our reflective judgement grasps what is already implicit. We have to presuppose that the world has been made in accordance with concepts by an intelligence, although not ours, and so to regard it in the way we regard a work of human making. The experience of beauty is the experience of the fit between the world and our intellectual capacities prior to our forming any particular concept. This issue of concept formation points to history, to change in the way life and the world are conceived by us, and for Kant this change has directionality towards an ideal, but one which we have to assume to be actual, to the already determined conceptual structure of the world. Now, just as concept formation involves our imagination playing around with different patternings of what is received in sensibility, so literature involves us in imaginative playing with the products of our understanding of the world. In this way we can make other worlds, ones which don't claim truth, but which make it possible for us to produce images of what is essentially beyond experience but which we have to believe is actual, the ideas of Reason. Literature as a creative form of language doesn't produce concepts to apply to the world, but rather 'aesthetic ideas', images and symbols which provoke us to reflection on transcendent things without a determinate thought corresponding to them. This gives to literature the power to provoke interpretation without any interpretation being final. Such images and symbols have an impenetrability that prompts the production of meaning without being absorbed by it. In this way, such poetic language suggests the nature of concept formation itself, that it is always a relation to a lack of meaning. Since determinative judgement and our current understanding of the world presuppose concept formation, such judgement and understanding always stand in relation to incomprehension. For Kant, however, although this is true of our human comprehension, we must suppose there is, as it were, a final reading of the world.

If we ask why we must, Kant refers us to reflection on the nature of our understanding of the world and ourselves as moral agents. The former presents the world as one of objects in temporal, spatial and causal relations with each other. There we can always ask for the explanation of whatever we provide as the explanation of some event, and science is the systematization of this possibility. The progressive nature of our understanding only makes sense if we assume there is a final state of knowledge, although one we can never experience. We have at least to believe in it. Similarly, he claims, we know we have moral obligations, but this only makes sense if we are free of the causal nexus of the world to act in it and if we have a moral goal where morality would not appear as obligatory, as something opposed to our inclinations. But need we find these considerations persuasive? We might, with the German Romantic, Friedrich Schlegel, suggest that the process of understanding is always a relation to incomprehension so that a final reading is unintelligible. We are involved in a process whereby all understanding, in responding to incomprehension, produces its own unendingly. And, he suggests, we can reject the moral law in favour of a parallel understanding of our own lives, constantly making ourselves anew. Or we might, with Nietzsche, see our understanding of the world not as grasping what is already there, but in terms of utility, a project of ever increasing our predictive and technological capacities, and ask why what we find useful should be 'true'. Like Schlegel, Nietzsche proposes our seeing life not in terms of submission to a universal moral law (why should we think we can speak for others?) but as a constant process of self-formation, of always venturing into the new, a law unto itself. In neither case would there be a 'final reading' of the world nor a moral law which applied to all.

But do these moves remove us from the transcendent standpoint? Richard Rorty would suggest not. Any attempt to deny this standpoint remains complicit with it, for it has to say its own preferred position is true. A position which asserts that the world is always coming into being and that life is to be lived in accordance with its nature as constant becoming, still claims to speak the truth.[6] Whether we remain complicit with the transcendent standpoint does not depend on whether we assert a final state of knowledge about the world or a final goal for life, but whether one's position is asserted as final, as 'the truth'. For that, as Rorty suggests, is to claim that one knows the true nature of the world and life, has grasped their own language, as it were, and how could one justify such a claim? The problem for the 'ironist theorists', Rorty's term for those who wish to mount a theoretical attack on the transcendent standpoint, is how to avoid this consequence. Rorty suggests that their characteristic strategy, since they cannot claim access to an eternal truth, lies in recounting a historical narrative which moves towards the overturning of 'truth'. Nietzsche's account of how the 'real world' became a myth[7] and Heidegger's History of Being are, he suggests, such moves. It is history itself, truthfulness overturning truth, for example, in Nietzsche, which announces the end of the reign of truth and the opening of a new possibility of relating to the world and life, which the theorist then begins to articulate. But such a strategy Rorty argues must undo itself since it must claim that its history is true. (He thinks this is the characteristic move made by Nietzsche, Heidegger and at least the earlier Derrida. Whether this is quite fair I will consider in a moment.) Hence Rorty's own response is to propose a new picture of our relation to the world and ourselves not as true but as inviting our acceptance of it as responding to how, partially through encountering the picture itself, we realize we see ourselves. The pragmatist picture seeks its audience in the way in which a work of literature does, creating its own taste.

The strategy of post-Nietzschean theorists like Bataille, Blanchot and Derrida is not, however, quite so straightforward, and 'theory' with its connotations of contemplation and the position of the spectator is not perhaps the relevant term. Rather, these thinkers in their 'theoretical' writings characteristically involve us in a process of reflection which involves itself in paradox and collapse. They do not assert the falseness of the perspective oriented towards the truth nor suggest we can do without its characteristic notions of truth, finality, determinate meaning, and so forth. But, at the same time, if we think through this trajectory, we find our thought about thought failing in a way which indicates that the possibility of thought directed at truth and determinate meaning depends, paradoxically, on its failure. The condition of possibility of truth and meaning is at the same time the condition of their impossibility, a paradox we find in one form or another in all three of these thinkers. As paradox, it cannot be grasped, it is itself a failure in thought. Through trying to make sense we are led into non-sense: we can no more avoid the one than the other. We are in our thinking involved in a para-doxical movement. 'The desire for the intact kernel is desire itself, which is to say it is irreducible ... despite the fact that *there is no* intact kernel' as Derrida puts it.[8] The movement of the texts puts us as readers into this position, one where we recognize that the assertions we seem driven to deprive themselves of sense, where we are implicated in a double and contra-dictory movement. For Bataille, this leads us into proximity to an experience of the loss of sense and so of the self as an identity, through a movement in which our drive towards finality reveals the complementary drive towards the overthrow of reason. Both Blanchot and Derrida reject this idea of an 'experience' as complicit with the drive to truth, for it might seem as if in this experience human life accomplished or lived its paradoxicality. Rather, we remain in the double bind. In Blanchot, we are implicated in a movement of thought aiming at finality, which becomes haunted by its repetition in the simple appearance and sound of the words. In this haunting, thought fails, and yet against the failure of meaning, which is signification without sense (it is, after all, the failure of words), it is exposed to its renewal in uncontrol-lable ways. The works enmesh us in this paradoxical movement, one which, therefore, ceases to be recognizably 'theoretical'. It is a movement which similarly characterizes Bataille's and Blanchot's 'fictions' and in this way the distinction itself between 'philosophy' and 'literature' becomes undecidable. Derrida's theoretical writings characteristically operate on particular texts in a double and paradoxical movement which leads to the new kind of writing found in later works like *The Post-Card*. Certain kinds of writing we think of as 'literature' can then be read as 'staging' this paradoxical movement.

Nevertheless, it's not clear that these thinkers quite avoid Rorty's suspi-cions. All three situate their thought historically, with the implication that we find ourselves in a situation which requires new forms of writing and living which would respond to this paradoxicality. It might then seem, as Rorty claims, that they are asserting the truth of these histories and revealing to us the necessity, if we are to affirm this truth, of thinking and living in a new way. It is difficult to avoid the feeling that even here the paradoxicality of life is being asserted and we are being invited to recognize what this now demands of us.

That the denial that there is an already determined order of the world and life may be used to justify a form of life, as in accordance with this truth, is shown in Iris Murdoch's philosophical writings. Life and the world are then 'for nothing', without determinate purpose or plan. To live this truth requires giving up living in terms of some conceived good. Since there is no plan, such a good could only be a projection of our will, but this could not satisfy our need to live in terms of the good. She refers to Plato's claim that we want the true good and not the mere appearance of it: even if we are satisfied with appearing virtuous we are so because we think it is really for our own good. But a good which was a projection of ourselves couldn't satisfy this since it would not be the good which determined the projection. We could alter the good we aimed at so that the question whether such alteration was good for us could not be answered. We are, Murdoch suggests, constituted as a movement towards goodness; but there is no given order and any we impose will not satisfy the requirements of this movement. We must, therefore, she argues, orient ourselves to the good as 'nothing'. Life becomes a movement towards a transcendent good which, as nothing, requires that we progress from attachment to determinate goods to a life lived 'for nothing', a life she interprets as 'love'. Good literature is concerned with this pilgrimage, as Iris Murdoch's own novels characteristically are, and plays its part in convincing us of this picture of life. In relation to the good life, intellectual argument is inadequate: at best, it can articulate the connection between concepts involved in a vision of life and the human's position in the world, but it cannot establish that vision. She agrees here with Martha Nussbaum, for whom such an inquiry must be both empirical and practical. The good, the truth of life, is the truth for us: it requires for its revelation submitting ourselves to the variety of views of life and recognizing in some alternative one which claims us, one which we can recognize as our truth, with all that that involves in action and emotion. Literature for Nussbaum, as for Murdoch, plays a central role in this inquiry in showing us in concrete detail what is involved in living according to different conceptions of the value of life. Yet the same procedures produce different results for each of them. According to Nussbaum, the life proposed as truth by Murdoch sees its value as immune to overthrow by chance since it involves a detachment from temporal goods in its orientation towards 'nothing'. She, however, proposes a form of life, which she calls 'Aristotelian' against the Platonism Murdoch explicitly subscribes to, which incorporates this possibility as essential. The value of our lives is indeed given by attachment to people, institutions and activities which chance may destroy or harm, so that that value is not immune to what is beyond our control. Both Murdoch and Nussbaum propose their visions as 'true', as valid for all, and both subscribe to an empirical and practical form of inquiry which involves essential use of literature. The intention is that through the articulation of their preferred conception and our exposure to their literary examples, we should recognize ourselves, come to a self-knowledge. We discover our nature through experiencing, in literary and theoretical forms, the alternatives. Yet their empirical and practical inquiries produce contradictory results.

Rorty suggests, however, that to reject the transcendent standpoint involves rejecting the idea of such a 'nature' which underlies Murdoch's and Nussbaum's procedures. But in order to avoid the problem he sees of 'ironist theorizing', of producing their histories and their results as 'the truth', he doesn't wish to argue that the transcendent viewpoint is false. One cannot argue with such a position without remaining complicit with it. But one can show that it conceives the human being as subordinate to a non-human authority, the 'order' of the world and life, and propose an alternative vision based on human self-reliance. He suggests that such a vision would abandon the idea that we have contact with a non-human reality and re-think the notions of 'truth', 'objectivity' and 'justification' in terms of relations between propositions which, being expressed in human vocabularies which are open to change, are always revisable. In terms of individual life, Rorty suggests that abandoning the idea of 'nature' and 'the truth' would lead us to conceive life as self-creation, the constant sampling of ways of life in a process of becoming without given end. This vision is not presented as 'the truth'. Its success would lie in its acceptance, by people finding it articulated how the world and life would look in terms of what they discover is their fundamental self-conception, that of self-reliance. In this way, the vision has the character of literature itself, showing us how life looks in terms of certain values, and whose success as literature depends solely on acceptance. Indeed, Rorty sees the novel (he cites Proust) as a safer way of conveying the view the 'ironist theorist' tries to present since, as 'fiction', it is beyond the temptation to assert its vision as 'the truth'. However, there may remain a hidden complicity with the transcendent position in his vision. It seems to accept, in its reinterpretation of intellectual life as subject to the permanent possibility of revolution and of life as constant self-creation, that position's claim that unrevisable truth and commitment to a way of life only make sense if one has a transcendent guarantee. But such a claim only seems plausible if we admit the intelligibility of the sceptical questions which give rise to the apparent necessity of the transcendent move.

Stanley Cavell suggests that Wittgenstein provided a new form of criticism in relation to scepticism. The sceptic purports to raise questions, and so to be questioning. Whatever we say, we *say, do* something with our words. But there are conditions for our 'questioning', 'doubting', 'asserting', and so forth, which the sceptic cannot satisfy. We can doubt, question, only where there is something questionable to indicate, yet the sceptic wishes to raise his questions where no such questionableness exists since, of course, he wishes to put in question the very possibility of knowledge. Knowledge has human conditions, those under which assertions can be made, doubts addressed, and justification given. In this way, Cavell suggests, our fundamental relation to the world and to each other is not one of knowing, but of acting and responding in a way which does not rest on beliefs and which provides the background against which we can understand questions being raised and answered. To learn the relevant forms of language is to be initiated into practices which develop from forms of reaction to each other and the environment which are not the products of thought but 'something animal' as Wittgenstein put it. To participate in such practices, we need to share both these reactions and those involved in learning and applying the relevant words. Intelligibility in this way rests on shared reactions, shared ways of going on in the same way as others. In this sense, when my reasons give out, I am thrown back on myself, on what I take to be the way to go on in relation to the words at issue. There is always the contingent possibility that this will not be shared, that I should prove unintelligible to others and they to me. But then my own intelligibility would itself be put in question. It is this which motivates the desire for a transcendent position, to put a stop to this fragility of intelligibility, to ensure that I am intelligible because I have a relation to the ground of intelligibility itself (the Forms, the logos of the kosmos and so forth). The sceptic thinks the ground is necessary but unattainable, the metaphysician that is it necessary and attained. Scepticism can only be treated by treating the desire, to reconcile ourselves to the human conditions of intelligibility and their necessary fragility.

Since I am a linguistic being, my intelligibility depends on my sharing with others common ways of using language. My existence as a linguistic being is, then, Cavell claims, constantly subject to proof, in requiring my successful sharing with others in linguistic practices. I depend therefore for my existence on others. Intellectual scepticism is one form in which the desire that this not be so appears. But it appears too, Cavell thinks, in other forms in which the individual rejects the necessity of sharing with others for the maintenance of their existence and so of regarding others in a way consonant with this recognition. Cavell sees Shakespeare's tragic figures, Lear, Hamlet, Leontes, Coriolanus and Othello, as manifesting in different forms the repulsion against this dependency, a desire for an autonomous existence. Shakespeare's theatre is a remedy for this desire, not only showing it in its consequences, but involving us as audience in re-enacting the conditions for community and individual existence.

But Cavell goes on to utilize the notion of our linguistic being to draw certain ethical conclusions. Having to prove my existence means relating to others as those upon whom I depend for this proof. An openness to others, a willingness to enter into communication and discussion with others and to revise one's views and life are required. This openness to change is what characterizes Cavell's 'perfectionism', the view that our existence as linguistic beings requires our relating constantly to what is other than our current self, but which at the same time speaks to us, a 'repressed self' which thus summons us to change. But this appears to ground a certain kind of ethical relation in Cavell's account of language. Yet he began, in his analysis of scepticism, with a rejection of the idea that our practices stand in need of grounding. In this way, he seems tempted to betray his insight into the origin of sceptical questioning and the metaphysical attempt to ground which flows from it.

The intelligibility of metaphysics, of the transcendent position, depends on that of sceptical questioning. But the latter fails to count as questioning: what we need is to return the sceptic's words to the contexts where we can understand them as questions. In this way, we return them from their apparent metaphysical use to their actual employment. Now, all the thinkers we've looked at wish to recognize the falsity or incomprehensibility of the metaphysician's claim to occupy a position from which he can judge non-philosophical human practices. They wish to return thinking and life to its humanity. But the way they do this, one may suspect, still maintains the metaphysical ambition, for the result of their attacks on metaphysics is then used to determine some preferred form of thought and life as in accordance with that humanity, however understood. Something like grounding reappears. But we need to recognize that to reject sceptical questioning is to reject the necessity for a philosophical grounding of our forms of life. Such an approach, which follows through the implications of Cavell's Wittgensteinian treatment of scepticism, I find in the work of D. Z. Phillips.

Cavell returns the sceptic's questions to the contexts where we can understand them *as* questions, to the lived context of the application of language. Against the sceptical questioning of morality and religion, and the philosophical theorizing which tries to respond to it, Phillips places the contextualizing of moral and religious concepts which takes place in literary treatments of life. Literature in this way can remind us of the lived application of such concepts as opposed to their theoretical misconstruction in philosophical attempts to justify morality and religion. Literature reminds us too of the heterogeneity of values, of the incommensurability of ways of valuing life, and that the determination of one as 'truth' is a matter of existential appropriation and not of intellectual argument. Literature explores the possibilities of living in terms of certain values under given social and historical circumstances. The very possibility of living in terms of moral and religious values themselves in the contemporary world is posed, for example, in the work of Samuel Beckett and, in a different way, in the poetry of R.S. Thomas. Through this, we may broach the question of whether some of the theorists we have considered may not be seen rather as part of the creation of new conceptions of life, ones which cannot be conceived as ethical (concerned with character) or religious, but which involve a new way of taking over the temporality of life, one which may be explored in its lived application in certain contemporary forms of literature. Whether this is so or not, the attempt to justify such a purported new conception of life in a way which would show that adherents to moral and religious perspectives were guilty of a failure of understanding (of, say, what our historical situation requires) would remain misplaced. The viability and attraction of such new forms of life is not dependent on philosophical views of language or history, nor does opposition to them rest on arguments binding on any disinterested party. We are none of us that. If it is difficult to remember this philosophically, literature continually reminds us.

1

LIFE AS ART
Kant, Schlegel, Nietzsche

The necessity for the appeal to the metaphysical lies in the apparent possibility of sceptical questioning, of subjecting our forms of thought and life to a general doubt. Yet, of course, there has always been a difficulty in understanding how the philosopher, who is, after all, human, can have access to a standard which could fulfil the metaphysical need, one which would be able to stand in judgement over all human standards. We must either claim, as Plato and Aristotle do, that we are, in a sense, more than human, possessed of the 'divine spark of the intellect', or that we have in some other way, through faith in the Creator, for example, access to the ultimate ground in terms of which our forms of life and thought could be judged. But what if we were to recognize that such a claim was an illusion, born, no doubt, as Cavell will suggest, of a real human desire to be more than we are? What would it be to give up this desire? And how then would the philosophical significance of literature appear to us? From Kant to Derrida we can trace the development of a tradition of thought which attempts to divest us of this ambition. Kant, in returning us to our finitude, nevertheless tries to maintain an essential role in our thought and life for the idea of a more than human position, and literature and art play for him a part in the articulation of that role. If, however, with Schlegel and Nietzsche we recognize that even the idea of such a role is itself illusory, life becomes in a certain way its own measure. But that is something, as we shall see, that Kant attributes to the nature of art and literature itself. Both Schlegel and Nietzsche are inclined to draw the consequence from their unmasking of this illusion that life must be understood as itself a form of art, which raises the question whether they have freed themselves as radically as they suppose from Kantian conceptuality.

I

Kant develops his account of the beauty of nature in the context of a critique of judgement, that is, of an examination of the presuppositions involved in the subsumption of a particular under a general concept. Philosophy had traditionally claimed that its reflections could show us the

1

general structure of reality as it is in itself, independently of human thought and experience, but Kant recognized the vanity of such a claim. All we can be said to know, he averred, were objects of human experience (contingent a posteriori knowledge) or the conditions for such knowledge: analytic knowledge (necessary and a priori) of the relations between concepts applied in that experience, or synthetic a priori knowledge of the principles in terms of which there can be such experience at all. What we take as the general structure of the world, that it is a world of objects having properties standing in causal and spatio-temporal relations to each other, is a result of the organizing principles of human experience and not a structure-in-itself to which we have access through thought. Nevertheless, the idea of things as they are 'in themselves', independently of the conditions of human sensibility, is not thereby redundant. When we reflect on our experience, Kant thought, we realize that we cannot avoid using it. Our experience is of being both knowers of the world and agents in it. As thinkers, we must presuppose that we are free of the causal nexus of the world since otherwise no distinction between true and false thoughts could be drawn: both would equally be the result of causal laws. Further, we have to think of ourselves as persisting through changes in experience and so as substantial egos which have thoughts and experiences but are never the object of them. Moreover, our experience is not of discrete items of knowledge: we strive towards connecting experiences in order to understand why things occur, and science is the systematic development of this. Such a project utilizes the idea of a totality of the world and of knowledge which guides the progress in our grasp of the world: we continue to ask for explanation and so presuppose there is one. We must, therefore, regard the world as ultimately intelligible and so as coming to be through the causality of intelligence, the supreme reason, God. As agents, we are aware of having to deliberate and decide, of being faced by the questions of what we ought to do and how we ought to live, and so of subjection to the moral law. This presupposes that we are positively free to intervene in the causal nexus of the world. We experience the moral law as obligation and so in opposition to our empirical nature. Morality holds out to us, therefore, a better state, holiness, in which this opposition between ourselves and what is moral would no longer exist, and which morally we are required to take as our goal. But we cannot do so unless we believe that it can be granted. It cannot be given in time, since no matter what our present state, deterioration is possible in the future. We must believe in the immortality of the soul and in a benevolent deity who will grant the goal by his grace. We must believe in the reality of these ideas of reason, and so believe that we are free, immortal souls embodied in a world made to fit our intellectual capacities and our capacity for action by a benevolent deity who will reward us according to our moral deserts in the afterlife. We cannot know this to be true: we have, however, to believe that it is. The ideas of reason have a 'practical reality'.

Nature is known by us only as phenomenon, as it appears through our sensibility and the application of the concepts of the understanding, and so as a causal nexus of events. Yet our consciousness of the moral law compels us to believe we are free, free from external causality, which includes that of our emotions and desires, our given motivational nature, and free to act because of duty. But here a problem of intelligibility arises, for how can we conceive such free action is possible in the world of nature governed by causal laws? As Kant says in *The Critique of Judgement*:

> Hence an immense gulf is fixed between the domain of the concept of nature, the sensible, and the domain of the concept of freedom, the supersensible, so that no transition from the sensible to the supersensible (and hence by means of the theoretical use of reason) is possible, just as if they were two different worlds, the first of which cannot have any influence on the second; yet the second is to have an influence on the first, i.e., the concept of freedom is to actualize in the world of sense the purpose enjoined by its laws.[1]

We need to show that free action, action for the sake of duty, is possible as an intervention in the causal world of nature: 'Hence it must be possible to think of nature as being such that the lawfulness of its form will harmonize with at least the possibility of [achieving] the purposes that we are to achieve in nature according to the laws of freedom.'[2] It is through a consideration of the conditions of possibility of judgement, the thinking of 'the particular as contained under the universal'[3] that Kant will try to show this compatibility.

We may in thinking the particular already possess the relevant universal and so judge that the particular satisfies the conditions set out in the empirical concept we already understand. But such determinative judgement is dependent on the primary formation of empirical concepts, of the seeking for the universal which will subsume the particular. Such reflective judgement requires for its operation a principle. Now the understanding determines that nature will appear in general as a causal nexus of events, but it does not determine the nature and range of actual empirical laws: 'the laws the pure understanding legislates concern only the possibility of a nature as such, but there are so many diverse forms of nature left undetermined by these laws. There must be laws for these too, which are empirical and contingent as far as *our* understanding can see.'[4] In searching for the universals of species and genera and the principles which unite the genera towards a systematic comprehension, bringing the diversity of empirical phenomena under them, reflective judgement is acting on a rule, that the 'diverse forms of nature' are such that they can be so subsumed, that they are intelligible, as if they had been formed by an understanding, though not ours, so as to be intelligible to us. Our understanding dictates the general lawfulness of nature as appearance, but this would be quite compatible with a general absence of intelligibility in the empirical diversity which nature shows. In our pursuing

3

intelligibility we act as if we believed nature to be intelligible through and through, an intelligibility which is not determined by the structure of our own understanding, but which we would have to regard as being already there, awaiting our inquiry. We act in reflective judgement on the principle that

> since universal natural laws have their basis in our understanding which prescribes them to nature, the particular empirical laws must, as regards what the universal laws have left undetermined in them, be viewed in terms of such a unity as [they would have] if they too had been given by an understanding (even though not ours) so as to assist our cognitive powers by making possible a system of experience in terms of particular natural laws.[5]

This concept is that of 'the purposiveness of nature', that the actuality of nature is the result of the efficacy of a concept. We regard nature as if it had been made by an intelligence in the way in which we regard a human artifact as the result of intelligent, concept-organized behaviour. Reflective judgement uses this idea of the purposiveness of nature merely for its activity and cannot claim to know it has reality. It must act as if nature were already intelligible but reflective 'judgement only uses this idea as a principle of reflection not determination'.[6] As with other ideas of reason, theoretical reasoning can merely establish its possibility whilst experience clearly cannot pronounce as to its reality.

Where reflective judgement is successful, we experience pleasure in being able to grasp nature.[7] The principle of reflective judgement is that 'nature makes its universal laws specific in accordance with the principle of purposiveness for our cognitive powers':[8] reflective judgement must believe for its activity in the harmony between nature and our understanding, a harmony which, of course, is beyond any possible experience. Such a harmony would be prior to and render possible any actual harmony in the successful operation of reflective judgement in grasping nature. Such a success, if it really is so, and this we cannot know, would be the actualization of the pre-existent harmony in which we must believe. Although we cannot know there is such harmony, we nevertheless have experience of a pleasure in a conceptless harmony, in the experience of beauty. Such an experience is occasioned where, in independence of the application of any concept, we experience an order in what we receive through our sensibility as if it were designed for apprehension by our cognitive powers. Such an order prior to the application of any concept can only be in the form of our intuitions, in spatial or temporal organization. What we experience is an order prior to the imposition of order which is therefore *received*. The 'subjective [feature] of the presentation which cannot at all become an element of cognition is the purposiveness that precedes the cognition of an object'.[9] But this is the very harmony of nature with our cognitive powers which cannot be known. Beauty is the experience of a general harmony of nature as what we experience and our cognitive powers, a harmony experienced, therefore, prior to the achievement of any actualized harmony through the application of concepts. What we receive in sensible intuition appears as susceptible to the ordering of our power of concepts, as having 'order' but without any determinate order. The experience of this conceptless harmony is pleasurable as is the successful operation of reflective judgement. But whereas the latter is a pleasure in our being able to grasp nature, and so in the exercise of our own capacities, the former is an experience of passivity. We have an experience, as it were, of the world and our cognitive capacities as being made for one another.

This 'purposiveness of nature', that we must regard it as already intelligible and so formed to fit our intelligence, 'mediates between the concepts of nature and the concept of freedom'. If we must regard nature not only in terms of the concept of cause given by the understanding but also through that of purpose, then we may consistently think the possibility of action in accordance with freedom as possible within the world and pursuit of what is commanded by the moral law.[10] But this purposiveness cannot be asserted as a reality. As an idea of reason it can only regulate activity in reflective judgement. The experience of beauty is not an application of reflective judgement: it does not contain a judgement. Rather, we experience, as it were, the possibility of reflective judgement, in contemplating a formal unity in terms of space or time, of what we sense which invites conceptualization: the imagination is able to form a unity in harmony with 'the understanding's lawfulness in general'.[11] In the experience of beauty what we receive appears as able to be structured but without any determinate structure. But the feeling of pleasure we take in this harmony of the given with our cognitive powers cannot take us any further towards asserting the actuality of the 'purposiveness of nature'.

In the experience of beauty, in which our sensory experience takes on a form appropriate to the notion of a lawfulness in general without any specific law being at issue, the imagination and understanding 'reciprocally quicken each other'. We experience the activity of reflective judgement at play and thus experience the harmony of the imagination with the understanding and the imagination with what it receives and so experience the purposive nature of such judgement, its being guided by the idea of a purposiveness of nature. Our cognitive powers are experienced for themselves rather than being used, and in their directedness towards the idea. The pleasure we experience in beauty is a self-recognition in feeling which involves our guidance by what is beyond our knowledge but on which we are dependent.

In the experience of beauty we experience nature as if it were art, that is, as if it were formed in accordance with concepts. Human artefacts are works of art involving the formation of materials into a product to perform some further function in terms of which their form is intelligible and may be assessed. But works of fine art are produced in order to engage the reader, spectator or listener in that disinterested experience of pleasure we call beauty. Since this judgement of taste involves no concepts, being the experience of the possibility of reflective judgement itself, it does not involve the estimation of the object in comparison with some independent concept (as the estimation of whether this is a good knife, say, would). Rather, the intention of the artist is realized in the work itself: if it is successful (that is, readers, spectators or listeners indeed engage in the disinterested contemplation of beauty in relation to it), then it is its own standard. A work fails, not because it doesn't live up to some independently specifiable concept, but because we cannot engage in the required way in relation to it: we don't find it beautiful. The production of fine art, therefore, cannot be taught; such works are not produced in accordance with determinate rules. Yet they are subject to estimation, in inviting our judgement as to their beauty. They involve a 'rule' in that sense, but the rule is that contained in the judgement of beauty itself: that is, in whether or not in relation to the work we have the experience of beauty, which, founded in our cognitive capacities, claims universality and necessity. Production of successful art, not being governed by a given rule and so not a craft, is a work of 'genius'.[12]

If successful, the work is its own standard, is 'exemplary'. And as such its 'concept' is itself. In this way what unifies the work, that through which we experience it as a whole, is something we cannot articulate and which nevertheless we must direct ourselves to in order to relate to its parts. We experience the unity of the work of art but cannot think it. In this way, the production and reception of the work involve the operation of our reason, our desire for unification, but without a rational idea. Encounter with the work activates the aspiration after unity, yet without a determinate thought. The work of human fine art as an intentional production is (if successful) the exhibition of a created harmony, whereas natural beauty is only the experience of a harmony as if the object were a work of art. In experiencing the beauty of a work of fine art we experience a harmony, a unity of its parts, which is the result of human activity. The experience of the beauty of fine art thus involves the play of our reason, our aspiration after unity, in the absence of a determinate concept.

Poetry has the highest rank of the fine arts.[13] It is an art of speech, and thus uses the products of the understanding, but where the imagination is utilized, not to provide the ordered materials to the understanding, but rather to re-order experience: 'it creates, as it were, another nature out of the material that actual nature gives it'[14] and so makes it possible to 'strive toward something that lies beyond the bounds of experience, and hence to try to approach the exhibition of rational concepts (intellectual ideas) and thus [these concepts] are given a semblance of objective reality.'[15]

Rational ideas cannot be exemplified in experience, but the re-ordering capacity of the creative imagination makes it possible to provide images of them. 'A poet ventures to give sensible expression to rational ideas of invisible beings, the realm of the blessed, the realm of hell, eternity, creation, and so on.'[16] The poet does this through 'aesthetic ideas' which provide a 'sensory embodiment' of rational ideas and idealizations. Genius exhibits aesthetic ideas[17] through the production of images and symbols which encourage the imagination to 'spread its flight over a whole host of kindred representations that provoke more thought than admits of expression in a concept determined by words'. Such aesthetic ideas give sensible expression to ideas of reason and also make it possible for the poet to take things 'that are indeed exemplified in experience, such as death, envy, and all other vices, as well as love, fame and so on' but then 'by means of an imagination that emulates the example of reason in reaching [for] a maximum, he ventures to give these sensible expression in a way that goes beyond the limits of experience, namely, with a completeness for which no example can be found in nature'.[18] Such aesthetic ideas provoke our contemplation and so 'much thought' but no definite thought. We are provoked to contemplate the symbol or image and its ramifications in relation to rational ideas, but without being confined to any determinate interpretation. The symbol or image appears indeterminate, as 'meaning' yet not in a determinate manner, and so cannot be paraphrased. It is 'a presentation of the imagination which prompts much thought, but to which no determinate thought whatsoever, that is, no determinate concept, can be adequate, so that no language can express it completely and allow us to grasp it'.[19] The creative imagination only succeeds in giving 'sensible expression' to ideas of reason or of 'ideal' pictures of human conduct which can be experienced (as opposed, that is, to the virtues) in so far as it expresses an aesthetic idea.

It is 'actually in the art of poetry that the power (i.e. faculty) of aesthetic ideas can manifest itself to full extent'[20] since poetry uses language. Poetry involves the concepts of the understanding, 'the material that actual nature gives', but not in order to make determinate judgements, but rather as material for the creative imagination, which itself, therefore, 'plays' rather than is employed in the service of the understanding. This play forms unities of image and sound, and is thus an exercise of imagination in the service of reason which in its usual employment tries to unify what the understanding provides. The expression of aesthetic ideas, providing an 'experience' of what is beyond experience, can attain an appropriate form of sensible presentation. In responding to aesthetic ideas and the unity of form of the poem, our capacities of imagination, understanding and reason are thus put into play but not exercised in the production of determinative judgement. This play allows us to experience our capacities for themselves, and so gives us, as it were, an experience of our humanity in the true form of the hierarchy of its capacities, in which sensibility and understanding are subordinated to the rational idea of our moral freedom.

II

The relation between the ideas of reason, of things in themselves, and those belonging to the human standpoint is in Kant asymmetrical. Whereas the latter require reference to the former, since Kant claims we cannot make sense of human experience without referring to them, the converse doesn't hold. The very idea of the way things are in themselves is of how they are quite independently of the human standpoint, and indeed of whether there is such a standpoint at all. Let us say that the notion of 'the way things are in themselves' is an 'absolute' notion to mark this asymmetry: other notions may need, for their sense, a reference to such an absolute notion, but it is intelligible in itself. But is such a conception of an absolute notion coherent? If not, we should have to jettison the idea of the 'way things are in themselves' and so of 'the truth' in the absolute sense it has for metaphysics and for Kant's God. And what would be the consequences of such a move for our understanding of the world, ourselves and literature? These questions are central to the writings of the Early German Romantic author Friedrich Schlegel.

Schlegel's writings do not take the form of the philosophical treatise. An unfinished novel, *Lucinde*, the *Dialogue on Poetry*, the *Critical* and *Athenaeum Fragments*, these are his characteristic productions. When he described what he called 'Romantic poetry', he said it would mix and fuse 'poetry and prose, inspiration and criticism'[21] and his friend Novalis indeed thought that this was what Schlegel had produced: 'Schlegel's writings are philosophy as lyric.'[22]

This poetry he characterized as 'transcendental' with reference to Kant's philosophy. Whilst transcendental philosophy showed its own possibility through a revelation of the conditions for the possibility of human experience in general, 'transcendental poetry' would 'In all its descriptions . . . describe itself, and always be simultaneously poetry and the poetry of poetry'.[23] But why should there be a 'reflexive' poetry of this kind? Why shouldn't the reflection on poetry be carried out by philosophy, and especially a transcendental philosophy reflecting on human experience in its totality and so on 'aesthetic' experience? But Schlegel's transcendental poetry is not to be subservient to philosophy. It is rather a transmutation in both what has been known as poetry and what has been known as philosophy. Such 'poetry' is not simply a continuation of what has been so called hitherto. Rather, it is what is pointed towards in the history of poetry. 'The whole history of modern poetry is a running commentary on the following brief philosophical text: . . . poetry and philosophy should be made one.'[24] Poetry heretofore has criticized reality in its totality in terms of the ideal (satire), mourned a past perfection (elegy), or proclaimed the identity at some stage of real and ideal (idyll).[25] In this, poetry had participated in the philosophical project of distinguishing the real and ideal and then attempting to relate them. But the philosophy appropriate to the poet today is different from one which could emerge out of this project itself. It accepts the Kantian transcendental turn: 'Kant discovered the table of categories and there was light in the spirit of man: I mean by this a real language, so that we can stop rummaging about for words and pay attention to the power and source of all activity.'[26] But this philosophy, unlike that of Kant, is one which finds its expression in a *transmutation of poetry*, and one which turns criticism on philosophy itself: 'Since nowadays philosophy criticizes everything that comes in front of its nose, a criticism of philosophy would be nothing more than justifiable retaliation.'[27] But how can such a 'criticism' of philosophy not itself be philosophical and so expressible properly in the form of philosophical argumentation?

But here, of course, Schlegel can point to the origins of philosophy. Plato writes in dialogue form and his works are saturated by 'Socratic irony'. The dialogue form involved the listener or reader in the movement of thought itself, rather than leading to memorizable results, whilst Socratic irony precluded taking away any such results as the dialogue seemed to produce. For what is said in irony is at odds with the way in which it is said or with the person who says it. What can therefore be communicated in irony is not so much a message as an awareness of what can be said, a sensitivity to the conditions of communication themselves. By 'its means one transcends oneself' arousing 'a feeling of indissoluble antagonism between the absolute and the relative, between the impossibility and the necessity of complete communication'.[28] Irony characterizes the 'transcendental poetry' by making relative anything said, whilst involving the reader or thinker in what is not relative, the conditions of communication. What is said will appear to be directly affirmed, and yet the manner of its saying will dislodge this affirmation by involving the reader in a development of the very concepts used in the affirmation itself. For example, 'poetry and philosophy should be made one' requires a transmutation in what is meant by poetry and by philosophy, and so makes a 'statement' which cannot simply be understood. It provokes our thought to develop the concepts to render what is said intelligible: it incites concept-formation. Irony 'is the form of paradox. Paradox is everything simultaneously good and great.'[29] But as paradox it shows us the nature of thinking. Thought, prior to arriving at statements to be affirmed, involves concept-formation, Kant's reflective judgement, and this requires paradox to incite it, give it life: 'isn't this entire, unending world constructed by the understanding out of incomprehensibility or chaos?'[30] Through this we can see how the 'criticism' of philosophy may proceed: ironically, by intervening in the very ambition of philosophy in order to show us, in terms of our own thinking, that that ambition is at odds with the process of thought itself. There is understanding only relative to incomprehension: there can be no such thing as a total comprehension which would remove incomprehension completely and make everything light and clear. The 'more one knows, the more one still has to learn. Ignorance increases in the same proportion as knowledge – or rather, not ignorance, but the knowledge of ignorance.'[31] The 'philosopher has only the choice of knowing either everything or nothing'[32] and so alternates between the system, which understands reality in its totality, and scepticism. But this alternation is undone by the ironic counterposing of absolute and relative to bring us to a self-awareness that knowledge and incomprehension are indivisible and must both be embraced: 'it's equally fatal for the mind to have a system and to have none. It will simply have to decide to combine the two.'[33] We embrace both where system and lack of system are transmuted into concepts of 'transcendental poetry' rather than remaining at the philosophical level of systematic and sceptical thought. 'Transcendental poetry' is the appropriate form within which the thought of life and the world as 'becoming', without origin and without end, and so without the possibility of system, is formulated so as to involve the reader in its own process. 'The romantic kind of poetry is still in the state of becoming [and] . . . should . . . never be perfected . . . It alone is infinite, just as it alone is free.'[34] However, although a new form of writing, it forms itself self-consciously in terms of what poetry always has been implicitly, although unrealized until now: 'The romantic kind of poetry is the only one that is more than a kind, that is, as it were, poetry itself: for in a certain sense all poetry is or should be romantic.'[35] Poetry which is 'always becoming' is what has always marked significant poetry and why it maintains its interest for and hold over us: 'A classical text must never be entirely comprehensible. But those who are cultivated and who cultivate themselves must always want to learn more from it.'[36] Great poetry, in its ultimate impenetrability, reawakens us to the nature of our lives and of the world of which we are a part and so recalls us to our true vocation, as we shall see: 'All the greatest truths of every sort are completely trivial and hence nothing is more important than to express them forever in a new way and, whenever possible, for ever more paradoxically, so that we won't forget they still exist and that they can never be expressed in their entirety.'[37]

But poetry in this sense is only possible because it is the manifestation of a poetry in a deeper, transmuted sense, one in which philosophical aspirations find their satisfaction beyond system and scepticism. There is an 'unformed and unconscious poetry' in all things and in us, a 'primeval poetry without which there would be no poetry of words'.[38] Poetry in the usual sense involves a production beyond rule: it isn't possible to 'impose upon [poetry] restrictive laws as the theory of poetics would like to . . . poetry bursts forth spontaneously from the invisible primordial power of mankind when the warming ray of the divine sun shines on it and fertilizes it'.[39] It is the production of something, therefore, essentially *individual*, which is its own law, its own standard, and cannot be referred to a species or a general notion for the specification of its measure. As such, it is a product of 'genius' and not of craft, and so emerges from what is essentially individual in the poet: 'the will of the poet can tolerate no law above itself'.[40] It is just this which distinguishes the human being, the capacity for individuality. What characterizes humanity is the capacity to go beyond determination by the species, to live as an 'individual', to make one's life a 'poem'. Every 'man .. bear[s] within him his own poetry which must and should remain his own as surely as he is himself, as surely as there is anything original in him'.[41] Yet this poetry of the human is at the same time part of the general 'unformed and unconscious poetry' that informs everything else; only humanity has the capacity for making it explicit and so creating their lives as individualities and for making poetry in the more usual sense.

Just as knowledge emerges only out of incomprehension, so what we have knowledge of only stands in the light because of an essential darkness. Order, and so what we can understand, emerges out of 'incomprehensibility or chaos'.[42] The world we understand is a creation, something we have wrested from an 'incomprehensibility', a darkness which cannot be directly addressed. The world is in constant becoming, without origin or end: 'Destruction and creation; one and all; and so may the eternal Spirit hover forever over the eternal stream of life and time.'[43] The 'unformed and unconscious poetry' of all things is their appearing only through this creative process in which humanity relates to an essential hiddenness, a process which involves the human capacity for language: 'It is the letter with which the irresistible will of that great magician, Fantasy, touches the sublime chaos of all encompassing nature, touches it and calls the infinite word to light, the word that is an image and a mirror of the divine spirit, and that mortals call the universe.'[44]

The human being can become aware of this creativity and so explicitly relate to its source in creative thinking. But humans are themselves part of this creation: they themselves are constituted in a relation to the always incomprehensible in themselves. We do not know ourselves, just as complete knowledge of anything is impossible: 'nobody has ever understood himself yet'.[45] Any self-knowledge takes place only in relation to the incomprehensible in ourselves. It is the possibility of living so as to relate to this which distinguishes the human.

> Other things cannot go back into themselves . . . [But man] can concern himself forever with himself and forever find new matter to occupy him . . . Just as every animal is attracted to its own native element as soon as it reaches maturity, so man's instinct leads him to his own depths; there he must be destroyed, perhaps by plunging headlong downwards, perhaps by sinking down calmly and beautifully . . . For a human being who is a human being, there is no other death than his own self-induced death, his suicide.[46]

The human being 'who is a human being' can relate to their own hiddenness, their 'own depths', through the constant venture into the unknown in relation to themselves: 'whoever desires the infinite does not know what he desires'.[47] As such, he or she *becomes*, exists as constant becoming, and so becomes their own law, their own measure: they become as individuals in a constant overcoming of their present self. 'Individuality is precisely what is original and eternal in man ... To pursue the cultivation and development of this individuality as one's highest calling would be a godlike egoism.'[48] In relation to our own depths we can do nothing directly. Indeed, philosophy, being blind to the 'poetry' of existence, its emergence out of the hidden, the unknowable, has characterized man's vocation in terms of activity, even if this is consummated in the form of contemplation. But 'industry and utility are the angels of death who, with fiery swords, prevent man's return to Paradise'.[49] A relation to the depths, to what is beyond consciousness and knowledge as its hidden source, can only be achieved in passivity, in a listening for what may emerge. Indeed, this is, since all knowledge and what is known have this character, true of all real thinking: 'talking and ordering are only secondary matters in all the arts and sciences: the essence is thinking and imagining, and these are possible only in passivity'.[50] Knowledge too is always becoming, and new thoughts emerge only through this passive openness to what may newly emerge. And with new thoughts, new things appear; the world changes too. Similarly, the human being who *is* a human being takes on the vocation of becoming, of allowing what is hidden in the depths to constantly appear so that they are *alive*. They can only be their own measure through rejecting all imposition of form from without. Lucinde, the heroine of Schlegel's novel, did not inhabit 'the ordinary world but rather a world that [she] conceiv[ed] and creat[ed] for [herself]', and 'she had renounced all ties and social rules daringly and decisively and lived a completely free and independent life'.[51] But the vocation of constant becoming involves more importantly being sensitive to the possibility of being enslaved by one's own habits, one's own past. Constant vigilance is required in order to maintain the sense of living, of being at one with one's activities and relationships, a relation Julius in *Lucinde* calls Love or the Word: having formed a relationship with Lucinde, he 'felt that he would never lose this unity; the mystery of his life had been resolved and he had found the word'.[52] This is that 'creative word' which allows the new to appear from 'incomprehensibility or chaos', in which, therefore, the individual as individual finds him- or herself. Just as the poem, as a work of genius, is its own measure and so an 'individual', so human life is to take on explicitly the character of poetry: 'so too', we are told of Julius, 'his life now came to be a work of art for him'.[53] Life as constant becoming never arrives and so is characterized as 'self-creation and self-destruction', and indeed, as Lucinde says, for such an individual 'there is no death other than his own self-induced death, his suicide' since even this must be taken up by the individual as part of his own permanent becoming. He declines to have a termination imposed from without and so incorporates it in the poem which is his life. 'Why shouldn't we interpret the bitterest whim of chance as a lovely witticism and an exuberant caprice, since we, like love, are immortal?'[54] Living as constant becoming disrupts the unity of the self. Rather, this 'unity' is to lie in the constant emergence of new life: 'of this only a mind is capable that contains within itself simultaneously a plurality of minds and a whole system of persons, and in whose inner being the universe which, as they say, should germinate in every monad, has grown to fullness and maturity'.[55]

Human life as art, as creativity and so as the constant becoming of individuals, each a law unto themselves, this is the 'religion of man and artist' that Schlegel announces.[56] 'God is everything that is purely original and sublime, consequently the individual himself taken to the highest power';[57] 'Every good human being is always progressively becoming God. To become God, to be human, to cultivate oneself are all expressions that mean the same thing.'[58] And it is this which determines the form of his writings.

At the beginning of *Lucinde*, Julius writes: 'No purpose . . . is more purposeful for myself and this work, for my love for it and for its own structure, than to destroy at the very outset all that part we call "order", remove it, and claim explicitly and affirm actually the right to a charming confusion.'[59] All order emerges only out of a relation to 'chaos', the incomprehensible, essentially hidden source of order and change: 'Confusion is chaotic only when it can give rise to a new world.'[60] We are not transparent to ourselves, any more than the world can become transparent to us. Living knowledge and a vital life require a constant positive relating to this source, a relation to the 'infinite', which gives to life and knowledge its character of constant becoming: 'create, discover, transform, and retain the world and its eternal forms in the perpetual variation of new marriages and divorces'.[61] The point of Schlegel's writings is to precipitate a relation to this source of creativity in the reader. This cannot be done by the discursive form of a philosophical treatise which makes things plain, gives us something to understand. The incomprehensible cannot be understood. We only relate to it in the disruption of our own thought and life, in so far as the order imposed from without or from within through habit and history is put again in motion, becomes not fixed and dead, but moving and living so that past and present and future are related as a process of constant becoming: 'Artists make mankind an individual by connecting the past with the future in the present.'[62] This disruption requires an interventionary form of writing: 'You're not really supposed to understand me, but I want very much for you to listen to me.'[63] To listen is to have the fixed order of one's thinking about oneself or the world disrupted and put into motion once again. The 'fragment' has its significance in this. 'A fragment, like a miniature work of art, has to be entirely isolated from the surrounding world and be complete in itself like a porcupine.'[64] The fragment is thus an 'individual', like a work of art, and one which resists us, like a porcupine, with its spikes that invade our body. The fragment is an antidote to 'spiritual sloth' or the *'fermenta cognitionis* [yeast or leaven of knowledge] for a critical philosophy',[65] precipitating thought, putting us again into relation with 'chaos or confusion'. The fragment, as individual, is not a part of an unfolding discourse which would invite understanding. It achieves its individuality, its separation from the outside, through its irony and wit, structures which resist understanding but which precipitate the movement of thought. Wit brings together notions which appear either to contradict one another or to be very distant and unrelated in order to provoke a movement of thought which will enable them to be held together. As, for example, 'Every good poem must be wholly intentional and wholly instinctive. That is how it becomes ideal.'[66] These notions of intention, instinct and ideality can be held together, but only by relating them to the hidden, the incomprehensible, to 'chaotic confusion', and the effort to think them together itself relates us to the source of the movement of thought. So *the fragment enacts and precipitates what it says.* Irony produces a paradox between what is said and its manner of saying. For example, saying in a fragment, which is a 'Romantic' form, that Romantic poetry is 'forever . . . becoming and never . . . perfected' sets up such a paradox, for how is this, which appears to be a final statement, to participate in such becoming? Irony 'is the clear consciousness of eternal agility, of an infinitely teeming chaos'.[67] That is, it is the manner of writing of someone aware that something is to be said but that whatever is said has a misleading semblance of finality denied by the character of thought and life as constant becoming. Irony is the mode of a writing aware of 'the impossibility and the necessity of complete communication'. The forms Schlegel adopts are what he communicates, one might say, since they are directed towards the reactivation of thought and life which is the only way we have of relating to the incomprehensible source of thought and life. He sees himself as a 'synthetic writer':

> The analytic writer observes the reader as he is, and accordingly he makes his calculations and sets up his machines in order to make the proper impression on him. The synthetic writer constructs and creates a reader as he should be; he doesn't imagine him calm and dead, but alive and critical.[68]

The reader as he 'should be' is not an ideal, but rather a reader ever moving into the future, as becoming: and it is to provoke the creation of such a reader that Schlegel intends his writings.

Schlegel has argued that the Kantian ideas of reason, as conceptions of the way things are 'in themselves', are unintelligible. There can be no such absolute notions. Knowledge, truth and reality need a reference to their lack, so we cannot have a coherent conception of final truth, ultimate reality or complete knowledge. Rather, we have to conceive the world as always coming into being in essential relation to our cognitive and practical activities, as a constant creation involving ourselves. Similarly, there is no 'truth' to which we can refer human life: we too must always be creating our own lives, preserving them as constant becoming, making them endlessly anew. Just as the work of art for Kant is its own measure, so here our individual lives are to be referred to no external standard. They are to be their own law: life as art, as a poem.

<h1 style="text-align:center">III</h1>

A similar movement occurs in Nietzsche, or at least in one of the main tendencies of his thought. Western thought, he argues, has been formed in accordance with the idea of the truth, that there is a final truth about 'reality' corresponding to which there could be a final knowledge. Knowledge of such truth, Nietzsche says in a brief summary of the career of the will to truth,[69] is, in ancient philosophy, assumed to be available to the human intellect. But where truth is the supreme value, assumptions are to be questioned and justified, thus requiring a justification for the assumption that our intellect is indeed in harmony with the truth about the world and ourselves. This leads to the further claim that, if this is to be so, then the world and our intellect must have been made for one another by a supreme reason, God. But life governed by truth needs a justification for this claim too, and finds no reason for believing that we can know the existence of such a God. The real world and God retreat to the status of ideas of reason with Kant, binding us as objects of faith but not knowledge. Positivism now, consistently with the value of truth, shows that unknown they cannot bind us since we cannot know if they exist or not. Nietzsche now steps forward and proposes, again in the name of truth, that we should abolish these ideas since they are manifestly of no use: 'Plato blushes for shame; all free spirits run riot.' They are 'no use' for human beings, since the application of the ideas of the real world and the final truth would presuppose a position transcendent to life. 'One would have to be situated *outside* life, and on the other hand to know it as thoroughly as any . . . to be permitted to touch on the problem of the *value* of life at all – sufficient reason for understanding that this problem is for us an inaccessible problem.'[70] Hence, a form of life governed by such ideas shows itself as rejecting the human position, whilst remaining, of course, human. Dissatisfied with human life, it seeks for something beyond it to give it significance and in terms of which it could live. Searching for the truth, it has looked for a ruler, something to obey. What is revealed when 'the truth' becomes unbelievable, and precisely through the pursuit of truth itself, is the very life-perspective which projected the ideas of truth and the real world in the first place, a life in revolt against itself. Value 'judgements concerning life, for and against, can in the last resort never be true: they possess value only as symptoms . . . the value of life cannot be estimated. Not by a living man, because he is party to the dispute, indeed its object, and not the judge of it.'[71] All valuations of life are by life on life itself. None can claim to occupy a position from which its valuation could assert a primacy which was anything other than its own self-assertion. But that is precisely what is involved in a life governed by truth. If we see, pursuing truth, that all valuations of life are perspectives on life by life itself, then we see the perspective based in 'the truth' as being one which cannot accept this: the supreme value of truth overturned, as Nietzsche says, by truthfulness. And if we then ask what sort of life is characterized by such a perspective, then the answer is that it is 'declining, debililitated, weary, condemned life',[72] a life dissatisfied with itself which seeks for something beyond it to give it significance: 'whoever is incapable of laying his will into things, lacking will and strength, at least lays some *meaning* into them, that is, the faith that there is a will in them already',[73] that there is some ultimate truth about the world and the human already, as it were, written into them. This revelation, that the ideas of the real world and the truth are part of the perspective of a form of life which denies itself, allows the manifestation of the opposite perspective:

> he who has really gazed . . . down into the most world-denying of all possible modes of thought – beyond good and evil and no longer . . . under the spell and illusion of morality – perhaps by that very act, and without really intending to, may have had his eyes opened to the opposite ideal: to the ideal of the most exuberant, most living and most world-affirming man.[74]

Having no external measure, such a life is its own 'law': 'We . . . want to become those we are – human beings who are new, unique, incomparable, who give themselves laws, who create themselves.'[75] The individual's life is to become self-creation, living art, 'conscious distinction, self-shaping'[76] as Nietzsche says, through which one imposes form on oneself only to overcome this when it threatens to subvert one's freedom from all imposed form, including that of one's own habits. Intellectual examination had revealed that all perspectives on life and the world are 'creative', are forms of art and not the revelations of a hidden truth. Perspectives which need to believe they embody such truth are thus illusions. The only intellectually honest life is the self-creative, accepting and affirming the very absence of any truth to which the individual is subservient: 'One could conceive of such a pleasure and power of self-determination, such a freedom of the will that the spirit would take leave of all faith and every wish for certainty . . . such a spirit would be the *free* spirit par excellence.'[77] Such a life would see that the forms which reality takes for us, and which even a free spirit must recognize, are themselves human creations, the product of the human will to self-preservation:

> in the formation of reason, logic, the categories, it was *need* that was authoritative: the need, not to 'know', but to subsume, to idealize,

16

for the purpose of intelligibility and calculation. No pre-existing 'idea' was here at work, but the utilitarian fact that only when we see things coarsely and made equal do they become calculable and usable by us . . . The categories are 'truths' only in the sense that they are conditions of life for us.[78]

IV

Metaphysics had tried to provide an ultimate justification for our modes of thought, and life based on it, by reference to *the* truth, the nature of reality, including ourselves, as it is 'in itself', independently of our thought and experience. Kant shows that such thought results in undecidable conflicts which are the result of our trying to transcend the human standpoint. We have no access to things in themselves; all we can do is to reflect on our experience to reveal its structure and conditions. Yet, of course, for Kant this internal critique shows that we must presuppose, for our empirical and moral experience to be as we take it to be, a belief in, but not knowledge of, the reality corresponding to the ideas of reason. We have to believe that we really are free immortal souls embodied in a world designed by a benevolent deity to fit our intelligence and capacities for action. We might say that from the human standpoint we have to believe that there is God's standpoint and that we do, to this extent, have access to the way things look, and so are, from there.

For both Schlegel and Nietzsche this latter claim is unwarranted, and indeed unintelligible. What both want to do, we might say, is to think humanly, in a way that doesn't pretend to some higher authority. For Schlegel, the notions of the truth, reality as it is in itself, are unintelligible since our notions of truth, knowledge and reality (and what other notions are to be used?) are inextricably bound up with their opposites: we only ever come to know in relation to what we don't know, and what is, as the object of knowledge, is only constituted in relation to 'chaos'. This precludes the intelligibility of a 'final' truth or 'ultimate' reality. For us, reality is always coming into being through an essential relation to our cognitive and practical activities. It is, and we are, in constant creation. Hence the form of life which reveals itself when we dispel the illusion of an appeal to a non-human standard is one of self-creativity. Nietzsche comes to a similar conclusion. Once we get rid of an appeal to a transcendent measure for our thought and life, once we restrict ourselves to our humanity (which is, after all, no restriction but a liberation from illusion), then we see the 'opposite ideal', that of life as constant self-creation, of the production of life as always new: life as art, its own law.

This might seem to give us the outlines of a human account of the world and life purged of reference to a transcendence, one couched in terms of 'becoming' rather than 'being'. Yet it may well prove to be subject to the same criticism it directs at metaphysics. The metaphysical appeal to 'reality as it is in itself' ignores the dependence of the notions of truth, reality and knowledge on their opposites for their sense in granting them 'absolute' status. But in attempting to remedy this, the same problem reappears here in the absolutizing of 'becoming', and the associated terms of 'creation' and 'art', which makes possible the formation of the account as the truth. If everything is 'becoming' then nothing is. The problem, it might appear, is one with the aspiration after a coherent account which has the same level of generality as the metaphysical (and, indeed, how could an account not aspire after coherence?). If metaphysics tries to tell us the truth about the way things really are, Schlegel and Nietzsche (at least when they are inclined to draw general conclusions in opposition to metaphysics) try to tell us how reality is given that there are no final truths. But any account which attempts this, and so implicitly claims itself as the truth, needs to appeal to certain terms which, as its principles of coherence, will be given an absolute sense, deprived of the contrast upon which their sense depends. The spectre of a 'final truth' is not so easily removed. As Rorty will point out, the aspiration after the 'transcendent' standpoint is seen not just in the projection of final states of knowledge or of the perfection of human life, but in the finality of the account offered to replace metaphysics, for such a final account will, as 'truth', involve the implicit claim to have contact with the 'essence' of the world and life. This is just as much the case if one claims that life is constant becoming which is lived self-consciously as art, as it is if one says that we are immortal souls who will receive our moral deserts in the afterlife. The 'absolutizing' of the concepts involved in the expression of the truth of 'becoming' is a mark of the fundamental complicity of this project with the metaphysical ambition, to occupy a position from which human life can (*pace* Nietzsche's explicit denials) be judged. Perhaps we should learn from this that no such coherent account of a generality to replace the metaphysical can be given. And perhaps that fact derives from a certain incoherence in thought, one which resists articulation in philosophical theorizing, but which more readily finds expression in other forms of 'literary' writing. This possibility emerges when language becomes the focus of philosophical attention. At least, Georges Bataille was inclined to think so.

2

GEORGES BATAILLE

The impossible

my thinking . . . is . . . in perpetual rebellion against itself[1]

Bataille's encounter with Nietzsche's writings in 1923 was, he says in an 'Autobiographical Note',[2] 'decisive'. What was decisive for Bataille was Nietzsche's account of the 'death of God', the impossibility of believing in access to a position transcendent to the human condition from which 'the truth' about the world and life could be pronounced. But for Bataille, Nietzsche's claim that in this revelation there appeared the opposite 'ideal' of the overman, a form of life which would be the creating of its own value, a conception based on the notion of the artwork which is its own law, remained complicit with the religion and metaphysics he wished to overturn. It was the further promulgation of a justified goal, even if its justification lay in the absence of an absolute. It represented the appropriate form for a human life which recognized it could not look outside itself for justification. In this way, it constituted an extension of rational goal-oriented life now liberated from the idea of a transcendent justification. But for Bataille the revelation of the unbelievability of the absolute follows from the structure itself of our experience of life and the world which shows us as divided or 'torn', desiring at the same time both selfhood and its annihilation, and so drawn, but not as to a purpose or goal, towards the annihilation of the conscious, articulate identity we take ourselves to be. In this way, 'The superman or Borgia side of things is limited and vainly defined in relation to possibilities whose essence is a going beyond the self.'[3] Exposure to the seduction of such possibilities was the result of the reflection that showed us the absolute's impossibility: 'No doubt I have more than Nietzsche dwelled upon the meaning of the night of non-knowledge (the "death of God").'[4]

The human is a linguistic being. 'In men, all existence is tied in particular to language.'[5] We relate to what is, including ourselves, only in language. Indeed, the very notion of 'what is', 'being', is itself linguistic. But words only have sense in relation to other words: the notion of a self-sufficient word which means in itself is unintelligible. And so 'being' itself can only be understood relationally: 'Being depends on the mediation of words, which cannot merely present it arbitrarily as "autonomous being" but which must present it profoundly as "being in relation".[6] As there can be no 'autonomous being', there can be no terminus which would fix meaning and so being: rather these are constituted only as differences without end. Constitution as differences depends upon 'difference', on 'relation', on the 'gap' between differences which prevents them ever constituting the 'final word' or 'reality'. It is this 'gap' which is Bataille's concern: it cannot become the object of thought, since this would constitute it as a difference rather than as the differing itself. (And so, of course, *this* thought must be in 'rebellion against itself'.) But although evading thought, Bataille believes it can, in a sense, become an experience.

'Experience attains in the end the fusion of object and subject, being as subject non-knowledge, as object the unknown.'[7] Bataille calls this 'inner experience'. It is an experience of 'continuity', that in which there are no longer the differences constituted as subject and object: 'There is no longer subject–object, but a "yawning gap" between the one and the other and, in the gap, the subject, the object are dissolved; there is passage, communication, but not from one to the other: the one and the other have lost their separate existence.'[8] To experience the 'yawning gap', differing itself, means the dissolution of subject and object. Here there can be no knowledge, therefore, nor lack of knowledge, but rather 'non-knowledge'. Since 'I' am only in relation to objects, this entry into differing itself is the annihilation of the self. I enter into 'the unknown which surrounds me, from which I come, to which I go'.[9] This 'unknown' is not potentially knowable but actually unknown: it is, as the condition of any knowledge or its lack, that which can neither be known nor not known. It is where all distinctions are obliterated in the annihilation of self and non-self.

We are 'discontinuous' beings, conscious of ourselves as identities standing in relation to the world and others. Yet we are only as such identities in so far as there 'is' differing, there is 'continuity'. This 'continuity', however, evades thought, since it underlies the very possibility of thought itself, the relation of subject and object. In so far as we address it, we fail. To speak of it as 'continuity' (as I shall continue to do) is to bring it within language, whereas 'it' makes possible the relational field of language itself. This 'world remains in me as that continuity from inside to outside, from outside to inside, which I have finally had to discover: I cannot in fact ascribe to subjectivity the limit of myself or of human selves; I cannot limit it in any way'.[10] I am in 'the unknown which surrounds me, from which I come, to which I go', and that unknown is me too, 'the unknown which we ourselves are . . . not the I sure of itself imagining itself necessary and undertaking to know'.[11] But this 'unknown', this 'continuity', cannot be addressed or revealed. Within language, within the relation of subject and world, the 'unknown' is what remains to be known, even if we cannot achieve this. But the 'unknown', which is the 'continuity' of the very relationality which constitutes language itself, evades language and thought at the same time as making them

possible: whenever thought turns towards 'it', it can only do so by incorpor-
ating 'it' within language and so failing in its task. Hence, prior to the development of Bataille's theory of religion, he says in the 'Introduction': 'in our
striving for cohesiveness, the incompletion is not restricted to the lacunae of
thought; at every point, at each point, there is the impossibility of the final
state . . . Philosophy responds from the start to an irresolvable exigency.'[12]
The 'continuity' which as differing constitutes language and meaning and so
makes possible thought in general, prevents the thinking which philosophy
aspires to of the identity of subject and object, the absolute knowing where
the totality of reality would come to its own self-understanding. The 'void'
of relationality makes impossible the attainment of 'being' as totality or
unity, and thus prevents either 'subject' or 'world' or their union attaining
completion, finality or unity.

Yet that is what, as subjects, we desire. 'Our existence is an exasperated
attempt to complete being.'[13] We desire to attain self-identity, a wholeness
which would come with the fulfilment and satisfaction of life, in the attainment of the Good. But this aspiration of ourselves as 'discontinuous' beings,
as subjects in relation to the world, is rendered impossible precisely by the
dependence of our being as discontinuous on the 'continuity' involved in the
relationality of language. 'Each being is distinct from all others. His birth,
his death, the events of his life may have an interest for others, but he alone is
directly concerned in them. He is born alone. He dies alone. Between one
being and another, there is a gulf, a discontinuity.'[14] But this 'discontinuity',
the individualization of ourselves in relation to others and the world, 'is not
the whole truth of the matter'.[15] 'It is a deep gulf [but] we can experience its
dizziness together.'[16] What makes possible our 'discontinuity' is the 'gulf', the
'void' of relationality which makes possible selves and world at all, but which
thereby makes impossible 'self' and 'world' as totalities, unities. The condition for the possibility of our being 'discontinuous' selves is at the same time
the condition for the impossibility of that self as discontinuous, as a separate
unity. The 'gulf' which is this condition 'can hypnotize us. This gulf is death
in one sense, and death is vertiginous, death is hypnotizing . . . for us, discontinuous beings that we are, death means continuity of being.'[17] In so far
as we are discontinuous beings, desiring our self-preservation and self-
formation, we are at the same time involved with the condition which makes
possible and impossible our selfhood, that 'continuity' which represents for
us the 'void' which evades consciousness and thought. Hence, we are not
'autonomous' beings, but are only in relation to what we are not. That relation is marked for us by birth and death, our coming to be and passing away,
which place our possibility in relation to a particular past and a future over
which we have no control. Anguish is the experience of the human being who
desires autonomous being, to be a self, an independent identity, but who can
desire it only on condition of its impossibility. 'Anguish is the fear of losing,
expression of the desire to possess.'[18] Anguish defines us as human: 'Anguish

is what makes humankind . . . not anguish alone, but anguish transcended and the act of transcending it.'[19] The movement towards its transcendence is eroticism, the movement into the differing which makes possible the desire to possess a self only by making it at the same time impossible of attainment. It is, therefore, the movement towards the destruction of the self. 'The whole business of eroticism is to destroy the self-contained character of the participators as they are in their normal lives.'[20] Eroticism 'presupposes man in conflict with himself'.[21] The condition for the possibility of what we desire, our self-identity, is at the same time the condition for its impossibility: desiring the one, we are fascinated by, drawn towards, continuity, death. 'At bottom, we actually want the impossible situation it all leads to: the isolation, the threat of pain, the horror of annihilation; but for the sensation of nausea bound up with it . . . we should not be satisfied.'[22] This fascination is towards violence, violation, the annihilation of the self. Eroticism thus involves a 'breaking down of established patterns, the patterns . . . of the regulated social order basic to our discontinuous mode of existence as defined and separate individuals'.[23] Yet this fascination with and being drawn by self-annihilation depends upon the drive towards self-preservation and self-formation of ourselves as discontinuous beings. The 'patterns of social order' necessary for the formation of our identities are affirmed precisely in their transgression: in eroticism 'we venerate the rule which we break. A series of rebounding oppositions lies at the basis of an instinct composed alternately of fidelity and revolt, which is the essence of man.'[24]

As discontinuous beings, as 'selves', we inhabit the world of discourse, the world of apparently distinct conceptions and beings. This world obliterates what it cannot contain but depends upon. It necessarily excludes 'heterogeneity', differing itself which makes possible the appearance of distinct beings whilst making them impossible as distinct. It excludes the experience of anguish and its transcendence which nevertheless mark us as human. In man there is 'an irresistible excess which drives him to destroy and brings him into harmony with the ceaseless and inevitable annihilation of everything that is born, grows and tries to last'.[25] This 'excess' in the human is the being drawn towards self-annihilation, the destruction of separate being, and so the destruction of what reason, thought, comprehends. 'In the domain of our life excess manifests itself in so far as violence wins over reason.'[26] This excess cannot be thought, but in desiring selfhood we are inescapably involved in it. It 'is by definition that which can never be grasped, but we are conscious of being in its power'.[27] Being depends upon, and is rendered impossible by, this excess, and so by the transgression of the limits which demarcate beings.

The human being is paradoxical, a living conflict. On the one hand, as human we are purposive beings and have to relate to a world of things in which our purposes can be enacted; on the other, precisely because we are purposive beings we are drawn towards the overthrow of rationality. As

purposive beings, we are distinct individualities addressing a world of distinct things; but just because of that, we are drawn towards a continuity with
'all that is' and towards the dissolution of the distinctness of things.

As self-conscious human beings living in the clarity and light of the world
of work these intimations of continuity fill us with terror and disgust, emotions associated for Bataille with the fundamental emotion of anguish.
Anguish is the experience of a being who desires selfhood, autonomous
being, the discontinuous I which for us constitutes our identity in the world
of things, of the possibility of the dissolution, destruction, of the self in a
recovery of our 'intimacy', our continuity, with all that is. In the face of our
complicity with continuity, we are, as discontinuous beings, repelled. That
which reminds us of the dissolution of the self, intimations of mortality,
human excreta, the corpse, for example, disgusts us or fills us with horror
(although as we shall see, our feelings are also, as befits our paradoxical
nature, in conflict). Around these intimations the purposive human being
forms taboos which remove such things from our practical lives. Such prohibitions essentially surround birth and death, the limits of the self which prevent the fulfilment of the aspiration towards the achievement of self-identity:
they concern sex, menstruation, childbearing, death in particular. Reproduction and death as limits mark the involvement of the discontinuous beings
we are as agents in that continuity which renders our achievement of the self
impossible. They are eruptions of violence affecting the integrity of the individual human being. Birth violently brings into being a potentially discontinuous consciousness from nothing, death destroys the identity of
individuals, returning them to the nothing from which they came, whilst in the
coupling of sex the individuality of the partners disappears in the paroxysm
of orgasmic pleasure. The taboos exclude these eruptions of violence from
our practical lives. The world of reason and the pursuit of identity is founded
on the exclusion of violence, of the disruption of that individual identity
through which we can address the world of distinct objects. This rejection of
violence is necessary for the ' untroubled clarity' of the world of action and
objectivity: prohibitions 'eliminate violence and our violent impulses which
would destroy the calm ordering of ideas necessary for human awareness'.[28]
The world of reason, the 'homogeneous' world of our common sense and
scientific understanding, of our purposive life, is thus founded on what is not
rational, on the unreasoning dread and horror of violence: the taboo is
'basically a shudder appealing not to reason but to feeling, just as violence
is'.[29]

These prohibitions exclude and set apart, however, what remains human
life. We are discontinuous beings, purposeful identities in the clear world of
our understanding, but just because of this we are implicated in continuity,
in that which disrupts identity, purpose and reason, in the 'heterological'.
The manifestations of our intimacy with continuity fill us at once with terror,
horror and disgust on the one hand, and fascination and desire on the other.

The 'sacred', that which is set apart intimating our complicity with the heterological, is the object of terror and desire. In relation to objects and situations which suggest the dissolution of the individual, the loss of the self and so of its world of rational order, we are filled by aversion and attraction at the same time. Moreover, and yet more paradoxically, we desire because we are repelled: 'repugnance and horror are the mainsprings of my desire . . . such desire is only aroused as long as its object causes a chasm no less deep than death to yawn within me, and . . . this desire originates in its opposite horror'.[30] Such reflections, Bataille says, 'go beyond reasonableness', since they reflect the paradoxical feelings of the paradoxical beings we are. The corpse is thus the object of both aversion and a horrified fascination. Our sexual desire too is complicit with an aversion. 'The sexual channels are also the body's sewers; we think of them as shameful and connect the anal orifice with them.'[31] If we did not feel repulsion at the sex organs our desire would not have the imperative form it does but would be akin to a desire for, say, ice-cream. The repulsion marks our recognition as discontinuous beings of what indicates a complicity with the desire for continuity, a recognition which threatens our identity. But our desire marks our recognition that this complicity is us too. The involvement of repulsion in desire, so that without the aversion there would be no attraction or not the same kind, indicates the paradoxical nature of our existence. On the one hand, we have a 'tormenting desire that our individuality should last'; on the other, 'there stands our obsession with a primal continuity linking us with everything that is'.[32] Continuity threatens our identity, but we should not have identity, discontinuity, unless we were implicated in continuity, with what disrupts identity. The condition for our identity at the same time makes it impossible. As discontinuous identities, we are already involved in continuity, drawn towards self-annihilation. Our very desire for our identity and its continuation involves therefore a desire for continuity. As identities we desire our self-annihilation.

> Man is the being that has lost, and even rejected, that which he obscurely is, a vague intimacy. Consciousness could not have become clear in the course of time if it had not turned away from its awkward contents, but clear consciousness is itself looking for what it has itself lost, and what it must lose again as it draws near to it.[33]

Self-annihilation can only be desired by a separate self–conscious being, a self; and that desire is part of being such a self who can only be separated on condition of being involved with continuity, with that 'unknown which surrounds me, from which I come, to which I go'.

We could, therefore, say that 'the taboo is there in order to be violated'.[34] Transgression is thus 'complementary to the profane world, exceeding its limits but not destroying it'.[35] The rational world of purposive activity and our lives as distinct individuals is possible through the exclusion of the eruption of violence which marks our intimacy with the unknown and unknowable. Yet the taboos which make possible our distinctness at the same time mark our involvement in continuity: we can be separate beings only in fascination with self-annihilation. What we desire, to be sufficient, complete identities, is rendered impossible by its very condition.

Archaic societies recognized the paradoxical structure of the human being by allowing the transgression of taboos an institutionalized place in social life, especially in the sacrifice and the festival. The taboo against taking life is institutionally transgressed in human sacrifice and in the forms of sacrifice which succeeded it. Sacrifice takes what is useful, and so characterized as a thing, an identity, and releases it from its rational ordering. Thus the first fruits of harvest or head of livestock are destroyed in order to remove the plant or animal, together with the farmer or stockraiser, from the world of things. Sacrifice draws the victim out of the world of utility, out of purposive life, and restores it to the 'intimacy of the divine world, of the profound immanence of all that is'.[36] The destruction of the identity of the victim takes place therefore in violation of the guiding principles of productive life, that we work in order to produce what is useful and to consume it in a useful way. The victims of sacrifice are consumed without concern for the future, and only such an unconditional consumption can restore the primacy of the moment which characterizes continuity. In the festival too the prohibitions surrounding rational productive life are overturned, in drunkenness, sexual orgies, the violation of authority relations (where servants rule masters, for example), and so on.

Religion, however, even in its archaic forms, is a compromised affair. It tries to regain continuity, but it does so in an institutionalized form, in a way that is socially useful. Sacrifices, for example, are held to be essential for the coming of the rains or the success of the crops. That is, religion responds to the desire for continuity in terms of the values of productive life, the values of the discontinuous world. It thus becomes the totality of prohibitions, obligations and partial freedoms 'that socially channel and regularize' the desire for self-annihilation and the destruction of the rational world. It thus 'betrays the needs that it was not only supposed to regulate, but satisfy'.[37] The guiding force of socially useful ideas creates in more 'developed' forms of religion the notion of divinity as protective of society and productive life, and understands divinity further and our relation to it in terms of the notions of discontinuity characteristic of rational life. Discontinuity thus survives death in the immortality of the individual soul who stands in relation to a discontinuous personal God. Socially useful religion thus makes a separation in what had been sacred between the pure (taboos, the individual soul, salvation, the personal God) and the demonic, the impure, whose presence is felt in the urge to transgress taboos. Christianity represents the ultimate development of socially useful religion in rejecting transgression entirely so that sacrifice, the festival and organized transgression are regarded as pagan and the work of the devil. Union with the perfect God becomes the goal of religious life, individual salvation from the world: in this we see Christianity's interpretation of the desire for self-annihilation. The possibility of transformation into absolute goodness means the possibility of rejecting evil totally and so occluding the paradoxical nature of the desire for goodness: that its strength is proportionate to the strength of the desire to transgress it. Only so can the good as the moral, the rational, the ordered have its force for us. Such a doctrine as Christianity's has only a weak hold on us, and one which, precisely because its structure is determined by social usefulness and so the criteria of rationality, will be overthrown ultimately by rational reflective criticism. Its destruction, however, opened the way only to profanation. Whereas Christianity had maintained the taboo and rejected all transgression as redeemable sin in the name of a possible perfection, now the taboos themselves become the object of rational critique. There are then no taboos, no transgression: all is subject to the clear light of reason. But the hold on us of the values of discontinuity, the values of rationality and purposive action, depends on the attraction of their violation. Perfect rationality which rejects irrational taboo as its foundation and the irrational violation of these taboos exercises no fascination. Life lived under its categories appears increasingly meaningless and boring whilst the desire for self-annihilation manifests itself in ever more incomprehensible and socially destructive forms, particularly in national wars. This is 'the death of God', the emergence of nihilism.

It is in this context that Bataille writes. Science, rationality, has achieved domination of human life in all its aspects. But in doing so, it has revealed the inadequacies of religion in all its forms. That religion was subject to rational critique showed its complicity with the values of reason, and the success of that critique uncovered religion at the same time as a way in which our desire for continuity, an essentially irrational desire, had been rendered into a socially useful form. 'The exclusion of mythology by reason is necessarily a rigorous one, on which there is no going back.'[38] Although this destroys rationalized religion, it at the same time makes possible the authentic expression of the desire for continuity freed of extraneous purpose. Human thought is 'everywhere and always ready to break loose', Bataille says, but in the past a purpose has always been imposed on this release. In archaic societies, sacrifice and transgression of taboo were required for the preservation of society, for the productivity of fields and flocks, the defeat of enemies; in modern religions, the end has been personal salvation. Rational critique has now liberated the human desire for immanence, for continuity with the unknowable, from all purpose and made possible Bataille's 'practical and theoretical heterology'.[39]

What we as discontinuous beings call 'good' is concerned with the maintenance and projected fulfilment of our discontinuity, with the attainment of 'autonomous being', selfhood. But this desire is, as we have seen, possible only through the impossibility of its attainment. Anguish, as the experience of this impossibility on the part of a 'discontinuous being', characterizes us as human. But the transcendence of anguish is the destruction of self: Bataille calls this 'summit'. 'The summit corresponds to excess . . . It . . . is a violation to the integrity of individual beings. It is thus closer to evil than to good.'[40] We are drawn towards 'evil', to the destruction of self, through desiring the good. The 'experience' which is the annihilation of self is liberation from limits, from distinctions, by entry into differing itself which is 'nothing'. It is, therefore, 'sovereignty', and the 'sovereign attitude' aims 'at nothing, wants nothing'.[41] It is a 'freedom' which involves the destruction of the 'freedom' of the distinct self. This is the entry into 'continuity' or 'intimacy': 'intimacy is violence, and it is destruction, because it is not compatible with the positing of the separate individual'.[42] Entry into intimacy is the destruction of thought and discourse and so 'Intimacy cannot be expressed discursively.'[43] It is 'expressed' only in violence, in destruction, in which the self becomes 'nothing': 'so unlimited is it that it is not even a thing: it is nothing'.[44] The self which aspires to complete being aspires to freedom. Yet this freedom exists only in the destruction of the limits of the self and so of language in which that self is constituted. Such freedom from language is freedom from reason and so from the future: 'free *existence* . . . is never bestowed except in the instant'.[45] 'Summit' can, therefore, never be taken as a project, a goal. It requires the relinquishment of the will. In breaking the orientation to the future, the experience 'cannot differ from ecstasy'[46] since it occurs solely in terms of itself and without reference to anything beyond the instant. Anguish is transcended in the loss of the desire to possess the self: 'should we give the slip to the need to possess – anguish just as quickly turns to ecstasy'.[47]

'Atheology' refers to an experience and the theoretical account of it, an experience of continuity, the void, within which the subject itself would be annihilated: 'it is in order to set myself before this *nothing* that I do talk of it . . . To this experience and to its accompanying reflection, I would want to give the name "atheology".'[48] Atheology is itself paradoxical, since it refers to an experience which goes beyond, violates, the very form of rational purposive life. Yet to 'set' oneself before this would appear only too like having a purpose, which the experience by definition cannot be, whilst to talk about it seems to bring it within the range of language which serves rational ends. As Bataille remarks, 'Inasmuch as "communication", evil, or summit are "the good of being" . . . they're reduced to the slavishness they can't be surrendered to. The very notions of *good* or *being* interpose a duration and concern that *essentially* are unknown to evil or summit.'[49] The experience cannot be taken as a goal and so as a 'good'. It rejects the characteristic temporality of purposive life, orientation towards the future which implies a past: it restores the temporality of immanent life, the instant, without past or future. Within the instant I

> lose all reason for existing, in fact, all reason period. I lose the possibility of *speaking*. Especially *speaking* as I am now of summit morality is something utterly ridiculous . . . the summit, when suggested as an end, is not the summit, since I'm reducing it to the search for advantage *when speaking of it* . . . the only possible way for dissipation to reach the summit is by not intending it.[50]

The experience within which subject and object would be annihilated cannot be spoken of, described, and it cannot be related to as an end. Rather, it must be kept in the form of a question: 'is there a moral goal beyond being I can reach?'[51] Activity can then take place in relation to the question. Such activity takes 'risk as a value', the chance of self-destruction which would be 'a thing of chance, outside will or movement'.[52] This activity lies in transgression, deliberate activity contravening the taboos and structure of rational conduct: in perverse (that is, non-reproductive) sex, love, drunkenness, gambling without prudence, and so on. If the summit experience occurs it 'is received and is not the result of searching for it; it is wholly and entirely governed by chance . . . If I can't make the summit an object of proceedings or intentions, I can make my life an ongoing evocation of possibilities.'[53]

This experience, as I remarked above, Bataille refers to as 'sovereign' since it is released from all reference to purpose. Paradoxically, through the overthrow of reason there is 'freedom'. 'Life is whole only when it isn't subordinated to a specific object that exceeds it. In this way, the essence of entirety is freedom . . . the practice of freedom lies within evil.'[54] Life is 'whole' only in the overthrow of self and reason and so in the loss of the goal of wholeness. It is closely related to mystical experience as recorded in historical religions. Mystical experience 'entails a complete detachment from material conditions. Thus it meets man's need to be independent of factors not chosen by himself but imposed from without. The aim is a state that can be called sovereign.'[55] In the mystical experience, there is 'indifference to what happens' and so indifference to the future. There is in this no desire (which has a future reference), and no activity: 'the subject becomes passive and suffers what happens to him with a kind of immobility'.[56] Removed from the references to future and past, the mystic 'ceases to belong to the passing of time . . . absorbed in the everlasting instant'. But then, the mystic ceases to be as an individual and ceases to relate to the world of objects, for both these forms of identity imply reference to past and future: one *is* for *a time*. Subject and object no longer exist: the mystic becomes 'lost in the indistinct and illimitable presence of the universe',[57] the continuity of the unknowable occurs, absorbing his discontinuous being. Nevertheless, such experience Bataille regards as still involved in religious categories: it is taken as a goal, and techniques are developed through which it can occur.[58] But then it is not truly an experience of the instant, devoid of references to past and future. Indeed, because it had as its aim union with God 'there is no reality to such ruin' of the self but only a 'representation'.[59] What is required is an experience without illusion (of God) and one entirely free of purpose and reason. Such freedom can be ensured only through the deliberate transgression of rationality and its moral rules where the possibility of the experience of the instant is held not as a goal but as a question. In such an experience, the self is lost not in the ascetic contemplation of the mystic, but in the violent paroxysms of perverse sexuality, drunkenness or crime. Such an experience is 'sovereign' in that it alone refuses all submission to rationality and purpose, and constitutes 'existing in the world with no end other than to exist'.[60] The nothing can become the 'content' of an experience in which, therefore, the subject too is annihilated, only through a 'chance' occurring in the course of a transgression of 'knowledge' itself: 'we reach ecstasy by a contestation of knowledge'.[61] The chance of the 'summit' is only recognized through transgression of rationality and purpose, the structure of human consciousness and knowledge.

This supreme experience, within which subject and object are annihilated and the continuity which makes possible subject and world in their relation is restored, is the unphilosophical resolution of philosophy's question. Philosophy seeks the identity of subject and object, the ultimate knowledge of the structure of reality within which reality would understand itself: here subject and object would pass into one another. But such a question aspires to 'the establishment of the homogeneity of the world',[62] rendering reality fully intelligible. There 'the truth' would be manifest. It thus averts its gaze from the heterogeneity involved in our having a conception of the world and of ourselves: that as differences these conceptions involve differing, the 'yawning gap' of a continuity beyond conceptuality. Philosophy's question finds its response rather where the discontinuous individual, the questioner, becomes annihilated, regaining 'continuity' in disappearance, and this is an experience and not knowledge. 'I believe that the supreme philosophical question coincides with the summits of eroticism',[63] the chance of which occurs only in transgressive activity. The supreme questioning is that to which the answer is the supreme moment of eroticism – that of 'eroticism's silence',[64] that experience beyond language in which subject and object, the condition for language, cease to exist. 'The pinnacle of being stands revealed in its entirety only through the movements of transgression.'[65] Philosophy aims at the totality of possibility. But what makes possibles possible is not itself possibility: it is the 'impossible', that which, in making thought possible, withdraws from thought. Relation to the impossible occurs only as the destruction of beings and in the contravention of what can be thought. The 'impossible is the distressing contrary of what we are, which is always connected to the possible'.[66]

Yet, of course, this account itself attempts to contain the impossible within discourse.

> Language substitutes the appearance of a solution for the insoluble, and a screen for violent truth. In short, any commentary which does not simply say that commentaries are useless and impossible moves us away from the truth at the very moment when it might come close to it in itself . . . even what I say is yet another obstacle which we must remove if we want to see.[67]

The only possible commentary on the impossible is one which annihilates itself, moves to transgress the limits of intelligibility and so draw the reader into the proximity of the experience which is the breaking of discourse. This is the movement of Bataille's theoretical writings.

> I should like to counsel my hearers the most extreme caution. I am really speaking a dead language. This language is the language of philosophy. Philosophy is also the death of language . . . I must caution you against my own words. I have been trying to talk a language that equals zero, a language equivalent to nothing at all, a language that returns to silence: that is, the suppression of whatever language may add to the world. This suppression cannot be rigorously applied. The experience of extremes has its own discipline – but this discipline is primarily contrary to any form of verbal apology of eroticism. Eroticism is silence.[68]

We shall see this movement of self-revocation by the text repeated in Bataille's fictional writings, rendering the distinction between 'theory' and 'literature' undecidable.

The 'task of authentic literature is . . . only conceivable in terms of a desire for a fundamental communication with the reader'.[69] 'Communication' is a relation within which distinct individuals to some extent recognize their lack of individuality so that a 'rent' is opened up through which they are united in a larger whole. The most fundamental form of communication takes place where the very integrity of individuals is disrupted so that they are led to an awareness of and participation in the sacred, continuity. 'Communication . . . takes place between two people who risk themselves, each lacerated and suspended, perched atop a common nothingness', as, say, when two lovers engage in mutual passion losing themselves in the fervour of the moment. With literature, Bataille says that 'in their major forms, literature and theatre . . . provoke dread and horror through symbolic representations of tragic loss (degradation or death); in their minor form, they provoke laughter through representations which . . . exclude certain seductive elements'.[70] Laughter is a response to a recognition of the impossibility of a final knowledge or control of the world which at the same time dispels the anguish this recognition causes. It occurs in situations in which the spectators can separate themselves from the incident that occasions this recognition, as in seeing another fall although I remain upright and stable.[71] The illusory nature of stability and of our control over the world is brought to consciousness but then dispelled. We respond to literary representations of such a fall in the same way; faced with representations of tragic loss or degradation, however, it is dread and horror we feel.

And such representations are able to show us the nature of human existence in an appropriate way. Human existence is paradoxical, characterized by conflicting fundamental emotions. Discontinuous individuals desire their own permanence, the maintenance of their own identity. Yet as discontinuous, they are implicated in continuity. They desire both the maintenance of self and self-annihilation, the latter repelling and attracting us at the same time. This cannot be accounted for, justified, by reasoned discussion, in terms of the principles of rational argument as in philosophy, since it shows us as, in part, irrational, and rightly so: 'Human life . . . is composed of two heterogeneous parts which never blend. One part is purposeful, given significance by utilitarian and therefore secondary ends; this part is the one we are aware of. The other is primary and sovereign . . . it evades the grasp of our aware intelligence.'[72] What literature does is to show us this in such a way that we can recognize for ourselves the rightness, the humanness, of what judged rationally is perverse, evil and to be condemned. Thus, discussing *Wuthering Heights*, Bataille remarks of Emily Brontë that what she shows is 'the tragic violation of the law' and whilst agreeing with the law, she 'based all emotional impact on communicating the sympathy which [s]he felt for the transgressor'.[73] 'The lesson of *Wuthering Heights*, of Greek tragedy and ultimately of all religion, is that there is an instinctive tendency towards divine intoxication which the rational world of calculation cannot bear.'[74] The transgression of the law is as human as its maintenance, and the attraction of the goodness of lawful behaviour depends on our attraction towards transgression, for our very separation marks our hidden complicity with continuity: we have to be so complicit in order to be the discontinuous selves we are. Literature shows us transgression and makes us feel its attraction. In this way it subjects us to the laceration of our own identity: it can fill us with dread and horror at the same time as fascinating us. 'Literature . . . is dangerous.'[75] Yet the attraction of the transgression is at the same time the attraction of the good: the strength of one goes with that of the other. It is thus at the same time the expression of 'those in whom ethical values are most deeply rooted'.[76] Literature shows us, by making us recognize ourselves through our responses, that 'the truth . . . is composed of opposites, Good and Evil',[77] that we are essentially and irredeemably attracted to both and that the attraction of one depends upon our simultaneously being attracted by the other. 'If the luminous intensity of Good did not give the night of Evil its blackness, Evil would lose its appeal';[78] 'had we not . . . longed for Good, Evil would provide us with a succession of indifferent sensations'.[79] We experience the truth of this by being made to feel, to experience, the fundamental attraction of what repels. 'Literature is not innocent. It is guilty and should admit itself so',[80] for it must, in being truthful, show us, make us feel, the attraction of evil, of the transgression of morality and the reasonable.

Poetry relates in a somewhat different way to the paradoxical nature of human life. It is, at its most significant, comparable to sacrifice. Sacrifice, as we have seen, removes the useful from practical life and destroys its nature as a thing, returning it to continuity. Poetry removes words, the very condition of our encounter with what is, from rational, purposive life and makes them the victims: 'poetry . . . is . . . the sacrifice in which words are victims';[81] 'poetry leads from the known to the unknown . . . poetry is sacrifice, but of the most accessible sort'.[82] Poetry renders the familiar and known into the strange and unknowable. In this way, it transgresses rationality and provides itself a transgressive experience. But in trying to make the unknowable present in the poem, to formulate the experience of the destruction of subject and object, it is doomed to failure; 'the poetic process wants the object to become the subject, the subject the object' and this 'transposes it into the realm of the impossible and the unsatisfiable'.[83]

Bataille, as we have seen, traces the trajectory of Western civilization towards an ever increasing dominance of the values of rationality to the point where religion itself is undermined. Literature has been one of the ways in which the contrary impulsion of our humanity has found expression: 'those arts which sustain anguish and the recovery from anguish within us are the heirs of religion. Our tragedies and our comedies are the continuation of ancient sacrificial rites'.[84] But now rationalism has reached its apogee, and in its triumph the new possibility of 'atheology' appears. One of the ways in which this possibility has manifested itself is in the movement of Surrealism. In Surrealism, literature and art break free of all social purpose. Surrealism 'brings about a free poetic release without subordinating it to anything and without assigning a superior end to it'.[85] It is not so much the products that are significant in Surrealism, but the activities themselves. The practice of automatic writing in particular is seen by Bataille as itself a form of transgressive activity which opens up the chance of the summit experience. 'What essentially characterizes automatic writing . . . is that it is an act of rupture . . . with the world [of practical activity]'. The individual forgets what exists and forgets himself and writes at random 'the most vibrant delirium which passes through' his mind. This is itself 'an act of insubordination' and 'in one sense he has performed a sovereign act . . . [and] has achieved the destruction of the personality itself'.[86] At the same time, this liberation from the subject results from the release of language from all practical purposes: 'the free activity of the mind would be betrayed if I subordinated it to some result decided beforehand'.[87] The will is relinquished in the rejection of the future, so that an occasion is made within which the instant can characterize experience: 'the seizure of the instant cannot differ from ecstasy'.[88]

Poetry in the past has always been subordinated to other purposes, social and religious, reflected in its subject matter. With the destruction of myth, of religion, and so the manifestation of the new possibility of an experience of continuity uninfected with illusion, poetry can itself become a way in which transgression can open up the chance for such an experience. In 'our time, poetry is no longer an expression of pre-established myths, it is itself the myth (or the "absence of myth", it doesn't matter which) which offers us the distracted, and so readily unleashed, movement that we are'.[89] It becomes itself a way in which we become free of all subservience in liberation from rationality and practical purpose. 'I cannot consider someone free if they do not have the desire to sever the bonds of language within themselves.'[90] This severing of the bonds of language takes place in one form in Surrealistic activity. It is 'an impersonal state of mind . . . constituted by denying the supreme value of categories of language'.[91] In this way it is 'mutism': and yet it must speak precisely in order to transgress, and so 'it must introduce a disorder or . . . an absence into the word'.[92] Surrealist activity invites us into the transgression of rationality through which by chance we may attain ecstasy, loss of self and the object world, the manifestation of continuity. This movement towards the transcendence of anguish is replicated in that required of the reader of Bataille's own fictions.

In the preface to the pseudonomously authored *Madame Edwarda*, Bataille says 'At the further end of this pathetic meditation – which, with a cry, undoes itself, unravelling to drown in self-repudiation, for it is unbearable to its own self – we rediscover God. That is the meaning, that is the enormity of this *insensate* – this mad – book.'[93] The word 'God' is 'the very word . . . which surpasses words'.[94] We 'rediscover God' in the sense of discovering what the religious concept of God has been an evasion of. We rediscover the 'power' which controls being in the 'nothing' of language, in the excess which attends all delineation of being, of all differences. Being is constituted in language, but just because of this 'autonomous being' is impossible: the 'yawning abyss' between differences prevents finality, totality. This 'nothing' is what the language of religion has repressed, the power of powerlessness which means that meaning is always collapsing, making possible new configurations. This 'rediscovery' takes place where the meditation unravels, repudiates itself where the collapse of intelligibility occurs, which both animates the reader's desire for meaning and shows that it can never achieve its ambition. The 'death' of the text and of the narrator signifies 'the unbearable process by which we disappear *despite ourselves* and everything we can do, even though, *at all costs* we *must not* disappear. It is precisely this *despite ourselves*, this *at all costs*, which distinguish the movement of extreme joy and of indescribable but miraculous ecstasy.'[95] The text narrates anguish and the act of transcending it through a form which leads the reader, in her desire to understand, to recapitulate this movement in her reading. In this way, the reader may be exposed to the chance of the transcendence of anguish just where the text disintegrates in unintelligibility. This is the 'underlying truth of eroticism' which the preface says *Madame Edwarda* shows us, here of physical eroticism.

The narrator begins with his experience of anguish, the experience of the desire to possess his self at the moment when its impossibility draws him, tears him away from himself. He is already, therefore, beyond the religious conception of God, of that which would give meaning and unity to his life. Rather, what that conception has been an evasion of now draws him (he has an erection) and the narrative will pass through a series of stages in terms of physical eroticism towards the 'truth', the 'nothing' which brings about the collapse of self (and text). He enters the brothel 'Mirrors'.

1   He is masturbated by Madame Edwarda and obtains an intimation of God: 'I became unhappy and felt painfully forsaken, as one is when in the presence of God.'[96] This would be so both in terms of the religious conception, since the presence of what gives meaning to one's life is an experience of one's nothingness, and in terms of the (future) rediscovery, where 'God' becomes that through which one must lose meaning and selfhood.

2   He has oral sex with Madame Edwarda who presents herself *as* God. She exposes her genitals and, when asked why, she says 'You can see for yourself . . . I'm God.' She commands him to come to her and kneel, whereupon he 'feverishly pressed [his] lips to that running, teeming wound'.[97] It is in terms of the 'wound' that Bataille in a bracketed paragraph a little later speaks of anguish, of the gap in ourselves which prevents our selfhood whilst making it possible as the object of desire: 'he only will grasp me aright whose heart holds a wound that is an incurable wound, who never, for anything, in any way, would be cured of it'.[98] This wound is to disrupt the sense of 'God': Madame Edwarda's declaration 'I'm God' makes no sense in terms of the religious conception.

3   They then ascend to a bedroom and copulate: 'our bursting hearts would strain wide open to welcome "the emptiness of heaven"'.[99] The copulation prefigures in the orgasm the annihilation of self, but the 'emptiness' is still objectified (the 'emptiness of heaven'), as if the experience were of a transcendence rather than an internal collapse. The narrative will now work against this objectifying tendence, obstructing the desire to know.

Madame Edwarda dresses in a hooded cloak and mask and rushes out into the dark street followed by the narrator. She appears to him now in progressively unknowable forms. The mask gives her first the appearance of an animal; she then appears to him as 'something alien' against 'a starry sky, mad and void';[100] and then, under the arch of the Porte Saint-Denis, she appears 'entirely black, simply there, as distressing as an emptiness, a hole'. He knows then 'that She had not lied, that She was God'. He feels 'as if face to face with black rock'. Madame Edwarda as God appears as an emptiness, but nevertheless one which he confronts 'face to face'. He consents, and desires, to suffer 'as far as the "emptiness" itself, even were I to be stricken, destroyed, no matter'. But this is prompted by his desire to know the nothingness which she as God appears to be: 'I knew, I wanted that knowing, for I lusted after her secret and did not for one instant doubt that it was death's kingdom.'[101]

On his finding her again, she asks 'Where am I?' His response shows he conceives her as God, as something to be known: he points to the sky. She strikes him, shouting 'You fake priest. I shit on you' and collapses. He had tried to set up Madame Edwarda as God, as the nothing he can know: he has become a 'fake priest'. The desire for knowledge, for appropriation, produces excreta: there is always something which the appropriation of knowledge, of reason, cannot absorb, which evades thought. And Madame Edwarda as that excess shits on the desire for knowledge which characterizes the narrator's relation to her.

Kneeling by the collapsed form, he is torn apart and experiences 'a power that would be mine upon condition I agree to hate myself'. Experiencing the wound, what had been an externality in Madame Edwarda's genitals, is experiencing the 'vertiginous sliding which was tipping me into ruin' and which opens 'up a prospect of indifference'.[102] Ruination, the annihilation of self, cannot be taken as a goal, as a matter of the self's power, but rather as a happening which takes place, if it does, in powerlessness. Madame Edwarda as the rediscovered 'God', as the excess which annihilates the self through its being drawn into that incurable wound which is our difference from ourselves, both is and isn't the narrator. As what precipitates the ruination of the self, she inhabits that self, and yet is other than the narrator who must appear in the narrative as 'I'. Hence, when she now copulates, straining 'to the final pitch of excess at which the heart fails' she does so with another. The narrator sees 'from her stare, then, at that moment' that 'she was drifting home from the "impossible"'.[103] This 'experience' of the 'impossible' is no one's since there the limits of the self are transgressed. From the position of the self, the first person, this 'experience' is already some other's. The narrator, in speaking of it, feels that his 'distress and fever' seem small things: 'those are the only great things in me which give answer to the rapture of her whom in the depths of an icy silence I called "my heart"'.[104] She is 'my heart' as the 'beloved' who gives the possibility of meaning precisely by preventing it, the wound in the self, the 'nothing' in meaning. In relation to what cannot therefore be presented or thought, the narrator can only feel that his distress and desire are 'small things': they, at least, can be narrated. And there the narration breaks off. We have been led to a point where the 'impossible' has been spoken of, that which cannot be encompassed in language, where the narrative must fail.

There then follows a bracketed paragraph which raises the question of the sense of the narrative. Does it make some kind of sense? Does it have a hidden meaning? Or, if we say it is meaningless, mightn't this be meaningful? The text rather is to lead, through the process of reading, of trying to make sense of it, to a collapse: 'understand it he who is dying and . . . the living self is there just in order . . . "not to know"',[105] a collapse which is that of the meaning of 'God'. 'But as for GOD? GOD, if He knew, would be a swine.' This 'God', that which cannot be appropriated, which represents the continuity of all that is, is less than human, that in which our humanity collapses, a pig rummaging in filth and excrement. At this point, the writer gives up ('how shall I go on with it?') and that is its completion, 'But I am done.'[106] The narrative fails, and in that it (perhaps) succeeds.

Nietzsche objects to the transcendent notion of 'the truth' about the world and life, the product of a 'God's eye view', as useless for us. Rather, we must understand our conception of the world in terms of utility for human purposes and life as the constant creation of art. But for Bataille the pursuit of such purposes is only possible in so far as, at the same time, we are drawn towards the overthrow of purpose. The human condition is paradoxical, drawn towards both good and evil in the sense of summit experience. Yet one may wonder whether Bataille's 'summit experience' does not rather betray the radicality of his insight into that which always evades expression but on which any form of expression, in thought, speech or action, depends. Even if it cannot be taken as a goal and has to be awaited in chance, it nevertheless is still brought within language, characterized as ecstasy, as the violent disruption of self-identity. Bataille speaks of it as an 'experience', and yet what is gestured towards here is, as the very condition of all language and so all experience, what cannot enter language, not even as 'the annihilation of language', or become an experience, even one of self-annihilation. Maurice Blanchot in a discussion of Bataille remarks on this: 'We speak as though this were an experience, and yet we can never say we have undergone it. An experience that is not lived, even less a state of our self . . . The experience of non-experience.'[107] But this should surely indicate that the reference to 'experience' is a false move, one still complicit with what it claims to reject, the totalizing move of intelligibility, of the reign of the possible as what can be comprehended: 'For this act of supreme negation we have just supposed . . . still belongs to the possible.' The 'impossible' which Bataille indicates as the condition of the possible cannot itself be 'experienced': rather, Blanchot will suggest, we must allow our thought to take, in relation to what evades thought, another form, one which relates to what always in a certain sense haunts all thinking, not as a prospective annihilation, the irruption into life of nothingness, of what he terms 'night', but rather as 'the *other* night, false, vain, eternally restless and eternally falling back into its own indifference'. To this 'indifference' of the 'other night' I will now turn, whilst knowing beforehand, of course, that this turn, for Blanchot, can never face its desired direction.

3

MAURICE BLANCHOT
Literature's space

> It may be (and are we not continually having this experience?)
> that the further thought goes toward expressing itself, the more
> it must maintain a reserve somewhere with itself, something like
> a place that would be a kind of uninhabited, uninhabitable non-
> thought, a thought that would not allow itself to be thought. A
> presence–absence with which thought torments itself.[1]

Blanchot's work maintains throughout its concern with this 'uninhabitable non-thought' and the relation of literature to it. Thought pursues 'the one, unity, sameness', it aims at 'a clear and defined coherence of actions and objects, relations and forms – the work of tranquil man'.[2] Thought is the very character of human life, and characterizes the 'speech of the universe, speech of knowledge, of labor and of salvation'.[3] Comprehension is thus 'a grasp that gathers the diverse into a unity, identifies the different, and brings the other back to the same'.[4] The life of the 'tranquil man' is the movement of establishing intelligibility, bringing the world and man himself to concepts and so creating knowledge, control and the purpose of his existence. Language is 'a power according to which when I speak, it is the world that declares itself, the clear light of day that develops though tasks undertaken, through action and time'.[5] When thought reflects on itself, it directs itself to 'the central question', 'the question of the whole'.[6] Directed towards unity, thought is governed by the notion of finality, the end, which gives it the power 'to limit, separate, and thus to grasp'.[7] In this reflection, addressing the 'central question', the 'day' of intelligibility appears in relation to the end, to finality, in which world and man would be brought into the daylight, and so in relation to 'the night', the 'exterior' or beyond of intelligibility. This exterior appears as the 'first night', the 'night of day', the night as end of the day, night understood from the side of day. 'Day makes the night . . . Night speaks only of day . . . Day is linked to night because it would not be day if it did not begin and come to an end.'[8] This night is 'welcoming' for here 'language completes and fulfills itself in the silent profundity which vouches for it as its meaning',[9] making 'of the world the future, the culmination of the world'.[10] Thought, what is said, the realm of language, tends towards finality and only so do we have understanding as determinate, or partial in relation to its fulfilment. There is only intelligibility because there is an end to it, and so a reference to its 'other side'. By the same token, what is thought, spoken of, 'being', what is, is only possible in relation to 'nothingness', the end of being and its 'other'. 'But when everything has disappeared in the night, "everything has disappeared" appears. This is the other night.'[11] For thought thinking the whole, the 'first night' is the 'nothing' which gives sense to illumination, that against which there is illumination, which cannot be illuminated. But in this thought, the 'nothing', the 'everything has disappeared' is itself thought as the necessary other of illumination. Its appearance as the 'other night', its repetition, marks the impossibility for thought to avoid thinking its 'other' which, according to thought's own project, should be beyond, exterior to it. Thought, language, is only possible in relation to its 'other': but this is now shown to be within thought, language, itself. When thought thinks everything has disappeared, then 'everything has disappeared' appears: the words themselves. The 'exterior' of thought, language and the world inhabits them, but for there to be thought, language and world, this must be forgotten. The 'exterior', and so the end of intelligibility in terms of which intelligibility has sense, must appear to the world of day as beyond it. In thinking this, however, it must appear within language. This 'other', this 'exterior', which is interior, is the essential failure of thought and world to be thought and world, to be oriented towards the unity that gives them determinateness. The condition of their possibility, the other, the exterior, is at the same time the condition of their impossibility. This is the 'presence–absence' with which thought torments itself. Thought, directed towards the whole, finds it cannot terminate itself. In its attempt, it passes beyond and so defeats itself. The very nature of thought is such as to defeat its own ambition (which means that there is no nature, essence, of thought, since its ambition is precisely to think the whole and so bring everything, including itself, within determinate limits). The 'other night' is not something beyond thought, as if there were something but thought couldn't think it. It is simply the appearance of what thought thinks when it thinks the whole, the end, the repetition of 'everything has disappeared' so that these words appear in their very resistance to understanding. Thought in thinking the whole defeats itself: that which makes thought possible, the idea of the whole, finality, makes thought impossible since thought cannot thereby avoid thinking the 'other' of the whole. This failure manifests itself in the repetition of what thought thinks, in the mere appearance of the words 'everything has disappeared' where they are deprived of sense. In this 'the very category of the whole – the one borne by the "general question" – is unseated and made to falter. We are here at the juncture where the experience of the whole is shaken.'[12] In thoughts and language aiming at unity, coherence and ultimately at the whole of the 'day', 'one shall always sense an entirely different speech, liberating thought from being always only a thought in view of unity'.[13] Thought, language, is indeed the realm of daylight and cannot be rejected since this work towards unity 'is the task of each one in working and speaking'.[14] But this thought, speech and language is haunted by another speech which repeats to thought 'everything has disappeared' or 'nothingness'. This is the concern of, not the 'central' or 'general' question of the whole, but of the 'ultimate question'. But this is not posed, it is 'the shadow of a question', 'it seems it can be thought and formulated only if we still question even when the whole is thought'.[15] One cannot understand this question, 'one can only repeat it, let it reverberate on a plane where it is not resolved but dissolved, returned to the void from which it arose. This is its solution: it dissipates in the very language that comprehends it.'[16] To comprehend it would be to bring it within the light of day. But it is precisely that in thought which disrupts it, in which 'everything . . . has collapsed in its identity as a thing, and the whole of things has collapsed in the slipping movement that steals them away as a whole'.[17] It is the appearance in thought, in language itself, of the impossibility of that finality and unity which governs them. It 'is repetition that will not leave off, satiety that has nothing, the sparkle of something baseless and without depth'.[18] This baselessness, lack of depth, is what repeats itself endlessly in language and thought, that which in concepts and their references in the world prevents finality, unity, determinateness, the very surface of words. It appears in the necessity in thinking 'day', the light of intelligibility, of thinking 'the first night', the completion, fulfilment and end of thought, and so of not thinking them, for in that 'nothing' they are exceeded.

> [The] speech of dialectics . . . seeks to include the moment of discontinuity: it moves from one term to its opposite, for example, from Being to Nothingness. But what is between the two opposites? A nothingness more essential than Nothingness itself – the void of an interval that continually hollows itself out and in hollowing itself out becomes distended: the nothing as work and movement.[19]

Thought thinks unities and ultimately aspires to the whole. But this is only possible in thinking 'nothingness' and so exceeding the whole. What appears to thought as its end is its internal failure to attain the unities, the whole, it aims at. It is the failure of thought, of language, which makes them possible. What must evade thought is precisely the failure which is the 'between' of the differences thought thinks. Unities of meaning are only as differences: the impossibility of completing the whole so that all differences would be subsumed under the Same is what is indicated in the impossibility of thought thinking its end. But then no difference is final. In the repetition of 'everything has disappeared' the 'between' contained in all thought is indicated but not thought, the 'between' between 'day' and 'night' which makes them both necessary and impossible. But if the end is impossible, then all concepts, unities, beings, must be such only in so far as they are other: they contain within themselves, in being the differences they are, the possibility of being other or of meaning differently. They differ from themselves, fail to stand still, to be the unities we (tranquil people) ordinarily take them to be. This is the 'doubleness of death'.

> That which produces meaning (nothingness as the power to negate, the force of the negative, the end starting from which man is the decision to be without being) is the risk that rejects being – is history, truth. It is death as the extreme of power, as my most proper possibility, but also the death which never comes to me, to which I can never say yes, with which there is no authentic relation possible.[20]

Meaning is produced in relation to its absence, its other, to what cannot be brought within meaning: death. This 'end' is what makes all understanding, interpretation, meaning possible in their (apparent) determinateness. But in this thought, 'death' appears within meaning. There is no end to meaning, we can't get outside it. This is the 'death' no-one dies: it ensures that those who cease to be continue nevertheless. Meaning is produced as determinate, but what makes this possible, the 'other' of meaning, makes it impossible. The other of meaning is within meaning itself, is that which disrupts it. Meaning is possible only through its failure. A word has meaning only in so far as it can mean differently. It 'differs from itself'. This 'nothing', the 'between' which is a 'nothingness more essential than Nothingness itself' is the impossibility of death, the end, 'Nothingness', which is heard in their repetition. For there to be what is, for there to be intelligibility, for there to be day, there must be night: but in that thought, the impossibility of night resounds, the 'other night': 'this outside which appears when even with ourselves, with our death, we no longer have relations of possibility'.[21] It is this absence of finality which thus inhabits self and world, all intelligibility, and thus destabilizes them. This difference from itself which characterizes language and thought is thus productive, making possible historicality, the movement of thought towards a mastery which is always denied. What 'speaks in things, and in words is Difference; secret because always speaking and because always differing from that which signifies it, but also such that everything makes a sign and becomes sign because of it'.[22] This 'other night' 'is empty, it is not; but we dress it up as a kind of being'.[23] We name it. The 'other night is the death no-one dies, the forgetfulness which gets forgotten'.[24] The death no one dies is the impossibility of death, of the end, of finality which is forgotten so that there can be meanings, intelligibility, the light of day of the world in which we live and have our being. The other night is always 'other', always 'outside'. It is inaccessible 'because to have access to it is to accede to the outside . . . to lose forever the possibility of emerging from it'.[25] To think 'it' would be to render present what makes anything present both possible and impossible. We 'hear' this speaking in the simple 'repetition' of anything said, where language ceases to say something definite, but where the power of signification 'speaks' in its very immobility and resistance to understanding. Such language in repetition appears both to have and to lack meaning. This 'speaking' of language has the character of a 'base impersonality'.[26] The impersonal is

> that which prevents, precedes and dissolves the possibility of any personal relation ... the They of which everybody and anybody is part, but who is part of it? Never anyone in particular, never you and I. Nobody is part of the They. 'They' belongs to a region which cannot be brought to light ... because it transforms everything which has access to it ... into anonymous, impersonal being, the Nontrue, the Nonreal yet always there.[27]

The summons of this speech takes place in a 'base eternity', 'which is only time become the loss of time'.[28] Here we can only gesture to a 'time without event, without project and without possibility; a kind of empty perpetuity'[29] which thought cannot grasp. The summons of this speech has always already taken place in any thought, in a 'time' beyond possibility. It can only appear to our thought as the empty perpetuity of the neutral, the incessant murmur which 'speaks' in language when language says nothing. The free human being works to master and understand the world, engaged

> in this enterprise of establishing a secure reign. We untiringly construct the world in order that the hidden dissolution, the universal corruption that governs what 'is' should be forgotten in favour of a clear and defined coherence of notions and objects, relations and forms – the work of tranquil man. A work that nothingness would be unable to infiltrate.[30]

We do this through the activities of work and investigation in which we form the world, bring what is to language where it can be thought, comprehended and mastered. But the difference of meaning from itself marks the infinite dissolution of all such projections: in relation to this, we are powerless, for it is the corruption of our world within which our power can operate. It marks that which at the same time makes language and thought possible and impossible. It is 'impossibility', that which cannot be thought; thought being of the possible, 'neither negation nor affirmation, indicates what in being has always already preceded being and yields to no ontology'.[31] From within the world, alterity which inhabits all meaning and being is what simply cannot be thought, it is nothing, and as such ignored: yet the very trajectory of the world shows a hidden recognition of its necessity. And as part of this trajectory, all words are marked by this alterity, this internal difference: it is what

41

makes possible meaning and the identity of the self whilst at the same time making them impossible.

Literature is language, but language not used to say what is, not used to live in the world. Rather, it is language which is now lifted from the world: so we say it is 'fiction'. Literature is 'to withdraw language from the world, to detach it from what makes it a power according to which, when I speak it, the world ... declares itself, the clear light of day that develops through tasks undertaken, through action and time'.[32] What makes it such a power is 'death' as finality, that which provides us with determinate meaning and being. But that 'death' is rendered impossible by the nature of language itself. The 'other night' is the repetition of the 'first night', 'death', in language itself. In withdrawing language from the world, literature draws us towards the realm of the 'other night' where language becomes appearance. Literature does this because it wishes to come into relation to that alterity, the 'nothingness more essential than Nothingness' which makes meaning, self and world both possible and impossible: 'art is linked ... to what is "outside" the world ... this outside which appears when even with ourselves, even with our death, we no longer have relations of possibility'.[33] But this 'outside' can only appear in language itself: it is the otherness of the world and of meaning, their essential failure which at the same time makes them possible, in relation to which we are rendered powerless. We have no relation to the outside, since we can do nothing in relation to it. It is the 'impossible', the impossibility of the possibility which the world represents for us. Yet art 'wants to be a power even in the region of the ungraspable, where the domain of goals ends'.[34] It is involved in an impossible project.

In 'Literature and the Right to Death' (1949), Blanchot identifies two 'slopes' of literature. In the first, characterized, for example, by Flaubert's novels, literature raises the language of the world from its representing function as if to regard the world from another place. In the second, to which most poetry belongs, literature desires to reveal the 'unknown, free and silent existence of things'.[35] It 'wants the cat as it exists, the pebble taking the side of things, not man, but the pebble, and in this pebble what man rejects by saying it'.[36] It turns here to the materiality of language, giving precedence to everything physical about language: rhythm, weight, mass, shape, the paper, the trail of ink, the book. Language is itself a thing: to present language is to present 'the thing' prior to its being raised to meaning. Literature aspires to be 'the presence of things before the world exists, their perseverance after the world has disappeared, the stubbornness of what remains when everything vanishes and the dumbfoundedness of what appears when nothing exists'.[37] But 'this wish to be a thing, this refusal to mean anything' fails, since this is now what literature shows itself as trying to mean. What appears in the destruction of the meaning of a name allows 'signification in general' to appear in its place, 'what asserts itself now is the very possibility of signifying, the empty power of bestowing meaning'.[38]

Literature thus discovers, by trying to say what is prior to language, that it just re-creates 'day' but now in the form of a fatality, as something it cannot avoid, and in trying to affirm 'night' it only finds it as impossibility. We discover that what is 'prior to the day is still the day, but in the form of an inability to disappear, not a capacity to make something appear . . . what we cannot escape from is day'.[39] The two 'slopes' of literature, one trying to show the nature of the world from a point outside it, the other the nature of things prior to language, both culminate in the same revelation: 'Literature is that experience through which the consciousness discovers its being in its inability to lose consciousness.'[40] We cannot get outside language: yet language is language only in relation to the outside, the other, but in the sense that this alterity is in language, that through which it always differs from itself. A literature which recognizes this fatality emerges with the collapse of metaphysical hopes, with the recognition of the impossibility of finality, of the 'last word' guaranteed by something outside, beyond language.

Here 'Literature is language turning into ambiguity.'[41] Ordinary language may not be clear, but it puts limits on equivocation and misunderstanding: this lack of clarity or misunderstanding is limited to meaning a or b or c, and that is quite definite. But in this literature language itself becomes ambiguous:

> the general meaning of language is unclear: we don't know if it is expressing or representing, if it is a thing or means that thing, if it is there to be forgotten or if it only makes us forget it so that we will see it; if it is transparent because what it says has so little meaning or clear because of the exactness with which it says it, obscure because it says too much, opaque because it says nothing.[42]

And this general ambiguity stems from an 'ultimate ambiguity' which is the ambiguity of language itself, so that the work can take on opposed appearances 'without its style, genre, or subject being accountable for the radical transformations'.[43] Literature presents language outside of its function in representing the world so that words change aspect, speaking to us but saying nothing, in a voice which is the voice of no one, of an impersonality, where what speaks is, as it were, the very power of signification which inhabits words 'before' they say anything. This 'original double meaning, which lies deep in every word' is the source of literature. In literature this double meaning shows itself behind the meaning of its words: and the question this ambiguity poses is 'the question asked by literature'.[44]

In relation to such literature, its very resistance to interpretation invites the question 'Is it literature?' But this question presupposes there is some essentiality to literature, some nature of literature in terms of which these works could be judged. But now 'what seems to be expressed in works is not the eternal verities, not types and characters, but a demand which stands against the order of essences'.[45] What is at issue in such works is 'perhaps literature, but not as an assured, definite reality, an ensemble of forms, nor even a tangible mode of activity'. Rather, one only engages with the 'question' which such works pose by turning away from 'literature', from the notion of literature as a determinate meaning, by 'eluding' literature 'to a point where all that seems to speak is impersonal neutrality'.[46] Such works 'question' and 'put at risk' the 'truth and essence of language',[47] that is, the very notion of 'essence', of 'meaning', which underlies the questions 'Is it literature?' and 'What is literature?' In them, language itself becomes a question, indicating 'that' which makes meanings both possible and impossible through its resistance to the comprehension it at the same time seems to invite. The 'signified can never be taken as being a response to the signifier, as its end' (the 'meaning' of the work cannot be understood as what gives the signifiers their sense), 'but rather as that which indefinitely restores to the signifier its power to give meaning and to constitute a question'.[48] The work thus affirms 'through the strangeness of this relation only the impossible becoming of signification in its infinite – . . . infinitely empty – plurality'.[49] What speaks in the impenetrability of the language of such works is the 'becoming of signification' itself, of difference as movement, an internal collapse.

Literature detaches language from its usual role in which it disappears so that the world can be revealed, it 'disappears behind what is said'.[50] Literature's language is removed from this referential function in which it is spoken or thought by someone about something. It therefore does not say anything, and is not addressed by someone to someone. This means, says Blanchot, 'that language doesn't speak any more, but is',[51] 'the milieu in which the name becomes being, but neither signifies nor reveals'.[52] Here we come into relation to 'a region which cannot be brought to light'.[53] Language presents beings in the world, but disappears behind this function. In literature, language itself becomes being, neither meaning nor meaningless. Art has its origin in relation to the 'outside of the world' or the 'other of all worlds'.[54] But art at the same time shows us the impossibility of any relation with this other, for whenever we turn our gaze, it remains within it.

The 'other of all worlds' is the 'blind spot of thought – this impossibility of thinking that thought is for itself in its reserve',[55] that internal difference in thought which makes it both possible and impossible. In literature, language becomes 'non-speaking speech',[56] the incessant murmur which is 'the secret of language where, outside of all power to represent and to signify, speech would come about as what always differs from itself, and, as difference, holds back'.[57] There 'is' always the other of thought and language, this difference of thought and meaning from themselves, so that there can be thought and language; and hence there can be no relation in thought and language with it. Yet we are compelled, precisely by thought, to 'recognize' it. Thus, any discourse in relation to it must betray it, must fail, so the writer 'devotes all his energy to not writing, so that, writing, he should write out of failure, in failure's intensity'.[58] Such writing can in this way indicate why it fails. Writing is active, continuous, strives for a certain coherence and so towards a certain unity. These are characteristics of what can appear: we can write and read it. But the 'other of all worlds' cannot appear, cannot be thought: it is not, doesn't exist, cannot be said to be continuous, unified, and so on. Yet although it cannot be said to exist, every time we use language, and so always, it 'is' as that thought and speech's other and our own: 'It is that in me which does not coincide with me – my eternal absence, that which no consciousness can grasp, which has neither effect nor efficiency and is passive time.'[59]

The work of literature stands in a certain relation to the alterity of thought and language to themselves. We think of the work of literature, a poem, say, as something we don't need to refer back to its author, or when and where it was written. It appears to be 'absolutely' and not in relation to something else (as a tool is which refers to its work). The 'literary work is neither finished nor unfinished: it is. What it says is exclusively this: that it is – and nothing more'.[60] It 'expresses nothing except the word being: the word which language shelters by hiding it, or causes to appear when language itself disappears into the silent void of the word'.[61] The work of literature resists reference to some 'essence' of literature which would give it its being as a work of literature and which would govern its interpretation. It appears to simply say itself, but without our being able to say what this is. To say the work merely 'is' means that it withdraws from us our power over it, to interpret it; it 'makes us weak and as if annihilated'. In relation to the work we are powerless: we can't do anything with it. But this isn't because of the superior strength of the work, but rather because 'It has no power, it is impotent' for 'it designates a region where impossibility is no longer deprivation, but affirmation'.[62] That is, it indicates the region of the other in thought, language, ourselves with which we can have no relation and therefore no power over or under: it is the impossible. The poem seems to escape comprehension, to even remove from us the power of speech itself: it seems 'the silent repose of a closed thing'. And it does so because it 'is eminently what it is made of', language, but not referring to anything, not in a representing relation to the world. Words here 'begin to become their appearance, and the elemental depth upon which this appearance is opened while at the same time it closes'.[63] Words become deprived of determinate sense, become their appearance as words and so indicate the power of signification prior to any determinate meaning.

Poetry does not say the 'other of all worlds' but 'simply answers to it, saying in responding'.[64] It does so in its form of existence rather than in terms of 'content' or 'form': 'It is poetry's existence . . . that in itself forms a response and, in this response, attends to what is addressed to us in impossibility (by turning itself away).'[65] The other in language and thought is 'foreign to every identity, unity, presence'[66] which are the characteristics of what can be thought. The poem resists these in resisting both comprehension and being put into relation with other things: it is 'made to disappoint all identity and to deceive comprehension as a power of identification'. The poem thus lacks identity.[67] Literary language seems to be characterizable in the negative terms which are the only ones we can use to indicate the other in speech and thought.

1   It appears to be always speaking but never saying anything, just as the other in language is both unspeakable and yet necessary for speech: it is 'a spoken word which cannot be interrupted because it does not speak; it is'.[68] The poet has heard the 'interminable and incessant' and 'rendered it perceptible', that incessant murmuring which is the speaking of language when language says nothing, the speech of the other.

2   Literary language is characterized by discontinuity and so cannot be made into a coherent whole: we have no centre in terms of which we could organize its unity. It resists interpretation in terms of some 'essence' of literature since it puts the notion of 'essence' in question. The other is pure difference, it is that which disrupts every unity.

3   The time of our conscious lives is one of a present with the future and past as horizons, so that the content of the present will be past in the future. But the other in language and thought is never present: it always already has been, it never is or will be. Literary narration stands in a relation to this time of the other. It is not an account of an event: it is the event which takes place solely through language. It narrates something (Captain Ahab's pursuit of Moby Dick, for instance) which takes place 'in' time: we can refer to when it began, what takes place on the journey, how it ends. But this 'taking place' happens only in language itself, so that Ahab is always journeying towards Moby Dick, has always met him, is always about to start. This lifting of language from its application to the world, and so to events in time, indicates the 'time' of the other. We speak language, use it in time: but the other never 'is' but has always 'been' when language is, just as the narrative never 'is' but has always already been: the strange character of something written which has the sort of existence ('absoluteness', not having an essential relation to other things for it to be what it is) which a literary work has. We cannot bring to language the other in language: literature allows language to present itself independently of its work in revealing the world and so 'points' to its difference from itself (although it doesn't show it, since what can be shown appears, and in appearance this 'difference' has always already been). The fictional narrative never begins and ends; it does not take place 'in' time. The story is written by someone at some time, but this is not the time of the beginning of the narration. That beginning is purely in language itself, and that beginning is never in time.

It is always beginning, always ending and always in between. The literary narration becomes a 'simulacrum' of the other time, 'a time peculiar to narration . . . where, in an imaginary simultaneity and as the space art tries to represent, different temporal ecstasies coincide'.[69]

4   Again, the other which speaks in the opacity of language is not the 'I' of the self for whom there is a world within which others (you, he, she, they) can be encountered. Yet it is necessary for there to be the I and so the others: it is the difference within the self, within the other person which makes their being both possible and impossible. What 'speaks' in language's difference from itself is 'base impersonality', the other in the person. Similarly, the voice that tells the story is neither you nor I nor he nor she. Even if the narrator has a name, the words are those of a fictional character: the voice of the 'writer' is anonymous, the speech of no one, and always addressed to someone else. It is a simulacrum of the other voice which always lies within our own. And when we read, it appears to be addressed to someone other than me, 'always awakening another person in the person who hears it',[70] speaking as if to my own difference from myself. Hence our relation to literature is not cognitive or one of knowing. It is rather 'fascination', for what fascinates us 'robs us of our power to give sense'.[71] In relation to the literary work, I am powerless to grasp its 'meaning' for its 'meaning' is precisely to disable sense.

In the past, works have served art by serving other values.[72] Western culture has been formed in terms of metaphysical values, in terms of the value of finality, however concretely understood. In works, these values were spoken, but thereby the very materiality of the work undermines the values it ostensibly promulgates. For the Greeks, the work bespoke the divine in so far as this is beyond thought and language. But the work marks the 'beyond' of the divine only in language, in the forms of man, so a work becomes statue rather than Zeus and contributes to the overthrow of the gods in the name of man's affirmation of himself, of his 'reasoned accomplishment of purposeful activity'.[73] Then the work speaks of this affirmation, but in a form where language is lifted from its world-revealing function and appears opaque. 'In the work man speaks, but the work gives voice in man to what does not speak: to the unnameable, the inhuman, to what is devoid of truth . . . Here a man does not recognize himself.'[74] This too contributes to the undermining of the metaphysical values of the ends of humanity. With the 'death of God', the works speak of disinheritance and despair and thereby show an attachment to values which at the same time are seen as impossible. But now 'what is left for the work to say? What has always eluded its language? Itself.'[75] Literature now can become the language 'no one speaks, which is addressed to no one, which had no center, and which reveals nothing',[76] rather than hiding this behind the speaking of metaphysical values or despair at their absence. Here 'language doesn't speak anymore, but is'.[77] Literature can now become explicitly the appearance of language within which the 'other' in language reverberates. 'Today the work has no faith other than itself. And this faith is absolute passion for that which depends upon the work alone to give it life.'[78]

There is no end to day (significance) and so no beginning either. We make sense by evoking a finality (that we are distinct beings and what we mean is clearly delimited) that this evocation prevents. Finality implies exteriority, what is beyond the end: but that is already within language, within signification. Day has no end: but then this utterance defeats itself, since day only has sense in relation to night, to its end. The 'exterior', the 'other' is *in* language but as *failure* of sense, as the necessary failure of sense which is sense's very possibility. We only make sense, and so we and the sense we make *are*, only in so far as we and our sense fail to coincide with themselves, fail to attain unity. Where there is such failure, 'There are no longer words, but the being of words'[79] and no longer someone who speaks, but only the 'immense faceless someone'.[80]

Our active making sense of our lives and world aims at coherence, and so takes place according to rules and in relation to a certain unity. It takes place in a time where the present of the self and its meaning is related to a future of our projected ends which gives sense to the past. In literature, this activity and its coherence of rules, unity and temporality, is transformed into a failure which shows itself to be at the same time necessary to them. In the light (if it is such) of this, we may look at Blanchot's *The Madness of the Day*.[81] It is a 'story' (*récit*) 'about' the impossibility of stories; it is an impossible story.

The *récit* begins in the present, expressing 'the remarkable truth, and I am sure of it: I experience boundless pleasure in living, and I will take boundless satisfaction in dying'.[82] The term 'boundless' (*sans limites*) renders this thought paradoxical, however, since the 'I' and its satisfaction can only be as limited. To think means to do so in terms of limits, and therefore in relation to the beyond of thought, to the exterior. But this thought of thought turns upon itself, the exterior appearing (as here) within language as its failure. This 'movement' is repeated in this sentence of the *récit*. 'I see the world – what extraordinary happiness! I see this day, and outside it there is nothing. Who could take that away from me?'[83] But here the 'outside' appears in language and so within the 'day'. The thought is taken away in its very expression (and the 'who' that does this is the impersonal they of the incessant speech that says nothing). 'Whatever ceases to be continues to be, . . . whatever dies encounters only the possibility of dying, whatever seeks to attain the beyond is always still there.'[84]

The 'story', which takes place in the past tense, seems to offer a series of stages towards this 'understanding'. The narrator's 'trials'[85] are an 'experience' of the inability to die: 'I was not able to walk, or breathe, or eat. My breath was made of stone, my body of water, and yet I was dying of thirst.'[86] Buried in the ground, he nevertheless arises: 'when I got up I could feel nothing'. He becomes a skeleton. 'At night my thinness would rise up before me to terrify me.'[87] In the night which is necessary for day to be day, he is still there, it is still 'day'. He comes out of this encounter with the impossibility of death 'with the strength of maturity'. 'I lived on, did not fall into nothingness.'[88]

He now has a 'vision', a brief scene in which a woman with a baby carriage passes through a door whilst a man passes in, but moves back and out again. This seems perhaps an 'image' of the paradoxicality of the 'day', the crossing into the dark from outside light which is always at the same time the reverse movement. In this vision, it appears he is on the point of *grasping* this impossible movement. 'I was sure of it, that I had seized the moment when the day, having stumbled against a real event, would begin hurrying to its end. Here it comes, I said to myself, the end is coming, something is happening, the end is beginning. I was seized by joy.'[89]

But then glass is crushed into his eyes: 'I could not look, but I could not help looking.' The glass removed, a thin film is put under his eyelids. Although asleep, he experiences 'the light of seven days' (the light of creation, perhaps), so that even when he ceases, the light continues. 'In the end, I grew convinced that I was face to face with the madness of the day. That was the truth: the light was going mad, the brightness had lost all reason.'[90] The light of intelligibility is only in so far as it fails: this defies reason. But this makes it impossible to come 'face to face with the madness of the day'.

After this, he is unable to read or write (which depend on a relation to finality, the end of the day) and is 'surrounded by a misty North' in which there is neither light nor dark. Yet this only makes him want 'to see something in full daylight . . . if seeing would infect me with madness, I madly wanted that madness'.[91] This desire, for seeing what evades thought, is removed by a sense of powerlessness: 'Reading tired me no less than speaking, and the slightest true speech I uttered required some kind of strength that I did not have.'[92] At the heart of interpretation, and so of the interpreter, is a failure in relation to which the interpreter is powerless. He sinks into destitution, poverty.

The doctors of the institution where he works, the men of knowledge, claim everything: 'Everything here belongs to us.'[93] He is given them to know, to bring fully into the light. 'In haste, I would rid myself of myself. I distributed my blood, my innermost being among them, lent them the universe, gave them the day.'[94] But in giving the 'whole of me', there is the 'nothing' which makes it possible (and impossible): 'when at last nothing was present but my perfect nothingness and there was nothing more to see, they ceased to see me too'. This offends the drive to know, that at its heart lies an impossibility: 'Very irritated, they stood up and cried out, "All right, where are you? Where are you hiding? Hiding is forbidden, it is an offense," etc.'[95] It is forbidden: nothing can escape the reach of knowledge, of day. But that can be read two ways. The failure at the heart of day, the 'other' side of day, is 'the silhouette of the law' which he sees 'Behind their backs'. This law is not the law which says 'hiding is forbidden'. It is the law of the 'other'. It credits him with all powers: but just in that, it renders him powerless. Its recognition of his right to be everywhere 'meant I had no place anywhere. When she [the law] set me above the authorities, it meant, You are not authorized to do anything.'[96] The law of the other both makes possible and impossible the law of the Same, the law which lays down limits and so forbids. It is the law which can never appear (and so not here or in *The Madness of the Day*).

He is asked who threw glass in his face. This 'was the crossroads to which all paths led', the key to the interpretation of the story. He is silent, dumb. Yet he too must join the search (the question torments thought). 'Who was being questioned? Who was answering? One became the other. The words spoke by themselves. The silence entered them.'[97] In this silence, words become their 'being', become the murmuring which says nothing. He is asked ' "just exactly" what happened. A story? I began' and the beginning of *The Madness of the Day* repeats itself so creating an impossible temporality: what was before is now, what is to come has already been. The beginning is at the same time the end which is the beginning, endlessly, like a filmed loop. ' "That was the beginning", they said. "Now get down to the facts." How so? The story was over. I had to acknowledge that I was not capable of forming a story out of these events. I had lost the sense of the story . . . A story? No. No stories, never again.'[98] Never. Again. There is only day: yet there is day only if there is night. We cannot stop telling stories (interpreting, producing meaning) yet each is meant to stop (to be the interpretation, the meaning, or on the way to it). The exterior, the other side of the story, is within, inside it in its repetition, in the sound of its words, their resistance, the murmuring which says nothing in relation to which we will once again begin the story.

It may appear that Blanchot's *récit* is betrayed by my commentary which attempts, impossibly, to bring the 'other' of thought and language into language itself. A writing which does not try to thematize this alterity may, in its very resistance, seem a more appropriate form. Yet we can't give up commentary: like all thought, its failure is integral to it. But in recognizing this failure, aren't we, just as much as in commentary, bringing this alterity to light? Blanchot objects to Bataille's 'experience' as remaining within the conceptuality of consciousness and light. But do we avoid this by asserting the impenetrability of language which makes conceptuality possible, or in writing in another form which invites a commentary within which such assertion is unavoidable? These are questions too which arise in connection with Derrida's works, and which raise issues Rorty will take up in his characterization of the 'ironist theorist' and his suspicion that such a theorist remains in fundamental complicity with the metaphysician they try to displace. Whether Rorty's response to this suspicion is adequate to free him of such a charge, however, remains itself a question.

4

JACQUES DERRIDA

The staging of deconstruction

Metaphysics tries to put a stop to sceptical questioning, to show why it is (really) unintelligible. It wants, therefore, access to something which would be able to stand in judgement over our forms of thought and life. Derrida calls such a ground a 'transcendental signified' and it occupies a paradoxical position in metaphysical thought. Its role demands that it should be able to judge human thought, even that of philosophers, and so it must be, in a sense, beyond, transcendent, to thought. On the other hand, to play its role, it must be thought, brought within the human thinking it is to be judge of, which immediately creates the possibility for it to be questioned. Metaphysics, against its intentions, unfolds as a history. Its ambition is to put a stop to fundamental questioning, to bring thought to its final truth, and in that sense either to show the historical appearance of metaphysics to be accidental, since reality is what it is independently of history, or to bring history to its end by appropriating, as Hegel does, this history as the unfolding of truth which has now reached its *telos*. What makes this history possible, however, is what makes the metaphysical ambition an illusion, and we come to see this when the linguistic character of human thought and life forces itself on philosophical attention.

The metaphysical ambition aims at a situation where we should be able to determine that certain forms of thought, and life embodying them, are in accordance with the way things are, as opposed to the ways they appear to us to be. The expression of this ambition, therefore, involves the use of distinctions, between reality and appearance, truth and error, knowledge and opinion, and so forth. The former notions are, metaphysically understood, concepts of what Derrida calls 'presence'. Reality here is the way things are, uncontaminated by any vestige of appearance, truth is its fullness without taint of error, and knowledge is complete grasp of the truth. These are notions of completion, of a 'full presence'. In this way, the metaphysical distinctions between reality and appearance, truth and error, knowledge and opinion involve the primacy of one term over the other. The secondary terms are dependent for their sense on the primary ones, as the notion of appearance seems dependent on that of reality, that of error on that of truth, and

51

the notion of opinion on that of knowledge. The primary terms in this way seem 'absolute', giving meaning to other terms but having an independence of sense themselves. It is this which makes possible the thought of 'reality as it is in itself', and the attendant notions of 'truth' and 'knowledge'.

Now, this train of thought takes place in language. But reflection about the nature of language shows that these notions of 'full presence' are unintelligible. Such reflection necessarily involves the distinction, which must therefore be presupposed by those used in the articulation of the metaphysical project, between the notion of a 'concept' or 'signified' and its 'signifier', the words or other perceptible medium through which the concept is conveyed. It might appear that the signifier is what it is only in relation to the signified and so is the dependent, secondary notion. The words 'table' and 'bord', for example, both indicate the same concept, the former in English, the latter in Norwegian, and are the words they are only through that relation. But when we try to say what is involved in the concept, we can only produce more words. The 'signified' is itself a signifier, in a particular relation to other signifiers. But then, if the identity of the signifier is given by its relation to a meaning, and if 'meaning' is simply another signifier or set of signifiers, then the signifier is what it is only in relation to other signifiers. If there is, however, nothing outside such relations which can determine the 'meaning' of any signifier, then meaning is always relational without there being a way of terminating the relations into which a signifier may enter meaningfully. (Hence the unintelligibility of the absolute notions of metaphysics which need a non-relational sense and one which can ground the notions of other forms of thought and life.) But then there is no way of determining the identity of any signifier and so we cannot speak either of them or of their relations. This thought is paradoxical. The condition of possibility of a *meaning* (namely, difference, its relation to its others) is at the same time the condition of the impossibility of *a* meaning (a distinct concept and its others). Concepts as we ordinarily understand them in their distinctions are the effects of a stabilization of a more general 'process' which, as the very production of meaning itself, can only be formulated in paradoxical fashion in terms of concepts themselves. These paradoxes indicate that any apparent meaning, reality, self, any seeming determined identity, is an effect of the repression of their essential relationality which, therefore, renders it impossible to speak of 'them' or their 'essence' or indeed their relations. This repression of the 'other' in the 'same' is shown when the dependence of the latter on predicates essential to the former is demonstrated. But this demonstration at once ruins both the notion of the 'same' and the notion of the 'other'. The paradoxes which emerge are the only way of addressing what cannot be addressed since it cannot be made an object of thought and so conceived. 'It' manifests itself only in the destabilization of the terms concerned, in rendering them 'undecidable'. This means, not that we can dispense with the notions of meaning, reality or the self, but rather that there is always more meaning, reality or self than could be thought. This excess is neither meaning, nor reality nor self, but is the 'absolutely other', the division in themselves of any manifest meaning, reality, self or other identity (their being subject to the logic of the 'other' in the 'same') which renders them unstable and so capable of another stabilization. Any identity is constituted only in its difference, its relation to its others, about which one can say the same thing. But then if identity is essentially relational, there is no identity and no relation. Difference is what makes (effects of) identity possible only by making identity impossible. Any apparent identity is thus divided in itself and only through this internal difference can the identity appear. This necessary internal difference which makes any identity possible at the same time makes it impossible: this is the burden of deconstructive thinking.

A sign which could only be used once would not be a sign: a word must be repeatable, 'iterable' is Derrida's preferred term. The reason for this preference lies in the difficulties of saying what 'repetition' might mean here. Repetition would be of the same term: but what gives it its identity so that we may speak of repeating the same term? Not a meaning over and beyond the use of signs. But if the sign only has its 'identity' relationally in a situation where these relations cannot be determined in principle, then it has no 'essence' in terms of which its identity could be established. But if this is so it cannot be 'repeated' in that sense. 'It' is 'iterable' only as entering into constantly different contexts and so meaning differently, whilst these contexts cannot be delimited. But then this openness to change, to becoming other, is what makes possible any occurrence of a term or any meaningful item, and so makes possible the 'first' occurrence which is to be 'repeated'. Such an item is never purely itself: it can be said to 'be' only by being 'divided' in itself, inhabited by otherness. Its 'sameness', its 'identity', is contaminated by 'difference'. This situation occasions the constant refrain of Derrida's thought. The conditions of possibility of any (apparent) identity are at the same time conditions of its impossibility. The meaningfulness of a sign or utterance is possible only if it can be repeated, put into other contexts, and so mean 'otherwise', differently. '*Différance* produces what it forbids, makes possible the very thing it makes impossible' as he famously remarks in *Of Grammatology*.[1] By '*différance*' Derrida is indicating the 'other in the same' which makes the same, any identity or meaning, possible, whilst at the same time making it impossible in the usual sense. For a sign to have meaning it must be capable of repetition and so meaning differently: but this destroys the identity of the terms 'sign' and 'meaning'. This doesn't make sense. 'Identity' is made possible by difference, by otherness, which thus makes impossible 'identity' as we normally think of it. 'It'. What?

For example. This text I am writing, if it is to be a text and so meaningful, must be readable, and so repeatable. But in the repetition it is other than it 'was': the commentary of the repetition, including my own reading as I go along, is necessarily other than what it commentates on. But it is just this possibility of reading which gives to the text its identity as text: but that is to say at the same time that it lacks identity. It is in relation to the otherness of the commentary that there is the 'sameness' of the text. The text has identity, is 'this text' only if at the same time it can be read differently. But the same thing goes for the reading itself: it 'is' what it is only if 'it' can become different in a reading of the reading. Endlessly. The text, we might say, is always 'open'. Its meaning is never present, finished, complete, but is always on the way, deferred. But 'deferred' not in the sense that it could be present but isn't, but rather in the sense that any meaning must contain the possibility of being 'other' and so isn't a full, final meaning.

Anything meaningful is inhabited by 'otherness', an openness which prevents full meaning, pure identity. Meaning is made possible by what makes it (as determinate) impossible. There is no meaning as such (and so no pure identity) of Kant's *First Critique*: its meaning lies in its readability, its possibility of repetition in which commentary will differentiate itself from the text. Commentary, interpretation, repetition is an 'ontological' necessity of the being of the text which prevents it from being *the* text. But this then applies equally to the reading itself.

This alterity, otherness, which inhabits anything meaningful cannot be thematized, addressed or grasped since it is what makes possible, and impossible, any theme, address or grasp. Rather, this other in the same, this *différance*, is nothing beyond particular 'meaningful items' and their possibility of iteration, interpretation. Addressing this is always a matter of attending to particular cases, for example the reading of particular texts in such a way that one shows that the reading which the text invites or proposes depends on features or aspects of the text which at the same time make that reading impossible. In this process, certain terms will take on a situated meaning, in that context of 'deconstructive' activity, which can mark the otherness of the text. Supplement, *différance*, iterability, trace – all are terms which take on this role in certain contexts. But they are not concepts, since we are attempting, and necessarily failing, to speak of what makes what we call concepts both possible, as effects, and impossible, as full meanings – let us say, their dependence on context for their sense but where context cannot be made determinate.

The impossibility of thematizing, grasping alterity means that it is beyond the possibilities of control. We produce meaning and intelligibility only in response to alterity which thus contaminates meaning with a radical contingency. Meaning happens, but in a way beyond the opposition between necessity and contingency in the usual sense, since this 'happening' is of what may appear necessary, relations of meaning, upon contrast with which the notion of contingency depends.

We see here the characteristic paradoxicality forced on our expression in relation to the 'other in the same'. Reflection drives us to speak of the condition of speech, of meaning. As soon as we try to do this we produce sentences which offend against the logic of identity precisely because what we are attempting is to articulate the condition of identity which is at the same time the condition of its impossibility. A 'translation' occurs, we might say, from sentences using the logic of identity to ones using that of differance. But the latter can only employ the words of the former since we have no others and a wilful attempt to replace them would inevitably simply repeat them in other words. But in using the former words we necessarily produce paradox. So 'The word is constituted by a signifier in its relation to a signified (concept)' becomes 'The trace is a trace of a trace, and so on'; 'A thing is what it is and not another thing' becomes 'A thing is what it is only by being other than it is'; 'Not both p and not-p' becomes 'p if and only if not-p'. All these second sentences are, of course, nonsensical. We are driven to them, however, because reflection, in terms of the logic of identity, forces us to realize that *meaning does not make sense*: rather, its not making sense is the condition of the sense it has.

The formulations which our reflection on alterity drive us to are, then, paradoxical. Let us continue with some more which will help, as it were, plot out the space of alterity, the space (or non-space) which, as we shall see, the literary may be said to 'occupy'.

1   We produce meaning only in relation to alterity and the alterity of particular meaningful items. And this means that there is only interpretation, readings of interpretations, without the possibility of reference to an 'original' text. And every interpretation is itself inhabited by alterity, the possibility of further interpretation. The 'other-in-the-same', *différance*, the difference from itself which inhabits any meaningful item is thus prior to identity, to conceptuality, to meaning. But this priority is not temporal, which qualifies items of reference, nor logical, which qualifies the relation between meaningful items. This priority refers to a time which never was nor will be.

2   Alterity is 'singular'. It is not a 'general feature' since it makes possible and impossible any generality and any feature. Nor is it singular as opposed to general, a singularity which could then be found elsewhere. The other is the other in *this*: it is nothing apart from the dependence of 'this' on its others which means that 'it' never manages to be 'this' and so is open to further interpretations which cannot be controlled or foreseen. It is singularity as the openness to interpretation of this item – which indicates, of course, that we cannot do without the language of identity, meaning and so on for our recognition of alterity.

3   We are ourselves inhabited by this otherness in order that we should be able to be the selves we are. The proper name and the first-person pronoun through which we mark our identity means that our identity is meaningful, bound up with language, and so involved in endless interpretability which precludes identity in the pure sense.

4   Our relation to any meaningful item (reading, interpreting, recognizing, and so on) involves a relation to what cannot appear, the otherness which makes appearance possible. We are 'already', in that time neither temporal nor logical, addressed, but not by anything, in a 'come, *viens!*', and at the same time we have already indicated that we stand to be addressed, a 'yes' to the possibility of address. That is, when I speak or think, I do so in language, and so in relation to what has been said and thought. This is only possible if I have already said, as it were, 'yes' to the gift of language. This 'yes' which Derrida, in a paper on Joyce's *Ulysses*, calls the telephonic 'yes' as when you pick up the receiver indicating your readiness to respond, is itself a response to the address of the otherness of what has been said. And the response to that address is to ask it to say 'yes', to respond to my responsiveness. All this has, as it were, 'gone on' in a time before time, for only then is there the time of particular responses to what I then count as past. And our 'yes', the telephonic 'yes', is itself divided, not unified and single. For there is no ongoing engagement with the other, but only endless repetition, since what I come to think or say will itself be inhabited by an otherness whose address I shall have to have already responded to in thinking again – and so on.

5   Such a relation to alterity, being to the interpretability of something, is, as we have seen, an exposure to chance. The meaningfulness of anything cannot be controlled since it is subject to contexts which are unforeseeable. So a relation to a text which recognized this would open it to chance, to the possibility, beyond our control, of new meaningful configurations emerging, and would do so in such a way that this response itself was open explicitly, as it were, to the possibility of new interpretation. Reading and interpretation in the usual sense, governed by the metaphysics of presence, tries to close down the text, to determine what it really means and its truth (as I am doing, of course, in relation to Derrida's texts). Reading in the 'other' sense, however, is a response to the alterity of the text which tries to preserve it. The text in its 'singularity' which Derrida calls its *signature*, that is, the otherness in itself which is ungeneralizable, needs 'counter-signing'. Reading as counter-signing means that 'Reading must *give itself* up to this uniqueness, take it on board . . . *take account* of it. But . . . for this rendering, you have to sign in your own turn, write something else which *responds* or *corresponds*, in an equally singular, which is to say irreducible, irreplaceable, "new" way: neither imitation, reproduction, nor metalanguage.'[2]

6   This structure, impossible to formulate in a coherent manner, is found in connection with anything and everything which can be spoken, written, thought: 'there is nothing outside the text'. Commenting on this in the 'Afterword' to *Limited Inc.*[3] Derrida says that it 'does not mean that all referents are suspended, denied, or enclosed in a book, as people have claimed . . . But it does mean that every referent, all reality has the

structure of a differential trace, and that one cannot refer to this "real" except in an interpretive experience.' All reality, anything which can be addressed in thought, speech and writing, has the paradoxical structure we have been 'addressing'. Identity is only possible as repeatability and so as the possibility of difference so that something is only 'the same' in so far as it is 'already' different. And the same goes for any interpretation, repetition, itself, endlessly. All reference to reality is therefore an interpretation, a relation to otherness which thus removes meaning from our control. In order that we should mean anything we must not know what we mean, and nor does anyone else. Derrida calls this structure of the 'differential trace' 'writing' or 'arche-writing': reality and ourselves have this structure of being as endlessly interpretable.

Understood in terms of the metaphysics of presence, the literary work is a unified text which has a meaning. It is the task of interpretation to bring out this meaning, whether this is understood in terms of literary critical interpretation, Marxist or psychoanalytical explanation, or whatever. At the same time, the text has a singularity which sets it off from other kinds of text: there can be many Spanish grammars but only one *Don Quixote*. In bringing out the meaning, literary interpretation must account too for this singularity, by remarking, for example, on the originality of the author's use of conventions, language, metres, and so forth. What interests Derrida is the way some texts called literary resist approaches of this kind and so put in question the terms they use: form, content, mimesis, meaning, interpretation, genre, and so on, all the various tools through which the 'meaning' of the text is to be exhausted. They are works which, Derrida says, put to work the questions 'What is literature? Where does it come from? What shall we do with it?' and they do this in a singular way. 'These texts operate a sort of turning back, they are themselves a sort of turning back on the literary institution'.[4] In putting the notion of literature in question, they do the same for the notions central to the metaphysics of presence in terms of which literature has been understood: meaning, truth, reality, the self, language, and so on. These forms of writing announce that there is no 'essence' of literature, no answer to the question 'What is literature?' in the sense that, first, literature is a form of writing whose concern is with the unthematizable precondition of the possibility and impossibility of 'concepts' or 'essences', and second, that this concern is always worked out singularly: 'every literary text plays and negotiates the suspension of referential naivety, of *thetic* referentiality (not reference or the intentional relation in general), each text does so differently, singularly . . . there is no essence of literature – that is, self-identity of the literary thing'.[5]

Language is 'a given . . . a system that is necessarily there before us, that we receive out of a fundamental passivity'.[6] But the gift of language, as we have seen, makes meanings and thoughts possible only to the extent that it renders them (as determinate meanings and thoughts) impossible. 'Language gives us to think but it also steals spirits away from us, whispers to us, and withdraws the responsibility that it seems to inaugurate; it carries off the property of our own thoughts even before we have appropriated them.'[7] This 'gift' stands, then, in essential relation to the 'exchange' of meanings, of thoughts, which constitutes communication and thought in language. But in so far as we think this relation, make it comprehensible, our thought depends itself on the concepts of 'gift' and 'exchange'. Yet as concepts (identifiable meanings) they are subject to deconstruction. If the gift is taken as the primary term (as language is given within which there is the exchange of meanings and thoughts) then it excludes exchange. But in so far as the notion of gift itself depends on that of exchange, it can be shown that exchange is necessarily involved in this notion of gift: there is 'some exchange' in the gift. Thus, Derrida argues that the notion of the gift involves ' "someone" giving "something" to "someone other" '. If the other gives me back or owes me or must give back what I give him, there is no gift. But then if the other recognizes it is a gift, if the gift appears as such, then this simple recognition annuls the gift since 'it gives back, in the place . . . of the thing itself, a symbolic equivalent'.[8] Similarly, if the donor sees it or knows it, he begins to pay himself with such an equivalent too, he begins to praise, to approve of, himself. Thus, 'The simple identification . . . of an identifiable thing among some identifiable "ones" would be nothing other than the process of the destruction of the gift . . . At the limit *the gift as gift ought not appear as gift: either to the donee or to the donor.*'[9] Hence, the revelation of the other (exchange) in the same (the gift) destabilizes both concepts, rendering them 'undecidable'. 'The truth of the gift', that is, its appearing or being as such, 'is equivalent to the non-gift or to the non-truth of the gift. This proposition obviously defies commonsense.'[10] 'Gift' and 'exchange' must be rethought beyond the sphere of presence within which we can have apparent distinct concepts. The gift would then rather involve forgetfulness, non-appearance, non-phenomenality, non-perception, non-keeping.[11] We cannot think this in the sense of making it present – a 'theory of the gift' is 'powerless'.[12] Rather, this deconstruction of the gift in its application to the 'gift' of language appears only as a necessary destabilization of manifest meanings and thoughts that language makes possible. The 'economy' of exchange of meanings must be shown to disrupt itself: the gift as event 'must interrupt the continuum of a narrative that nevertheless they call for'.[13] It opens the narrative, the text, in disrupting its apparent sense, and in this way makes possible 'aleatory events', giving 'exchange' its 'chance': it opens the manifest meanings to the generation of new meaning which is beyond our foresight or control.

Baudelaire's short story 'Counterfeit Money' stages this deconstruction of meanings made possible and impossible in the 'gift' of language. In the story, the narrator and his friend leave a tobacconist having purchased some tobacco. The friend scrutinizes a two-franc piece he has received in his change. Outside, they encounter a beggar to whom they both give, but the friend more than the narrator, who then says 'You are right; next to the pleasure of feeling surprise, there is none greater than to cause a surprise.' (The text is given in the endpapers to *Counterfeit Money*.) But the friend replies calmly that it was the counterfeit coin he had given to the beggar, 'as though to justify himself for his prodigality'. It then occurs to the narrator that such conduct was excusable only 'by the desire to create an event in this poor devil's life, perhaps to learn the varied consequences, disastrous or otherwise, that a counterfeit coin in the hands of a beggar might engender'. It might lead him to prison if he were accused of passing counterfeit money, or it might accumulate wealth for 'a poor little speculator'. The friend, how-ever, interrupts this reverie by saying, 'Yes, you are right; there is no sweeter pleasure than to surprise a man by giving him more than he hopes for.' The narrator sees he is candid. 'I then saw clearly that his aim had been to do a good deed while at the same time making a good deal; to earn forty cents and the heart of God, to win paradise economically; in short to pick up gratis the certificate of a charitable man.' The narrator could almost forgive him for the 'criminal enjoyment' he had previously assumed motivated his deed. But he cannot forgive 'the ineptitude of his calculation. To be mean is never excusable, but there is some merit in knowing that one is; the most irreparable of vices is to do evil out of stupidity.'

Baudelaire's story, according to Derrida, stages the formation of meaning (its readability) only through its impossibility (of communicating a determinate, final meaning) and in this way shows the 'gift' that is language. In having meaning only through the impossibility of a unitary sense, Baudelaire's text is 'delivered . . . up to a dissemination without return'. I will briefly consider this in relation to the frames of the narrative and the central critical issue in the narrative itself.

The question of the identity of the text, of what we are addressing or talking about, is, Derrida claims, undecidable. It might be thought that this identity was sufficiently demarcated by the frames of the text, its title and dedication, yet both can be shown to render that identity essentially prob-lematic. The title, 'Counterfeit Money', immediately refers to two things: what is called 'counterfeit money', on the one hand, and the text. This div-ision then produces others. The 'thing' called 'counterfeit money' is 'a sign whose signified seems . . . not to correspond or be equivalent to anything, a fictive sign without *secure* signification'.[14] It is a fiction. The text is a narrative that presents itself, in the narrator's voice, as non-fictive, whilst being really fictive, since Baudelaire is not the narrator. So the text is counterfeit money, fiction passing as non-fiction. Yet, of course, we are in no way deceived by this since this is the character of a literary text in the first person. But further, the narrative's subject is fictive money, so it is a fiction of fiction. In this way, everything that can be said in the narrative about counterfeit money can be said of the narrative itself. 'Everything that will be said *in* the story, *of* counterfeit money (and in the story of counterfeit money) can be said of the story, of the fictive text bearing this title . . . It is as if the title were the very text whose narrative would finally be but the gloss . . . on the counterfeit money of the title.'[15] Which is the text (that is, the one requiring commentary)? Perhaps the title turns on itself: it is itself 'counterfeit money', only feigning reference to what is called 'counterfeit money' and to this text, only feigning to be a 'title'. And should we look to its dedicatee to delimit the text, as if this could limit the 'proper' reading to that of a particular addressee, Derrida says 'from the moment [Baudelaire] let it constitute itself in a system of traces, he delivered it – and that was giving it – above and beyond any determined addressee, donee . . . The accredited signatory delivered it up to a dissemination without return.'[16] A text must be readable in the absence of any actual addressee and so reference to one cannot determine the interpretation.

This undecidability can be shown to inhabit the narrative itself. The movement of the narrative is what occurs in the narrator's friendship so as to surprise it. This takes place as a meditation on itself: the narrator tells us, this is happening to me, to my friend and me, and I can't forgive him. 'It is as if the narrative condition were the cause of the recounted thing, *as if* the narrative produced the event it is supposed to report.' We only have his word. (But then, this is all we ever have: our own words, which may be the repetition of those of others.) Now, the central issue in reading the text is the question of why the friend confesses to giving the counterfeit coin. The text seems to provide various possibilities.

1 He does it to be excused from any sense of competing with his friend. He does it, then, out of friendship.
2 It is a boast that he had bought himself the greatest pleasure at the lowest price.
3 It is an expression of innocence. In using the counterfeit coin, he had withdrawn from the cycle of the gift as violence towards the poor man, giving nothing whilst giving him the chance to make it bear fruit.
4 Or perhaps the response is counterfeit. He gave real money but said otherwise to produce a certain effect in the narrator.

Our reading of the text will turn on the interpretation of this confession, yet all these (and no doubt others) are possibilities. The 'readability of the text is structured by the unreadability of the secret, that is, by the inaccessibility of a certain intentional meaning or of a wanting-to-say in the consciousness of the characters'.[17] The text 'gives to be read that which will remain *eternally* unreadable, absolutely indecipherable, even refusing itself to any promise of deciphering or hermeneutic'.[18] Here is indicated 'the secret about which literary fiction tells us the essential or which tells us, in return, the essential concerning the possibility of literary fiction'.[19] The 'secret' is that there is no secret, nothing underlying or beyond the text which can determine its interpretation. The 'secret' in literature is revealed in its possibility only to the exent that 'it is spread on the surface of the page'.[20]

Fiction tells us the secret that there is no secret, no key which will determine once and for all its meaning. The gift of the text 'must interrupt the continuum of a narrative that nevertheless [it] call[s] for'.[21] The narrative, the text, is interrupted by its making its readability depend on its essential unreadability and in this way disrupting the appearance of unitary sense and making possible 'aleatory events', the happening of meaning which cannot be foreseen or controlled. The theme of chance is central to the narrative itself of *Counterfeit Money*: 'the stakes are those of *chance*, of the *luck of the draw* (fors, fortuna) that presides over this whole essay on gift and forgiveness, over this whole attempt at gift and forgiveness'.[22] For example: the narrator believes that pleasure always has its cause in a surprise, in the sudden coming of the new, of that which cannot be anticipated; the friend is excusable only if he had wanted to create an event in the beggar's life whose consequences are unforseeable;[23] the meeting with the beggar is chance, as is the presence of the counterfeit coin (if it is one) itself; as far as the narrative is concerned, the narrator and friend have their fortunes, which enable them to be alms-givers, by chance, since no account of how they acquired their prosperity is provided there.

Yet even though the text enacts the dependence of readability on unreadability, the narrator judges. He can't forgive his friend for doing evil out of stupidity. The friend ought to want to understand, and the evil he does is not trying to understand it: 'It is finally for his failure to honour the contract that bound him to the gift of nature', that is, to our intellectual or hermeneutic power, 'that the friend is accused'.[24] This hermeneutic power is always engaged in producing interpretations that essentially embody their own possibility of re-interpretability. But the narrator, then, in judging, exudes 'that stupidity of which he speaks . . . which will always hang in the air around a sentence and a judgement'. The 'narrator has the last word, of course, and that is perhaps the greatest lesson of this literature'.[25] The narrator here occupies the place of 'nature', determining the truth underlying the signs his friend gives. Yet at the same time the narrator is fictional. This might suggest an interpretation of literature or fiction as nature, an interpretation '(perhaps) as fictive as the counterfeit money that it uses'.[26] That is, it might tempt us to an absolutizing of the notion of 'fiction', as if we could do away with the notions of reality, meaning and self and conclude 'there is only fiction'. But this privileging of 'fiction' is as subject to deconstruction as is that of 'reality'. Baudelaire thus, perhaps, shows us the fiction of such a naturalization of literature, of such an absolute privilege accorded to fiction and so 'invites us perhaps to suspend the opposition between nature and institution, phusis and nomos, nature and convention, nature and all its others'.[27] His text stages for us both the necessity and the impossibility of meaning, reality and self.

Baudelaire's text occupies historically a place in relation to a romanticism that, perhaps, sought to privilege fiction in an absolutizing moment, and deconstructs this privilege. Modernist texts, occupying the historical juncture when 'language invaded the universal problematic . . . when everything became discourse',[28] can be read as staging the general deconstruction of the notion of 'nature', of the appeal to what could determine meaning in a final way. The concern of this writing is 'writing' in the above sense of arche-writing.

Of Kafka's short story 'Before the Law', Derrida says 'The story . . . does not tell or describe anything but itself as text.' This doesn't mean it is self-referential so that an interpretation of this reference could be forthcoming in a commentary. The story does not operate 'with an assured specular reflection of some self-referential transparency'. Rather it carries out its concern through insisting on its own unreadability and thus on the 'otherness' which makes its coherence both possible and impossible. It must have a conceptuality, here, a narrative, but at the same time this narrative is rendered unreadable and in such a way that this unreadability is what makes possible its narrativity. 'The text guards itself . . . speaking only of itself, that is to say, of its non-identity with itself.'[29] And again: 'Kafka's story operates across the naively referential framework of its narration which leads us past a portal that it comports, an internal boundary opening on nothing, before nothing, the object of no possible experience.'[30] As the peasant waits before the doorway desiring to come before the Law, so we desire to interpret the story, to come upon the meaning. Without an absence, a lack, we wouldn't desire meaning. But this absence, this nothing, is not the opposite of a presence which could satisfy our desire. Rather, there is only meaning, Law, in so far as there is not, in so far as it is inhabited by the very alterity that provokes our search for meaning. The darkness of the threshold is essential to the illumination there is. It is only when the peasant gives up his quest, dying, that 'a radiance . . . streams inextinguishably from the gateway of the law'.[31] Our desire for interpretation, for a whole coherent meaning, is both enacted by the narration and involves that desire in its necessary defeat, for we cannot speak coherently about alterity. In this way, Derrida tries to rebuff the obvious charge that this is itself just such an interpretation as has been claimed to be impossible. It is not an interpretation in the sense of an exposition of the 'meaning', but precisely because we find we cannot coherently formulate a response, the very possibility of interpretation is itself disrupted. The story is thus 'the Law, makes the law and leaves the reader before the law'. That is, the story is non-identical with itself and only so does it have its coherence; it stages this rendering possible and impossible at the same time; and this involves us in our own non-identity in reading it, demanding as it does our countersignature. 'In its very act, the text produces and pronounces the law that protects it and renders it intangible.'[32]

Or let us look briefly at Derrida's treatment of Francis Ponge's poem 'Fable'.[33] The poem 'stages' deconstruction,[34] that is, the paradoxical situation of language in which the condition of possibility of meaning is at the same time the condition of its impossibility. Meaning is made possible by difference, and so by context. But since there is no end to difference, no saturable context, there is no final, determinate meaning. Meaning is made possible, paradoxically, by being always other than it is. Any apparently present meaning is always an interpretation, a re-contextualizing, of past meanings, and the same applies to them too. This is an impossible situation: there is no beginning, meaning is always under way as repetition, but where there is nothing original to repeat. It is this impossible situation which is staged in Ponge's poem. The first line speaks of itself: so it is immediately in a second language, a metalanguage. But there is no first language for it to be about. It 'is an inevitable and impossible metalanguage since *there is no language before it*, since it has no prior object beneath or outside itself'.[35] There is no metalanguage: but that is all there is. This instability affects all language and 'disturbs normally, as it were, the norms, the statutes and the rules'.[36] It is not a total disturbance, not an abandonment of rules, since it needs those rules for its operation. What is staged is the paradoxical situation of language which deconstruction marks: there must be meanings, rules, laws, but there cannot be. There is thus an inbuilt instability in meaning which cannot be coherently expressed since it inhabits anything we would call coherent expression. It can, however, be staged, enacted, as Derrida himself does in relation to philosophical works. 'The interest of deconstruction, of such force and desire as it may have, is a certain experience of the other as the invention of the impossible, in other words, as the only possible invention.'[37] The impossible is the paradox, the necessity for and impossibility of meaning. This impossibility is what makes any meaning other than itself and so is an 'experience' of the other (without, of course, being an experience of any determinate difference).

Our thinking and experience take place ostensibly in terms of concepts, and these are themselves organized around concepts of presence: reality, self, meaning. Indeed the concept of a concept is such a concept of presence. In this way, the concepts which structure our lives privilege concepts of presence, which privilege produces dependent concepts of appearance, the unconscious, absence of meaning and so on. A deconstruction of these distinctions undermines this appearance of privilege by showing that the privileged terms are themselves dependent on predicates associated with the former secondary terms. But this move ruins the appearance of distinct concepts, and produces, when we try to understand the new application of these predicates, paradoxical expressions. A paradox is one for thought, and so for the logic of distinct concepts. The expressions produced, therefore, cannot be thought: they remain as disruptions of 'coherent' thought and experience, but disruptions which that 'coherent' thought or experience is dependent on.

They are what prevent there being fully coherent thought or experience, what prevent presence's claim to privilege, and which therefore produce more 'reality', 'meaning' and 'self'. The paradox cannot do without the concepts of presence, just as these cannot do without the paradox.

The realm of ethics is that of presence: the promulgation of responsibilities and duties derivable from some apprehensible ground (which varies historically). Here, as with all forms of thought which privilege presence, the 'manifest is given priority over the hidden or the secret'.[38] Now, in the sense that this is so within such forms of thought, the secret or the hidden is a notion dependent on that of the manifest. It is a secret or the hidden which could be manifest, but isn't (at this time, or for finite beings in general). In so far as this opposition is subject to a deconstruction, however, we must think the hidden or the secret in the manifest, that which can in no way either be manifest or lack manifestness. This 'secret' (which we have seen is the concern of literary writing) in relation to ethics is that which ethics as a field of manifestness depends on whilst being unable to encompass. Ethics shows us in general life appropriate to the self, however understood. The self as a privileged notion, involving immediate self-consciousness, gives us a dependent concept of 'others', other selves whose consciousness is only mediately known by the self. But in so far as we deconstruct this opposition, and so undermine the privilege of presence and so of distinct concepts, we must think the other in the self, that which one can be neither conscious nor unconscious of. This is the 'secret' upon which the experience and consciousness of the self depend but which it can never encompass: its essential disruption. It is 'this' Derrida 'calls' 'singularity' and which is suspended in speaking or thinking, in making present. It gives the unethical in the ethical, that which the ethical can neither do without nor address: the irresponsible in responsibility. This 'absolute' responsibility, responsibility which is 'beyond' responsibility yet within it, the internal *différance* of responsibility, is that which prevents us ever being fully responsible in our responsibilities.

> Absolute responsibility is not a responsibility, at least it is not general responsibility or responsibility in general . . . it is as if absolute responsibility could not be derived from a *concept* of responsibility and therefore, in order for it to be what it must be it must remain inconceivable, indeed unthinkable: it must therefore be irresponsible in order to be absolutely responsible.[39]

'Absolute responsibility' is the relation of the self as singularity to singularity. 'These singularities represent others, a wholly other form of alterity: one other or some other persons, but also places, animals, languages.'[40] It is the 'relation' of what prevents me from being 'a self' to what prevents whatever becomes manifest in language from being wholly manifest. It is that which always summons me to thought, to responsibility and action but which can never be exhausted there, an excess which means there is always more responsibility or thought than responsibility or thought can encompass. It is why I always fail to be responsible or to think adequately, it is what necessarily disrupts the fields of consciousness, action or thought. It is this necessary failure which makes ethics and thought in general possible, and therefore, impossible. 'I owe myself infinitely to each and every singularity'[41] so that responsibility is not limitable. 'I cannot say with good conscience that I have made a good choice and that I have assumed my resposibilities.'[42]

> If I conduct myself particularly well with regard to someone, I know that it is to the detriment of an other; of one nation to the detriment of another nation, of one family to the detriment of another family, of my friends to the detriment of other friends or non-friends, etc.[43]

'I know that I have not done enough, and it is in this way that morality continues, that history and politics continue ... The relation to the other does not close itself off, and it is because of this that there is history and one tries to act politically.'[44] Respecting singularity means recognizing the necessity of failure, that thought and action are possible just because they can never be complete. It means letting thought and action be a response to the 'come', the address of the absolutely other, that which prevents, whilst making possible, any conception (of the self, of the other, of the world) whatever.

> It calls for a betrayal of everything that manifests itself in general, the very order of universal generality, and everything that manifests itself in general, the very order and essence of manifestation, namely, the essence itself, the essence in general to the extent that it is inseparable from presence and from manifestation.[45]

This requires allowing there to be history, of the self, of the other, of whatever can be manifest. To allow there to be history is to allow the future to be future, to be essentially what cannot be manifest, cannot be contained within language or thought. 'There is the future. There is something to come. That can happen ... that can happen, and I promise in opening the future or in leaving the future open.'[46] It requires a relation to the manifest which keeps the manifest, whether myself, the other, the text, and so forth, *open*, which respects that which makes the manifest possible by making it impossible (as complete). It is this which, in relation to the text, is 'countersigning' or the 'invention of the other'. It is the response to the manifest, of whatever kind, which allows the new to come forth, but in such a way that it preserves the otherness in whatever becomes manifest and so keeps the future as essentially open.

For both Blanchot and Derrida, the 'literary' has always been a 'notion' subversive of conceptuality in general. From the moment when language is removed from its invisibility in practical and intellectual life in an apparent articulation of the world and self in terms of an understanding of them, this understanding is presented in its linguistic resistance to interpretation, both inviting and preventing it. In this way, this very removal undermines the appearance of finality of that understanding. Hence the opposition of those who invest in finality, those whose interest seems to lie in setting a limit to understanding, including, of course, philosophy in its history as the pre-server and demarcator of such limits, to this aberrant activity. Of course, those involved in this activity have not understood themselves in this way, producing defences and apologias for what they do in terms of varying understandings of the good for the human being. But the nature of their activity defeats the intention of these justifications: history, in the sense of the inevitable movement of understandings of world and self, opens with the lifting of language into the aberrant condition of a writing that contains within itself the opacity which provokes and defeats final interpretation. We have now, through this history, come to see ourselves and our world as con-stituted in language and so as essentially bound up with this opacity of the hitherto deviant practice. The literature of the twentieth century, in its revo-lutionary forms, shows language, no longer in apparent subservience to a final understanding of world and self, but explicitly in this opacity, showing what its past forms knew only in their silence. In the paradoxical understand-ing of ourselves which this gives, literature and its attendant forms of reflec-tion no longer show us an understanding of world and self, but summon us to an intervention into the conceptual oppositions which such understand-ings have bequeathed to us, to liberate them towards a response to the 'singu-larity' they depend upon but occlude. No doubt the breakdown of our understandings of gender, social, political and ethical relations is symptom-atic of this, as we move into a world in which the privilege of finality, of the truth and the good, is undermined, replaced by the endless conditionality of our judgements (which we cannot do without), a conditionality which is the necessary response to the essential alterity of ourselves and the world. We must remake ourselves and our relations to each other and the world without end. The 'literary' as the aberrant notion, no doubt, will itself dis-solve with the conceptual structures it opposed, dissipating into an endless multiplicity of writing for which the appellation 'fiction' as opposed to writ-ings concerned with 'the truth' will no longer be relevant. An exciting, or for those still enamoured of the truth, a daunting, prospect.

A brief recapitulation

Metaphysics tries to provide an ultimate justification for thought and life based on it through showing us the nature of reality 'as it is in itself', and so what we really 'are'. Whether access to such a position is through reason, faith or the self-unfolding of history, the significance of works like *Oedipus*

the King, *The Divine Comedy*, or *King Lear* will be determined by their relation to such 'truth'. They cannot play a part in the work of reasoning
towards such truth since they are non-discursive, and they are not works of
scripture. At best they may be regarded, as they were by the neo-Platonist
Proclus or by Dante himself, as providing allegories of what is more properly
apprehended by reason or faith. And since truth is to be apprehended intellectually, their historical role for Hegel in creating the situation for such
apprehension has now been superseded by philosophy itself.

Kant tried to show that all such claims to apprehend the way things are 'in
themselves' lead to irresolvable conflicts which are the result of our trying to
transcend our own human standpoint. We have no access to things in themselves, the way things are over and beyond our human experience. We cannot
know the nature of reality in itself, all we can do is to reflect on our own
experience to reveal its structure and conditions. But this internal critique
nevertheless shows, he claims, that the idea of the way things really are is not
redundant and that we must believe in the reality corresponding to the ideas
of reason. Poetry here can play a subordinate role in giving us a quasi-
experience of what cannot be experienced through the creation of images of
these ideas embodied in works of art whose appreciation involves our
imagination, understanding and reason in a play through which we have, as it
were, an experience of ourselves, of our humanity. Yet this relocation of the
metaphysical from a matter of knowledge to one of belief still requires
the intelligibility of the notion of 'the way things really are' transcendent to
the human standpoint. This intelligibility is questioned by Schlegel and
Nietzsche who endeavour, in their different ways, to rid our thinking and life
of such a conception of transcendence. They raise, therefore, the question of
what it would be to think and live in a purely human way, one which would
be its own measure. It is, of course, just this that had characterized Kant's
conception of the work of art as a work of genius and which demarcates
for him the realm of human creativity as opposed to technical production.
Schlegel and Nietzsche (at least in one of the dominant trends of his thinking) attempt to think the world and human life in terms of constant creation,
the process of unending becoming. Life now becomes itself conceived in
terms of (a Kantian conception of) art, as a 'poem' as Schlegel puts it, so
that actual poetry becomes, as it were, an image of life. This attempted
transmutation to a purely human view founders on the incoherence of its
absolute generality: if everything is 'art', then nothing is. Thought (as Schlegel
and Nietzsche themselves often know) depends on difference which thus
preludes the intelligibility of a final account whether metaphysically in terms
of 'being' or humanly in terms of 'becoming'. Thought can no longer aspire
to either a metaphysical or a 'human' account of life and the world: the
thinking of 'difference' must embody, if it is not to betray itself, a form other
than that of a general, coherent account, a 'theory'. Such thinking addresses
what must evade thought whilst at the same time making it possible, so that it

must in a certain sense fail (as when we try to 'identify' what is at issue in the 'between' of differences, the 'gap' or 'abyss').

It is just here that what had been seen metaphysically or 'humanly' as literature's deficiency moves to the forefront of attention. It is language used in the absence of a point of (apparent) reference which could (seemingly) determine its interpretation. The opacity of its language, which is this divorce from an apparent point of reference, both invites and resists interpretation. Seen in this way, literature appears to already know what both incites and resists thought. It becomes the place where the 'fascination' of dissolution can operate on our discontinuous selves (Bataille), where the 'incessant murmur' of language which always differs from itself 'speaks' (Blanchot), or which stages the deconstruction of sense (Derrida). Literature in the past has raised apparently final interpretations of life and world into their linguistic opacity and so prepared their transformation. It has been, as Bataille says, 'dangerous'. Literature now liberates itself from such interpretations, concerns itself with itself, with its own impenetrability. Thought, as the heir of metaphysics, now appears as a reflection on literature and one which, in order not to betray its task, must render the distinction between itself and literary work undecidable. Which is *Madame Edwarda*, *The Madness of the Day*, or *The Post-Card*? Such thinking and literary work show what is incumbent on us now, the dismantling of the fixed conceptual oppositions which have structured thought and life, to make possible life lived in relation to an open future within which we could make ourselves constantly anew. And doesn't this indeed speak to us now in a time of the decline in religious belief and the rethinking of ethical, gender, social and political relations?

And yet, as Richard Rorty will suggest, this position still seems to share a commonality with the metaphysics it seeks to distance itself from. All three authors offer us a certain history which determines our current situation, with the claim that recognition of this would require a certain way of life. But then this history must be claimed as the truth, the measure for our non-philosophical practices, as though it reads history's own language, and what could justify such a claim? Doesn't this imply that history has an 'essence' when the appeal to historicality was intended precisely to disabuse us philosophically of that notion? Whether Rorty's solution to this problem of the 'ironist theorist' is acceptable, I will consider in the course of tracing how a position in close proximity to that of the European theorists may be reached within an Anglo-American tradition of thought.

5

IRIS MURDOCH
The transcendent good

'Art, especially literature, has in the past instinctively operated as a form, the most profound generally accessible form, of moral reflection.'[1]

In *The Sovereignty of Good* Iris Murdoch identifies a picture of the human which she claims underlies contemporary moral and political philosophy and which is too 'the hero of almost every contemporary novel'.[2] In this picture the human being 'ought to know what he is doing' and so aims at 'total knowledge of our situation and a clear conceptualization of all our possibilities'. This knowledge is of 'reality' which is potentially available to different observers, an impersonal world of facts. Within the facts as he apprehends them, the individual must choose to act. Our essential being is the 'overtly choosing will' which is independent of what is the case in the external world or with ourselves. 'Will is pure choice, pure movement' essentially to be distinguished from 'thought or vision'.[3] Morality is 'a matter of thinking clearly and then proceeding to outward dealings with other men'. Since morality is concerned with action and so with the operation of merely the pure will, its vocabulary requires fundamentally only the most abstract of terms, 'good' and 'right'. This conception of morality as concerned with publicly observable action is supported by a theory of meaning for mental concepts, that they 'must be analysed genetically and so the inner must be thought of as parasitic upon the outer'.[4] That is, we learn concepts, and can do so only by watching other people. I learn, for example, 'decision' by observing someone who says 'I have decided' and then acts: the term can only have for me such a publicly observable sense. 'A decision does not turn out to be, when more carefully considered, an introspectible movement. The concept has no further inner structure; it *is* its outer structure.'[5] Similarly, anger is distinguished from jealousy not by reference to private mental experiences. I had to learn these notions and I could only do so by referring them to outward behaviour and publicly observable contexts. From this conception of the meaning of mental terms, and, therefore, of moral ones concerned with the operation of the will, two conclusions are drawn about the nature of morals. First, morality must be action, a matter of publicly observable activity, since this is

69

required for moral concepts to be learnable. 'Salvation by works is a conceptual necessity.'[6] It is, therefore, not possible 'to take up an idle contemplative attitude to the good'.[7] Second, reasons are essentially public and derive from the rules of public institutions and their purposes. They become reasons for the agent through his own free choice.

Against this picture, Murdoch poses another which draws its inspiration from an interpretation of Plato's Form of the Good. We are constituted as a movement towards goodness. As Plato said, we all desire the good and are not content with its mere appearance. We may be content with appearing virtuous, but in that case need to believe that being so content is in fact good for us. This movement towards goodness Murdoch often calls, following Plato, eros. Initially, and commonly, this impulsion towards goodness latches on to particular ends, identifying them with the individual's good. In this way, individuals appear to achieve a unity of self in which their lives attain a direction and goal. Yet this is self-delusion. To think of one's life in this way, as given meaning in the pursuit and obtaining of particular goals, is an unconscious turning away from the reality that whatever we have may at any time be taken from us. Thinking of our lives in this unified way conceals death and chance 'by the invention of forms. Any story which we tell about ourselves consoles us since it imposes a pattern upon something which might otherwise seem intolerably chancy and incomplete. However, human life is chancy and incomplete.'[8] To recognize the reality of chance and death, the movement towards goodness, eros, must be redirected, away from particular, and so false, goals to the Good itself. Nothing can be said about the Good other than it requires turning away from all temporal goals and the quasi-temporal consolations of rewards 'after death' of conventional religion.

> 'All is vanity' is the beginning and end of ethics. The only genuine way to be good is to be good 'for nothing' in the midst of a scene where every 'natural' thing, including one's own mind, is subject to chance, that is, to necessity. That 'for nothing' is indeed the experienced correlate of the invisibility or non-representable blankness of the idea of Good itself.[9]

Life, seen in this way, is a task of redirecting one's eros and engaging in the consequent struggles with one's attachment to particular goals this entails, the transformation of 'base egoistic energy and vision (low Eros) into high spiritual energy and vision (high Eros)'.[10] We are concrete historically situated individuals, born into a particular historical and social situation with abilities and temperament not of our choosing. As embodied eros, we have always already formed attachments in terms of which our lives appear to us as meaningful (or meaningless if those attachments fail). From this position, in which we have constituted a (false) self, identity, we can take over our own contingency through re-orienting our drive to goodness, liberating ourselves from attachment to particular goods, present and projected, to attachment to the nothing which the Good must be for us. 'This is a progressive redemption of desire . . . patiently and continuously (effecting) a change of one's whole being in all its contingent detail, through a world of appearance toward a world of reality.'[11] It is a world of 'reality' in the sense that only in so far as our movement is away from self, an 'unselfing', do we recognize that we are contingent transient beings living in a world which has no, as it were, built-in purpose. We see ourselves and the world as it is in turning away from ourselves; in directing our energy towards nothing, the world in its contingency and pointlessness is recognized. This is something which we show an implicit awareness of in our everyday lives, devoted as they may well be to the pursuit of false goods. In that pursuit, we nevertheless have to suspend our attachment to these goods in order to see the way things are and so determine what to do. The intending bankrobber must turn away from his projected goal and how he wishes things to be in order to determine, for example, what the actual routine of the bank is. The ability 'to perceive what is true . . . is automatically at the same time a suppression of self. *The necessity of the good is then an aspect of the kind of necessity involved in any technique of exhibiting fact.*'[12] Orientation towards the Good, away from the projected goods of the self, is our only access to the reality of the world, to what is. Our own reality as the transient contingent beings we are can then be lived through the transformation of our attachments from illusory goods to the Good itself, to living 'for nothing'. To relate to others, to activities and intellectual disciplines 'for nothing' is 'love': hence, life lived in orientation to the Good is the life of love. 'It is in the capacity to love, that is to *see*, that the liberation of the soul from fantasy consists.'[13]

Seen is this way 'Life is a spiritual pilgrimage inspired by the disturbing magnetism of truth.'[14] This is not a progress towards grasping *the* truth but rather towards an increasing truthfulness, towards a freeing of ourselves from those intellectual and emotional ties which bind us to illusory goods and which prevent a recognition of, and motivation by, the Good: towards a living in truth. This process is itself, of course, always incomplete. It is 'a progressive redemption of desire . . . the overcoming of egoism',[15] of the projection upon the world and on life of an illusory finality which 'fits' them to us. Egoism, whether individual or in a general human sense, projects its own good upon the world. Spiritual development is directed towards accepting the absence of such finality and an embrace of human life and the world in its essential otherness to human projections of significance, towards what, as we have seen, Murdoch calls 'love'.

Understood in these terms, the essential features of human life appear quite differently from those embodied in contemporary literature and philosophy. What is central to morality is the notion of the individual, and the individual, as opposed to the abstract 'agent' characterized by pure will, has a history, the 'progressing life of a person'.[16] A main characteristic of such a history is the constant 'reassessing' and 'redefining' of moral concepts. That is, although the individual initially learns these concepts from others, they are those concepts only in so far as they permit this form of development which is at the same time a development of the individual herself. Such concepts, to be really learnt and so made a part of the individual, have a personal use, which means, for example, that 'Repentance may mean something different to an individual at different times in his life, and what it fully means is a part of this life and cannot be understood except in context.'[17] This undermines the genetic account of meaning, for 'we have a different image of courage at forty from that which we had at twenty. A deepening process, at any rate an altering and complicating process, takes place.'[18] This process, in so far as it is a spiritual development, lies in the progressive erosion of egoism, one which itself is never complete and in relation to which we are forced here to 'speak of an inevitable imperfection, or of an ideal limit of love or knowledge which always recedes'.[19]

Reasons are not, therefore, necessarily public here. 'They may be reasons for a very few.'[20] What reasons we find depend on our development of the moral concepts and so on our own moral development itself. At different levels quite different 'reasons' will be seen as obvious and compelling. 'I can only choose within the world I can *see*, in the moral sense of "see"' and that will depend on my moral development. Such 'seeing' is, therefore, already morally structured. Individuals do not find themselves in neutrally specifiable situations. Rather, what their situation is depends on how they see it and this in turn depends on their development. Since perception in this sense is already evaluative it can result itself in action. 'Choice' marks an exceptional moment in this process and 'at crucial moments of choice most of the business of choosing is already over'.[21] The individual is 'not a combination of an impersonal rational thinker and a personal will. He is a unified being who sees, and who desires in accordance with what he sees, and who has some continual slight control over the direction and focus of his vision.'[22] It is this latter which makes development possible. What is primary, both in respect of moral 'action' and development, is vision and not 'will'. In so far as we speak of choice, it is an event situated in a constant process of seeing and acting in accordance with what one sees. Such sight, as moral seeing, is already structured in accordance with the extent of our moral development. Development takes place not primarily in terms of will in the sense of choice of action, but through a more basic exercise of freedom, the attempt at 'attention'. Development implies a lack, a situation of imperfection which may be reduced. Morally, and so humanly, this imperfection is egocentricity and its mode of vision, its seeing the world and others in terms of its own projections of finality and so not as they are, that is, as always to preclude such finality. To try to 'attend' is to try to submit oneself to what is 'there', the always 'other' nature of the world and human beings, including oneself. Moral development is a progressive liberation from the self and its fantasy vision: 'fantasy, the proliferation of blinding self-centred aims and images, is itself a powerful system of energy, and most of what is often called "will" or "willing" belongs to this system. What counteracts the system is attention to reality.'[23] Freedom is not, therefore, the exercise of will, but rather the selfless seeing which occasions, of itself, action (for perception of our situation is always evaluative and occasions our constant activity). Such selfless seeing, which is itself motivation, is love. Development is a progressive alteration in our orientation, towards perfect attention in which there would be no question of choice. 'If I attend properly I will have no choices and this is the ultimate condition to be aimed at',[24] although, once again, this is impossible of attainment.

This process of development, which embodies an orientation to the absolute good in terms of which all temporal goods are seen as imperfect, is 'an acceptance of the utter lack of finality in human life'.[25] All such patterns, whether projected by the individual or social convention, or produced by philosophy and theology, are themselves products of fantasy, of the desire of the ego to impose its own meaning on reality. 'This is to say that there is, in my view, no God in the traditional sense of that term; and the traditional sense is perhaps the only sense. Equally the various metaphysical substitutes for God – Reason, Science, History – are false deities.'[26] The self imposes its conception of its own unity upon the world, sees the world in terms of itself. But seeing this clearly, abandoning the centrality of one's self, involves the recognition that 'there is no general and as it were externally guaranteed pattern or purpose'[27] to the universe or therefore to life itself. Such philosophical or theological attempts to impose meaning derive from the same source as all egocentric visions of the world: they are forms of human self-assertion, of the desire to impose our own sense of a good upon life and the world. In giving up this ambition, we do not give up the idea of good. Rather, relation to the good requires giving up all projections of goodness. It appears therefore as the 'nothing' which can give meaning to life and the world and which can therefore be said to be 'transcendent': ' "Good is a transcendent reality" means that virtue is the attempt to pierce the veil of selfish consciousness and join the world as it really is. It is an empirical fact about human nature that this attempt cannot be entirely successful.'[28]

Moral development involves a 'change of one's whole being . . . through a world of appearance towards a world of reality'. Such a transformation, as she remarks of Plato, 'involves a desire for and achievement of truth instead of falsehood, reality instead of appearance'. Hence, whenever we can speak of 'getting things right' and so of truth-seeking (she cites meticulous grammar or mathematics), there we have 'truth-seeking as virtue'.[29] Morality, and in its highest form as demythologized religion,[30] is concerned with the progressive achievement of truthfulness, of that condition of individuals and so of their vision and motivation which is freed of 'methodical egoism, the barrier which divides the area of our interests and requirements from the rest of the world'.[31] As we have seen, Murdoch regards such truthfulness as encountered as a requirement in the apprehension of what is the case in everyday life and in intellectual disciplines: we must divest ourselves of our desire that something be the case and see, submit ourselves, to what is there. Morality is making this truthfulness the nature of our lives, and not just a requirement we submit to now and then in the pursuit of our egocentric desires.

It is in terms of this picture that Murdoch attempts to provide an account of the nature of art and literature. There is no externally guaranteed purpose to the universe or therefore to human life. 'Our destiny can be examined but it cannot be justified or totally explained. We are simply here.'[32] To live in full recognition of this, to embrace it in an orientation to the Good, is to live in truth and not through the 'appearances' we project upon the world in order to live. 'Art is about the pilgrimage from appearance to reality (the subject of every good play and novel).'[33] It relates to this pilgrimage in several ways.

The relation of the reader, spectator or listener to the work of art is one of contemplation which requires our seeing 'what is there' independently of our desires. Such relating is itself, therefore, a moral activity: 'The appreciation of beauty in art and nature is not only ... the easiest available spiritual exercise; it is also a completely adequate entry into (and not just analogy of) the good life, since it is the checking of selfishness in the interests of seeing the real.'[34] This appreciation of the artwork requires its separation from the items of everyday life in terms of which it appears 'pointless'. But 'The pointlessness of art ... is the pointlessness of human life itself, and form in art is properly the simulation of the self-contained aimlessness of the universe.'[35]

Form is that through which the artwork achieves a certain self-containedness, unity. But this is precisely what is involved in the egoistic projection of purpose upon life which is illusion. Bad art provides us with the most perfect forms of unity since these are what egoistically we fantasize our lives could be: 'the bad story is the sentimental untruthful tale of how the brave attractive ego (and of course he has his faults) triumphs over accident and causality and is never really mocked or brought to naught'.[36] But good art shows us 'not only the (illusory) unity of the self but its real disunity ... Good art accepts and celebrates and meditates upon the defeat of the discursive intellect by the world. Bad art misrepresents the world so as to pretend there is no defeat.'[37] In this way, good art shows us our propensity to live in illusion: as fiction, it shows us the fictions we make about our lives. And in making us aware of them and their illusory nature, it provides us with an antidote. It redeems us of 'our tendency to conceal death and chance by the invention of forms'.[38]

Good art thus uses form but 'to isolate, to explore, to display something which is true'.[39] What is true is the absence of purpose, of form, in life which we recognize in orientation to the transcendent Good. We must come up against the fact that 'We are simply here.' Art does this through its concern with what breaks the illusions of purpose we project upon our lives. It shows that only in our fantasies are we unitary beings. Literature shows us as we are, 'unfinished and full of blankness and jumble; only in our own illusioning fantasy are we complete'.[40] It shows us the 'randomness of the world through which good purposes are checked', that randomness which continually upsets the best laid plans. It reminds us of the 'hardness of the real properties of the world', that dealing with the world requires work which may always miscarry, and that what has happened is irreversible. And most crucially, it shows us death as the ultimate prevention of a conception of one's life as an 'aesthetic' whole. Art's concern with these features of our condition is to show us 'the place of necessity in human life, what must be endured, what makes and breaks ... so as to contemplate the real world (usually veiled by anxiety and fantasy) including what is terrible and absurd'.[41] Art shows us the world and ourselves without the illusions we project, and shows us projecting them and their defeat. 'Good art shows us how difficult it is to be objective by showing us how differently the world looks to an objective vision.'[42] In this way, art shows us how the world looks from the selfless position where we are rid of our ego's projected illusions: it shows us how the world looks to the good. 'We are presented by a truthful image of the human condition in a form which can be steadily contemplated . . . [Art] is a kind of goodness by proxy.'[43]

It is in these terms that Murdoch understands the nature and significance of tragedy. Tragedy essentially involves death: 'In tragedy the compulsory nature of death is an image of its place in life.'[44] Tragedy shows us death breaking the ego, 'destroying the illusory whole of the unified self . . . Tragedy must break the charmed completion which is the essence of lesser art, revealing the true nature of sin, the futility of fantasy and the reality of death.'[45] Yet in doing this, tragedy involves us in an acceptance, even a welcoming, of this destruction of the self's projected unity: we enjoy the spectacle. In this enjoyment, we occupy, albeit transiently, the place of one who truly embraces the otherness of life and the world. 'Perhaps one could say that the art form of tragedy is the *image* of a (rarely achieved) moral condition . . . What does it all look like to a saint?'[46] For a brief time, we can contemplate the world from the point of view of the good. But this ambition of tragedy involves it in a kind of contradiction with its status as art. Art 'cannot help, whatever its subject, beautifying and consoling'[47] since it brings life into a graspable form which speaks to our desire that it be intelligible and controllable. Tragedy, however, must reject all consolation in order that in its spectacle we should engage in a certain rapture which transcends all egoism. The 'form' of tragedy militates against its aim. 'Great tragedy then has to be some sort of contradiction, destroying itself as art while maintaining itself as art.'[48] Great tragedy (and I imagine she is thinking of Shakespeare rather than Sophocles or Racine) breaks its own form, encompassing what resists interpretation in the inclusion of the apparently inconsequential and pointless.

Art has, therefore, a close relation to philosophy. It is an 'image of metaphysics'.[49] It shows us 'deep conceptual connections' like those between truth, justice and love through getting us to see that, for example, seeing the world truly is seeing it selflessly and so in love. Philosophy appears as the intellectual articulation of what we experience in art, a self-recognition. 'It is the height of art to be able to show what is nearest, what is deeply and obviously true but usually invisible. (Philosophy attempts this too.)'[50] Art shows us a 'truthful image of the human condition' in which we recognize ourselves; philosophy articulates this picture and brings out the conceptual connections which art manifests or shows. Metaphysics 'sets up a picture which it then offers as an appeal to us all to see if we cannot find just this in our deepest experience'.[51] Philosophical 'proof' thus rests, in the last resort, on whether we do find the picture one which makes sense of our lives: '[the philosophical proof] if there is one, is the same as the moral "proof". I would rely especially upon arguments from experience concerned with the realism which we perceive to be connected with goodness, and with the love and detachment which is exhibited in great art.'[52] There is an essential circularity in all such proofs, since the phenomena are described in terms of the fundamental picture itself. What metaphysics does is to present a unified picture of human life and the ultimate principle of unity involved appears as simply presupposed: it gains its force through its ability to explain and hold together the other phenomena.[53]

> Plato makes the assumption that value is everywhere, that the whole of life is movement on a moral scale, all knowledge is a moral quest, and the mind seeks reality and desires the good, which is a transcendent source of spiritual power, to which we are related through the idea of truth ... The 'proof' of [this picture, as with Kant's alternative] is provided through numerous examples.[54]

Plato, and Murdoch following him, takes the Good as the fundamental unifying principle of his picture, the 'story' he tells. Its 'proof' lies in its ability to account for the range of our human experience.

> The transcendental proof of it is from all the world, all our *extremely various* experience. The Form of the Good ... may be seen as enlightening particular scenes and setting the specialized moral virtues and insights into their particular patterns. This is how the phenomena are saved and the particulars redeemed, in this *light*.[55]

Murdoch's picture is one which appeals only to what we can find within human experience: that we are constituted as a desire for the good, which as transcendent can only be related to in giving up all projections of good upon the world. And in this it is a form of naturalism: 'I offer frankly a sketch of a metaphysical theory, a kind of inconclusive non-dogmatic naturalism, which has the circularity of definition characteristic of such theories.'[56] And part of the 'proof' of this theory lies in its account of the nature of literature, one which appeals to our own experience as readers or as members of a theatre audience.

Let me, then, consider the experience of reading one of Iris Murdoch's own novels, *The Black Prince*, published in 1973 midway between two of her major philosophical statements, *The Sovereignty of Good* (1970) and *The Fire and the Sun* (1977). The work contains a story by Bradley Pearson, 'The Black Prince: A Celebration of Love' framed by two forewords (by Pearson and his editor) and six postscripts (by Pearson, his editor and four dramatis personae). Pearson, who has understood his vocation as that of a writer of literature, has written the story, which claims to be of his own recent life, whilst wrongly imprisoned for life for the murder of his friend Arnold Baffin. In his postscript, he says that now he can see his life 'as a quest and an ascesis',[57] a quest that has led him to his friend and teacher P. Loxias, who becomes, after Pearson's death, the editor of his story, providing a foreword and postscript. The postscripts by the other four dramatis personae all contain hypotheses about Loxias's identity, but his own postscript suggests that only one gets near the truth, although in too crude a manner. The wife of the murdered man, who still denies her own guilt, says that Loxias is a fellow prisoner with whom Pearson was fixated, a notorious rapist and murderer who, some time ago, killed a fellow musician in an appalling manner. Now, Loxias is one of the names given to Apollo who flayed the musician Marsyas when the latter claimed to be able to better the god's own music, and this myth plays a central part in two of the decisive events in Pearson's story, his realization of his passion for Julian, Arnold Baffin's daughter, and his near rape of her. Apollo, god of law, harmony and music, is, too, imaged as the sun, Plato's own symbol for the Good. Pearson's quest, in his recent life and as a writer, involves his undergoing an ordeal (his trial and imprisonment) which leads him into a communion with Loxias which enables him to write again. The resulting story is thus both about the quest and its product. Loxias, at least in Pearson's view, is a teacher of the truth of life's quest. Pearson makes explicit reference to Plato's account of the ascent of the soul in the *Symposium* in his own postscript: 'Human love is the gateway to all knowledge, as Plato understood.'[58] Loxias thus appears as the teacher, communion with whom illuminates for Bradley the moral change his life has undergone, a teacher of the doctrine of the Good. Pearson's story (in his own view) is of his redemption through love for Baffin's daughter, Julian. He passes through this gateway and enters 'into another world'. 'The Black Prince' is 'a celebration of Love' in being both a love story and one which shows that, as Loxias says, 'Man's creative struggle, his search for wisdom and truth, is a love story.'[59] All this, one might say, is familiar to us from Murdoch's philosophical writings. Yet in so far as the life of love, of coming into relation to the Good and living that relation, is to be lived by a historically and socially situated indidividual with her or his own personality, any account which claims to be of such a life will raise certain questions for the reader. What is the lived nature of such a life, how does it manifest itself in the conduct of relations with others and in the contingencies of everyday life? To what extent are we to take Pearson's account (or Loxias's, for that matter) at face value? How do we determine this? Questions, that is, about the possibility of the embodiment of this view of life and its manifestation here, in Bradley Pearson's life, and about how we as readers can answer them.

The story Pearson tells is divided into three parts. The first shows us his life before his love for Julian, climaxing with the realization of his love for her. The second details the course of that love over a few days culminating in their escape to a cottage, 'Patara', by the sea. The third shows us their discovery by the father, Arnold, Julian's disappearance, and the murder of Arnold by his wife for which Pearson is arrested and charged.

Pearson shows us his earlier self as a man obsessed with order and control. He detests disorder, lives in a meticulously tidy manner, and fears the irruption into his life of the accidental and unpredictable. Contingency as an essential character of life fills him with fear and disgust. Trains, for example, upset him as they 'image the possibility of total and irrevocable failure' and being 'dirty, rackety, packed with strangers' they are 'an object lesson in the foul contingency of life: the talkative fellow traveller, the possibility of children'.[60] Indeed, the thought of desiring children, physical, demanding presences who would upset the ordered, hygienic tenor of his life, fills him with incomprehension.[61] He attempts to immure himself against the physicality of human life, experiencing bodies 'involuntarily and without positively shuddering in crowded tube stations'.[62] His life is devoted to art. He is a writer, although he has published little by the age of 58. Art for him aspires after perfection, the 'condensing and refining of a conception almost to nothing'.[63] Nothing satisfies this desire, so his life has largely consisted in the destruction of failed attempts. He now has writer's block, unable to write anything at all.

All other aspects of his life are subordinated to this goal of artistic perfection. He fails to see other people as individuals, seeing them only in terms of their relation to his own ordered existence. Whilst married to her, he never realized his now ex-wife Christian was Jewish. When his sister, having fled an abusive and adulterous husband, arrives at his flat, his response is to condemn her as 'in a thoroughly silly state. Women of your age often are. You're simply not rational.' His solution to her predicament is for her to return to her husband, selfish and tiresome as he is, and to forgive him, declaring that women must just put up with selfish men, 'it's their lot'.[64] Pearson tends to see others in terms of generalities and in any case only in terms of their capacity for disturbing his pursuit of artistic perfection. He does not relate to them, see them, as the individuals they are. He is shown to us as identifying the good with his goal, and in terms of it attempting a mastery of his life circumstances which is, in Part One, interrupted by an ever increasing series of events which culminates in his falling in love with Julian, the daughter of Arnold Baffin, his friend and rival author (who unlike Bradley Pearson is prolific, popular and wealthy). When he realizes his passion, whilst discussing *Hamlet* with her, it announces itself in his finding her physicality attractive ('I could smell her sweat, her feet, her breasts')[65] and, throwing open the window of his flat, he lets in the confusion of city life, a 'massed-up buzz of various noise filled the room, cars, voices, the endless hum of London's being'.[66] Embracing physicality and the disorder of everyday life, his love appears to transform his vision. He has, through apparently losing the obsession with imposing the form of a willed order on his life, come into contact with reality. He is, he believes, released from his self. His love for Julian is not desire but a simple gratitude for her very existence. He does not intend to tell her of his passion. He becomes on that first day, he tells us, 'a saint', vitalized by sheer gratitude and overflowing with charity and compassion. He is incredibly nice to his sister's husband and his mistress, forgives his ex-wife when she asks him to, and even goes so far as to worry about whether he may not have misjudged his rival Arnold's books and promises to re-read them. But this condition is revealed as a 'false loss of self' on the second day when he discovers the need to be with Julian and sets about planning how to achieve this. The future reappears and his life becomes valuable, once again, in terms of the goal he now identifies as his good, union with Julian. When Julian seems to reveal she already has a boyfriend, Bradley is thrown into despair, looking forward only to a life of permanent jealousy. When he declares his love and Julian says it is reciprocated (although she says she has loved him since she was a child), he walks away 'blindly, grimacing with joy'.[67] Reality has disappeared. He had seen the world and life in terms of the pursuit of artistic perfection; he now sees them in relation to his passion for Julian. These passions are now, however, to be revealed as one.

United, the pair escape to 'Patara'. Bradley tries to have sex with Julian but unsuccessfully until, on returning to the cottage, he finds her dressed as Hamlet, the Black Prince. He tears her clothes off and has violent sex, hurting her. He had, as mentioned, discovered his passion for Julian in talking to her of Hamlet. In this discussion, after dismissing psychoanalytical interpretations as true but trivial, he suggests (in an increasingly excited prose which mirrors his passion) that Hamlet is 'the tormented empty sinful consciousness of man seared by the bright light of art, the god's flayed victim dancing the dance of creation':[68] Hamlet as Marsyas, achieving art as the celebration of creation through his own self-destruction. At the cottage, he can only be aroused by Julian when she appears in the guise of Hamlet/Marsyas, in the guise of what he loves, the artist who achieves the highest art through self-destruction. His passion for Julian is revealed as part of the unfolding of the desire which characterized his earlier self but now liberated from its obsession with control: the desire of the artist as worship of the god, as self-sacrifice. He doesn't love Julian, he doesn't see her as she is, nearly forty years younger, inexperienced in relationships, and having known him all her life. Rather, Bradley's relation with Julian appears as part of an unconsciously willed path to self-destruction which is the trajectory of the transformation of his artistic drive from desire and its projected object to erotic worship of the god of art. This path achieves increasing clarity in the events which follow Julian's disappearance. Bradley, apparently unthinking, leaves a letter from Arnold Baffin declaring his love for Christian where Arnold's wife Rachel is bound to see and read it. Rachel kills Arnold and when Bradley arrives summoned by her to help, he cleans the murder weapon but leaves his own fingerprints on it. Rachel, who had previously declared a love for Bradley which is mocked by his relation with her daughter, has her revenge by failing to confess when he is charged with the murder. But Bradley's drive to self-destruction achieves self-recognition when he doesn't try to defend himself and is sentenced to life imprisonment, his reputation and his previous life destroyed.

Through this transformation of his artistic drive, he is now able to write. His desire for art, blocked by appearing as directed towards a determined object (his conception of the art object) which is to be produced through his controlling will, is released into worship of the god. The self of the artist is sacrificed. He writes *this* book about that very progress from self-absorption to self-sacrifice. In being driven through desire to a point where he is divested of what he thought he desired, he discovers a point beyond 'the fruitless anxious pain which binds to past and to future our miserable local arc of the great wheel of desire' and this becomes his story, his work of art. But it is a story which has a more general significance: 'Art is a vain and hollow show, a toy of gross illusion, unless it points beyond itself and moves ever whither it points.'[69] His journey from self-absorption as an artist to worship of the god and so loss of self becomes the subject of his own art and at the same time exemplary of a spiritual journey which has general human relevance. The work he now produces is far from being 'a conception refined almost to nothing'. It is rather one which encompasses through the form of a thriller (a form the previous Bradley had held in contempt) his own spiritual journey culminating in that absence of self in which the reality of the world becomes manifest. For him, his prison wall has the beauty of 'a glory beyond words, the world transfigured, found. It was this, which in the bliss of quietness I now enjoy, which I glimpsed prefigured in madness in the water-colour-blue eyes of Julian Baffin.'[70] Bradley presents his recent life as a spiritual progression, from self-absorption to selflessness, and so from a world of appearance (where people and things are seen in terms of the ego's objectives) to one of reality, where all is seen in the light of the Good.

This is, of course, to take matters at Bradley Pearson's word. But if we put these words, apparently articulating the achievement of a lived relation to the Good, love, into the context of his life, they may appear more problematic, 'ambiguous' as Loxias suggested in his foreword. Pearson portrayed his earlier life as involved in an impossible project of protecting himself from the incursions of contingency whilst comically being shown as its constant victim. The love which strikes him is preceded by his imminent departure for the cottage being constantly interrupted by people and events which require his response. This project, like his conception of art whose pursuit it ostensibly protects, seems a response to fear, a refusal of the world which is seen as threatening his identity as an 'artist'. He sees his love for Julian as ridding him of such fear, purging him 'of resentment and of hate . . . of all the mean anxious fears that compose the vile ego'.[71] This love, willing another, brings with it a vision of selflessness, the all-embracing love of the saint: 'why cannot this release from self provide a foothold in a new place which we can then colonize and enlarge until at last we will *all* that is not ourselves?'[72] Yet, his love for Julian is shown to be itself an illusion. She is not loved for herself but as an image of Bradley's own desire for artistic creativity: she can be fully embraced only in the guise of Hamlet/Marsyas. She serves her part in his unconscious drive to sacrifice himself to the god of art, to undergo the ordeal[73] which will make writing possible once again for him. But the strange thing about this ordeal, his imprisonment which brings the loss of his relations with the characters in his life, is that it gives him as near as possible what the earlier Bradley desired. His life in what he calls his 'monastery' is cut off from the world, as immured from chance as may be, and his relations with Loxias seem to operate at a purely cerebral level. The quest and ascesis which he now sees as his life, and which form the story of his book, may appear as the ultimate flight from the world, the desired goal of his fear, rather than the attainment of a state in which eros is transformed into love. That he should append at the end of his postscript the desire not to be seen as forgetting the 'real being' of the others in the story, and in particular Julian, while not wishing to know anything about them (which might, one wonders, disturb him), may well seem indicative of a further ego-induced illusion.

The possibility of this reading suggests it might have a more general relevance to the notion of love of the Good in Murdoch, or at least in the understanding of it Bradley Pearson articulates. 'The world', he says, 'is perhaps ultimately to be defined as a place of suffering. Man is a suffering animal, subject to ceaseless anxiety and pain and fear . . . the endless unsatisfied anguish of a being who passionately desires only illusory good.'[74] He points out that what I am attached to may be damaged or taken away at any time and certainly one day will cease to be. Attachment to such transitory goods inevitably brings with it anxiety and fear at their future prospects and regret and sorrow in relation to their past. These are painful emotions and ones we would wish to be without. We cannot then call these things truly good, and surely we desire what is really and not merely apparently good since we can be content with the appearance of goodness only where we judge that this is in fact good for us. Only by turning away from transient particular goods can the desire for good find what it is looking for, that attachment to which does not bring suffering in its train. Only so can we 'forswear the fruitless anxious pain which binds to present and future our miserable local arc of the great wheel of desire'.[75] That I suffer (or may do so) in relation to the goods I am attached to shows, since suffering is undesirable, that my desire seeks something else. Hence the necessity of giving up the pursuit of such good in a relation to the Good.

But this train of thought implies a motivation by fear of suffering which would make the 'willing for nothing' an illusion. It would be (what one may suspect Pearson's is) a willing for the sake of avoiding suffering. (This is, of course, part of Nietzsche's charge against Christianity and Buddhism.) Now, Pearson claims that only what transcends time can constitute the good for me, attachment to the temporal can only be to an illusory good, and that only through the former relation do I encounter people and things as they are and have a relation to 'the real'. But these claims seem unpersuasive. Let us say that I identify my good in terms of my attachment to certain people and relationships, to certain forms of activity, to a certain social and cultural context, to a certain place, with an understanding of their relative significance for me. If it is suggested that these are illusory goods since they may, indeed will, be taken from me and so relation to them must involve suffering which precludes them from constituting my good, it might be replied that this very temporality is in fact intrinsic to their goodness for me. How otherwise could I love this person if it is not the love for someone who ages and will die? How otherwise could I love a place if it is not a place situated in time and so subject to change? How otherwise love an intellectual activity if it is not a human activity subject to the creative reinterpretations which keep it alive and interesting? The point, it might be said, is to love people and things in their contingency, not to love the eternal and only through that return to the world. That would be not to really love what one finds there at all but rather to find it significant only in its relation to the eternal, in pointing beyond itself. It is not surprising we wonder about Bradley's love for Julian. His passion for her was a stage in his spiritual ascent to the good, not a love for her in her individual particularity. Having achieved his ascent (if indeed he did), what can now be meant by his claim that his love for Julian remains undiminished even though he wishes to know nothing of her life?[76] Real love, it may be said, for real people cannot avoid the reality of suffering and to be that love it must accept, even embrace, this fact. Far from the relation to the Good (at least in Bradley Pearson's understanding of it) revealing things as they 'really are', it may appear rather as a flight from an involvement with their contingent particularity.

This is, indeed, Martha Nussbaum's perception in a discussion of Murdoch's notion of love which addresses Bradley Pearson's case. Murdoch's account of the transformation of lower eros, directed towards illusory goods, to higher eros, directed towards the Good, means that one's love in the latter sense for an individual is always a love for 'the human particular in spite of itself'.[77] What we truly love in the higher sense is the Good and only through this do we love particular individuals. But this is not to love the particular individuals for themselves; it is to turn away from their reality. As she says of Bradley, in so far as he loves in this Platonic way, he looks 'beyond the real people [he loves] to the obscure image of a metaphysical source of that reverence and awe'.[78] Indeed, Martha Nussbaum sees this avoidance of attachment to and love of individuals in their contingent particularity as a characteristic of much Western ethical and religious thought, one motivated, as with Bradley, by the desire to eliminate or at least minimize the possibility of moral suffering, the possibility that contingency can determine the moral value of one's life. Nussbaum finds the antidote to this tendency in Aristotelian philosophy and in certain forms of literature. It may be, of course, that Bradley Pearson's understanding is presented as defective in its connection with the fear characteristic of his earlier life and in its development and articulation in his 'monastery' cut off from life. In that case, he would not show us concretely what love of the good means; rather, the deficencies in his understanding would prompt us to reflect on what this would be. This is suggested, for example, by Murdoch's remark that 'The great artist, while showing us what is not saved, implicitly shows us what salvation means.'[79] Love of the good would then involve embracing the pointlessness of the world and life and so the contingency of individuals Nussbaum emphasizes here. Even so, although not motivated by a desire to eliminate the individual's suffering, it might be said that the 'saint's' position still appears to be one beyond suffering and so opposed to a view of life which sees its value as essentially bound up with the possibility of suffering. To such a view, and its connection with literature, I now turn.

6

MARTHA NUSSBAUM
Moral fortune

'there is a distinctive ethical conception (which I shall call the
Aristotelian conception) that requires, for its adequate and
complete investigation and statement, forms and structures
such as those that we find in these novels'.[1]

Plato, according to Murdoch, sees life as a spiritual journey from attachment
to particular temporal (or quasi-temporal in the case of the rewards and
punishments of conventional religion) goods to attachment to the transcendent good. Contingencies, what happens to an individual rather than what
she does, have significance within this vision in their capacity to disrupt the
pursuit of illusory goods which is why such pursuit is inevitably enmeshed in
suffering. In so far as we maintain a relation to the transcendent Good,
however, they do not have the power to affect the value of our actions or
lives: hence the 'rapture' Murdoch speaks of in our experience of tragedy
where even the power of death itself is overcome. Now, as I have noted, her
'proof' of the truth of this vision lies in an appeal to self-recognition, to our
finding that we can make sense of our multifarious experience in its terms.
This appeal is a necessary feature for her of the pursuit of the truth about the
good for human beings. We are ourselves at issue in this question: the truth
of our condition must be what can precipitate such recognition and can lead
to our living in terms of the measure it provides. The 'proof' is to that extent
both 'empirical' (we recognize our lives in the vision) and 'practical' (the self-
recognition is at the same time that of the measure for our lives and so
involves us emotionally and practically). Now, Martha Nussbaum agrees
that the 'proof' of the truth about the good life must be both empirical and
practical in this way. Yet she will suggest that Plato's characterization of life
is provoked by what he regards as unacceptable features of an alternative
vision, called by her 'Aristotelian', which would in fact more readily pass the
empirical and practical tests. These features concern the Aristotelian acceptance that contingency can affect and indeed determine the ethical value of a
life. 'Plato's elaboration of radical ethical proposals is motivated by an acute
sense of the problems caused by ungoverned luck in human life.'[2]

What, then, is the Aristotelian conception according to Nussbaum? The good life for Aristotle consists in activity according to the excellences: these activities are what is ultimately valuable and for which we do everything else. There is a multiplicity of such excellences, and each one is distinct: a life lacking one is incomplete in a way which cannot be recompensed by the presence of other aspects. It is this, Nussbaum claims, which is meant by saying that such an activity is an end in itself – there is 'no trade off without loss'.[3] The variety of valuable activities are in this sense incommensurable with one another: there is no common standard or measure in terms of which they can be weighed. Excellences are states of character – justice, courage, moderation, generosity, friendship – in terms of which one desires in appropriate ways. Having such concerns, one will see particular courses of action as being possible in concrete situations. The ability to choose rightly, to determine the right action in the circumstances one finds oneself in, is practical wisdom, and is part of having the other excellences themselves. Such insight into what to do in terms of excellent activity is not something summarizable in general rules. Rules may be useful as summaries of past particular actions in particular circumstances, but their relevance to any new case must itself be judged. More significantly, practical choices cannot in principle be completely captured in rules. The world of change confronts agents with ever new situations so that they need to improvise what to do; situations are 'indeterminate' in the sense that one has to determine in each situation what the salient features are and respond accordingly: they don't come ready labelled; and concrete ethical situations may contain ultimately particular and non-repeatable elements – in love and friendship features of shared history and family relatedness are not even in principle repeatable.[4] Rather than rules, what we have before us as a standard is a kind of person, the phronemos, the person of practical wisdom, an individual who has all the excellences, who is just, generous, temperate, friendly, and so forth, and who responds to their situation in an appropriate way in terms of their essential ethical concern. This 'appropriate way' involves the choice of appropriate action and the having of the appropriate emotional response. To truly have an excellence is to have a disposition to feel in a certain way in certain kinds of situation and to act through the motivational force of that feeling. Thus, to have the excellence Aristotle calls 'gentleness' is to feel anger in the right way at the right time in relation to the right people. It is to feel anger at insulting behaviour and thus to have a disposition to act in relation to it.

All the excellences, Aristotle says, have a social aspect. Thus true courage is shown in battle in defence of one's city, true moderation shows a respect for the communal customs relating to eating, drinking and sexual activity, generosity a concern for the welfare of the recipients.[5] In fact, the excellences appear to be those of essentially social beings, individuals who are respectful and dutiful towards their parents, who value friendship especially with other good people, who care for the well-being of their city and its citizens and are ultimately willing to sacrifice themselves for them. At the same time, as thoroughly socialized individuals, they are sensitive to other people's attitudes towards themselves, having a marked sense of self-respect and expecting appropriate behaviour towards themselves from others. The human being is, Aristotle says, an animal who by nature lives the life of the polis and will have the excellences required by such a nature. As a social being, he values communal relations and activities for their own sake: family life, the sharing of concerns and conversation with friends, the active participation in the community's institutions for the maintenance, defence and celebration of city life. And he desires to spend lavishly on communal projects. Aristotle thus repeatedly stresses the role of habituation in developing the excellences of the social being. One is made into a social being by being surrounded by examples of good social behaviour and by being encouraged to do likewise. The point of such training is to turn the capacities for liking and disliking, the emotions, *pathe*, towards love of family, kin and polis, so that one comes to feel and act in appropriately socially concerned ways. As Aristotle says, 'The complete good seems to be self-sufficient. But by self-sufficient we mean not a life for the individual alone, living a solitary life, but for parents as well and children and wife and in general friends and fellow citizens, since the human being is by nature political.'[6]

If the good life is activity in accordance with the excellences of an eminently social being, then it is subject in various fundamental ways to disruption by chance, *tuche*, to what may happen over and beyond the possibilities of control by an individual. The very development of the excellences themselves depends on propitious circumstances. One needs to be surrounded by exemplars of good family and social life and to be encouraged to act in socially concerned ways to develop the appropriate habits of emotional response which are the basis for the excellences through which later one will choose to act in these ways. Assuming one has developed the appropriate character dispositions, their activity is dependent on external factors. In order to act generously, one needs resources and appropriate objects of one's generosity, and either one or both of these may be lacking; temperance requires the necessities for eating, drinking and engaging in sexual activity. Activities which flow from one's love of polis, political activities, or from friendship or love of family, are obviously subject to disruption from external factors. The political structure of the polis may render political activity in the normal sense impossible, through the institution of a tyranny, say, or through civil war, friends and family may perish or be taken from you. Or, most fundamentally, the very institutions of civilized life may collapse, depriving one of the total environment in which the excellences may be practised. We shall see Euripides investigating such a possibility in *Hecuba*. Furthermore, we can be placed in situations in which action required in terms of one excellence conflicts with that required by another, as when love of city and of family require incompatible courses of action. Since the excellences are incommensurable, such a situation precludes the possibility of acting well. Whatever one does, the possession of the relevant excellences will, since they are emotional dispositions, result in regret, remorse or even despair.

If the point of life is to live well, then a gap opens up between the excellences and their activity so that it is possible to be a good human being possessing the excellences of the human form of life, and yet fail to live well, to be *eudaimon*, through circumstances beyond one's control or intention. This dependence of the possession of the excellences, of their activity, and of their harmonious employment, and so of the very possibility of living well, upon external contingent factors, and the consequent gap between living well and being a good human being, can appear monstrous. Nussbaum sees Plato as engaged in a substantive ethical project directed towards remaking our values in order to remove this offence. The experience of offence comes from the very desire to live well and so have an end, a *telos*, for our lives. Such an end would provide a rational structuring to life so that we can act in a purposeful way. In terms of what counts as living well, we can see the ethically relevant aspects of situations and choose to act in the right way thus exercising the appropriate excellence. But if both being directed towards the right end and being able to engage in the appropriate activity are subject to circumstances beyond our control, then how can such a conception of an end satisfy our desire to organize our lives in a rational way? What is needed is to identify the *telos* of human life as lying in activity which is as immune as possible to the predations of chance so that the gap between being a good human being and living well should be narrowed to the greatest degree possible. At the same time, it must be an activity which would satisfy our desire to organize our lives, which would be chosen by our desire for and love of order. The philosophical activity of contemplation satisfies these requirements. Its concern is with truth, with the order of reality and thus represents the supreme activity corresponding to our desire for order and form, and so would be chosen by the desire which is itself the motivation for ordering our lives. And such contemplation is least dependent on external contingencies. Its objects are eternal unchanging objects of thought: their availability is therefore not dependent on changing circumstance. A life ordered in terms of the priority of such contemplation achieves a maximal self-sufficiency. Like all human lives, it still needs the necessities for life's continuation, but these are now seen as regrettable deficiencies. The activity of pure thought appears as the ultimately desirable form of life, although one we can engage in only periodically. A life aspiring in this way does so for a 'detached and extra-human standpoint':[7] it aspires for a non-human life, one beyond need and dependency on contingency. And so, of course, it renders its *telos* absolutely unattainable since we are after all humans, even if we have the capacity for philosophical contemplation. Nevertheless, it may be said that although it makes perfect, in the sense of permanent, *eudaimonia* impossible, it nevertheless ensures for those capable (possessing the relevant intellectual excellence) a participation in *eudaimonia* through the exercise of their excellence where this is not itself subject to upset by external factors. It thus better satisfies our need to organize our lives, and ensures, as far as is possible, that a good human being lives well, and so responds to our sense of justice.

This obviously raises the issue of how such a disagreement between Plato and Aristotle is to be resolved and so of Aristotle's method. Nussbaum's account of this seems to be as follows. Aristotle is engaged in the search for truth, here about the good life for human beings. But this search is conducted by one human being amongst others; there is no access to a non-human standpoint from which truth could be seen. Acceptance of the human stand-point requires an inquiry that is both empirical and practical. It is empirical in that it begins from the varied reports of human experience, considering the alternative views that have been given by 'the many and the wise' about the good life. Since it is an inquiry directed towards truth, it involves com-mitment to the principle of non-contradiction, and since it is conducted by one human being amongst others, what has generally or universally been accepted cannot be entirely rejected, even if we have to show its truth in a different light (as when we show that pleasure is indeed a good but not a self-guaranteeing one, and that the good pleasures are those of the good human being). Reviewing the various conceptions of the good life, we see conflicts between them which, directed as we are towards determining what the good life really is, we must remove, whilst preserving 'the greatest number and the most basic' of the original judgements. And it is here the essentially practical nature of the inquiry makes itself felt. For we are ourselves human beings inquiring about our own good. In examining the different views we uncover certain conflicting essential characteristics: for example, the Aristotelian view sees the good life as involving the activities of incommensurable excellences whilst Plato's measures all values against that of the contemplative activity itself. The only way of assessing such a conflict is to imagine 'vividly what a life would look like both with and without that belief, allowing us in imagin-ation and emotion, to get a sense of what the cost for us would be if we gave it up'.[8] And it is one philosophical role literature can play in providing such vivid imaginings, into which we emotionally enter as readers. But, provided, of course, that one can imagine the alternatives coherently, ultimately we as individuals must 'simply ask what looks deepest, what they can least live without – guided by their sense of life, and by their standing interest in consistency and community'.[9] Literature has an essential part to play in the search for the truth of the good life: in itself literature is 'a source of a human sort of truth'.[10] We as humans are essentially implicated in the search for the truth of the human good. It is for us both an intellectual and a practical inquiry, and the ultimate test for each of us is whether we find here what we 'can least live without', whether the conception of life, when imaginatively worked out, speaks to our deepest intuitions in terms of which we ourselves could live. And yet the inquiry is one into truth: what we find we offer not as an individual but as a human result, claiming universal validity.

One may wonder whether this account is true of Aristotle, and also whether anything produced by it would warrant calling 'truth'. As to the first, Aristotle himself seems explicitly to recognize philosophical contemplation as the highest form of human activity in the *Nicomachean Ethics*, the *Eudemian Ethics* and in the *Politics*, and elsewhere by implication. Nussbaum is, of course, aware of this, but sees it rather as an expression of the power of the desire for a simpler, less conflictful life that is itself only too human. (We shall see this desire portrayed in tragedy together with its insupportable consequences.) But I suspect this does not do justice to Aristotle (nor to Plato, for that matter). I am inclined rather to think that both Aristotle's and Plato's positions in relation to the good life derive from their resolution of fundamental metaphysical problems, and it is this which gives those positions the accolade of 'truth'. And this applies also to the extent to which the life of active social excellence can be held to be 'true' for human beings.

In order to provide the justification for thought and life in response to sophism's sceptical questioning, Plato hypothesizes the Forms as transcendent standards available to the intellect so that the world becomes a 'copy' in spatio-temporal and so material terms of the purely intelligible. This seemed to Aristotle to be merely metaphorical. Plato in the *Timaeus* had utilized the image of the *demiourgos* making the world from a blueprint, but this remained an image and could do nothing to make the talk of 'copy' any the less figurative. Further, the nature of the metaphor required a contrast between the temporal world, of which we too are a part, and the eternal, unchanging forms. But how could there be a connection between the temporal and the timeless, and how could we, as temporal beings, ever come into contact with the latter? Aristotle's response to these difficulties is to find the intelligible structure of the world implicit in it, as a potentiality which ultimately finds its proper actualization in thought. The mind grasps forms and these *are* the things of the world without matter, that which cannot be thought but which gives to beings their particularity. And from these further forms themselves can emerge, in the actualization of thought, the most fundamental notions of reality's intelligible structure, the laws of logic, the notions of form, substance, end, and so forth, which we find Aristotle concerned with in the *Metaphysics*. Our experience is of the real world since it brings to actualization potentialities that were already there, the potentialities of appearance (perceptible form) and thought (intelligible form). The world, as Jonathan Lear puts it, 'as such is meant to be known and it invites man to fulfill his role as a systematic understander of the world'.[11]

But humans do not just understand their world in different degrees of clarity, but utilize their capacity for thought, for form, to act in the world and change it. The craftsman has the form of the table within him and actualizes this in making one, so that the order the table exhibits is a result of this actualizing. But we don't just form utensils and works of art; we form ourselves. This is, of course, manifest in the explicit asking of the question of the nature of the good life. But form is emergent first in the unreflective process through which human life becomes ordered. The sexes come together for the purpose of reproduction, in the family unit; families come together for the maintenance and safeguarding of life, in the village. But higher than such orderings is that found in the polis where a social ordering which is not for reproduction or the maintenance of life (although both these functions are still fulfilled) emerges. Here social ordering is for its own sake, so that the good citizen is indeed characterized by the excellence of social living. But the human capacity for form, the intelligence which makes us what we are, is capable of pure activity, and not merely an application within materials, even human ones.

> Eudaimonia is an activity, but the active life is not necessarily active in relation to other men, but far more those speculations and thoughts that have their ends in themselves and are pursued for their own sake: for the end is to do well and so is a form of action.[12]

Philosophical contemplation is the highest human activity as the full actualizing of our capacity for form, our reason. In so far as we have to live as social beings, the character excellences are indeed required to live well socially. But human life can aspire to a higher form of life, the activity of pure thought, philosophy, which is 'higher' as the actualization of our reason which is otherwise only 'embodied' in the ordering social life takes. We can see here that the justification for the social excellences does not just derive from the study of the views of 'the many and the wise' through an internal resolving of conflicts. Such views are, of course, important, since reason for Aristotle is emergent: our experience of the world and of ourselves is never (in so far as it is generally shared) illusory, but rather is 'of' a reality in some way. But in order to see what that way is, one has to understand the particular appearances in relation to the development of form from potentiality to actuality, and so through the actualizations of previous potentialities which are themselves potentialities for further actualization, and so on. What guides Aristotle's inquiry is the telos of understanding, of the active and pure exercise of intellect in terms of which we can then regard human life, and indeed all animal and plant life, and inanimate things, in their hierarchical ordering. Without this fixed point, the dissolving of conflicts which ultimately seems to appeal to our experience (we find ourselves reacting in this or that way and so recognize what we really value) would have no claim to truth. It would be possible (and most likely) that we react in different ways with only a minimal level of agreement in values. But even if this were not the case, the common experience could not show its truth: it would remain an experience whose significance remained to be shown. Its claim to truth can only be shown by situating it in the process of the emergence of the truth of the world, so that we can then see it as the truth of social human life, and true because it is the expression of form in that medium. But to say that is to see the possibility of a higher type of human activity which would be the exercise of intelligence for its own sake. With these reservations let me return to Nussbaum's account of literature.

Literature no more than philosophy speaks with one voice. Literature, like moral philosophy, shows us ways life is seen. Life 'is never simply *presented* by a text; it is always *represented as* something', and this 'as' appears not only in what we could paraphrase as content, but in the 'style' of the writing, its shape and form, its structures and terms, which require of the reader a certain kind of activity.[13] And it is in relation to the Aristotelian conception of ethics that she refers us to Greek tragedies and certain novels, particularly those of Henry James: 'there is a distinctive ethical conception (which I shall call the Aristotelian conception) that requires for its adequate and complete investigation and statement, forms and structures such as those that we find in these novels'. This Aristotelian conception involves, as we have seen, the following features. The good life lies in a plurality of activities having no common measure or even a small number of measures: rather, these activities are each good as an end in themselves. Hence, there is a pervasive possibility of conflicting attachments. Living well involves discerning the relevant features of one's situation and this is itself valuable, is itself the expression of a moral excellence. Such responsiveness to one's situation involves taking account of three features which preclude thinking of this response in terms of the application of rules: new and unanticipated features; context-embeddedness of relevant features so that the relevant moral aspects must be determined in situ; and the ethical relevance of particular persons and relationships. Whereas one might still say that the first two aspects could be incorporated, however merely formally, in a rule, so that if this situation were to be repeated in the relevant aspects, then the same response would be appropriate, the third feature absolutely precludes this. There, what matters is that it is just this person she is responding to, not a bearer of repeatable properties, and since both their lives are lived only in one direction, we cannot imagine that just this encounter could be repeated. To imagine otherwise 'is to imagine that life does not have the structure it has'.[14] Within this Aristotelian view, emotions have ethical significance in themselves. For Aristotle, the excellences are dispositions in relation to emotion. Hence it is morally significant what one feels as well as what one does. That the emotions should have this significance is a mark of the ethical significance of contingency, since emotions involve beliefs about contingencies and their importance. Uncontrolled happenings have ethical significance in that they can destroy or make possible living well.

Now, we can outline this conception, but we need

> to show forth the force and truth of the Aristotelian claim that 'the decision rests with perception' ... texts which display to us the complexity, the indeterminacy, the sheer *difficulty* of moral choice

91

and which show us . . . the childishness, the refusal of life involved in fixing everything in advance according to some system of inviolable rules.[15]

Such a conception requires a certain kind of literary embodiment for its proper presentation. The novel or play can show us what can't be encompassed within the generalities of philosophical prose, the uniqueness of the situation, in which individuals encounter one another in terms of their unrepeatable histories. The narrative of individual histories alone makes this possible. Further, literature is needed to 'convey the way in which the "matter of the practical" appears before the agent in all of its bewildering complexity without its morally salient features stamped on its face'. If we give philosophical examples, we do so having already determined what is relevant. The novel or drama, however, can show us individuals actively engaged in this perception itself, and thus convey 'the active adventure of the deliberative intelligence'.[16] It is part of the Aristotelian view that this very perceptiveness is itself the work of an excellence and so has value in itself. The novel in showing us this deliberation and responsiveness can give us a sense of its own value, 'the peculiar value and beauty of choosing humanly well'. And, of course, the novel requires of the reader just such an exercise of perception, thought and emotion in following the story. We are emotionally involved with the characters, seeing the world from their perspectives, and actively engaged in this interpretive activity in following their thoughts and perceptions. At the same time, this enforces our recognition of our own incompleteness, that we have no access to a more than human standpoint but that there can only be individual human perceptions and interpretations of their situation. But this engagement of our faculties, emotional and imaginative, takes place outside of our own practical engagement in our lives: 'we are free of certain sources of distortion that frequently impede our real-life deliberations . . . our personal jealousies or angers or . . . the sometimes blinding violence of our loves'.[17] There is, Nussbaum believes, 'something about the act of reading that is exemplary for conduct'. Our attention to James's characters, if we read well, is itself 'a high case of moral attention'. In this way, the novel not only shows what moral attention is but elicits it[18] and under conditions most favourable to it, since we are removed from the practicalities of our own life. 'We find here love without possessiveness, attention without bias, involvement without panic.'[19] Through this experience we not only attain understanding of our own deepest values, but do so through a morally valuable form of experience itself.

It is this significance Nussbaum sees in Greek tragedy and which explains Aristotle's concern with it. The tragic poem, she writes,

is a carefully crafted working through of a human story, designed to bring certain themes and questions to each reader's attention. It can therefore advance the conversation among readers that is necessary to the completion of the Aristotelian project, whose aims are ultimately defined in terms of a 'we', of people who wish to live together and share a conception of value ... it can therefore promote self-inquiry while also facilitating co-operative discussion.[20]

Aristotle said that tragedy effects 'through pity and fear the catharsis of such emotions'.[21] For Aristotle, an emotion is a composite of the feeling of pleasure or pain and a particular kind of belief about the world where the belief is the ground of the feeling.[22] With both pity and fear the belief concerns the significance of chance for the human good. We pity another in recognizing the importance of what has happened to him beyond his control or intention for his well-being, and what we pity in others we fear for ourselves.[23] To pity others we have to identify with them, and so, as Aristotle says, they must be 'like us', not perfect paradigms of virtue. (Nussbaum notes how Oedipus' shortness of temper helps the tragic response since it aids our identification with him.)[24] 'The great tragic plots', she writes,

explore the gap between our goodness and our good living, between what we are (our character, intentions, aspirations, values) and how humanly well we manage to live. They show us reversals happening to good charactered but not divine or invulnerable people, exploring the many ways in which being of a good human character falls short of sufficiency for eudaimonia.[25]

This 'vulnerability of good people to ethically significant reversals'[26] includes, as I noted above, the dependence for the development of the excellences on the right social environment, for their practice on the maintenance of such an enviroment and the possession of other resources, and the potentiality for circumstances to produce situations of fundamental ethical conflict where one can only do evil. Aeschylus' *Agamemnon* shows us a case of the latter, and in doing so reveals the tragic vision of human life as embodying an Aristotelian conception of value. Agamemnon is required by Artemis to sacrifice his daughter if the Greek fleet is to cease to be becalmed. No fault of Agamemnon is given in the play for his predicament, although such attribution is given in other tellings of the story: Aeschylus' omission of it would seem to be to stress the sheer contingency of the circumstances which have produced his dilemma. Agamemnon, whilst recognizing that as king and so leader of the Greek forces commanded by Zeus to avenge a crime against hospitality, the sacrifice of his daughter is to be chosen, nevertheless regards both alternatives as involving evil. The two relationships, of Agamemnon with his people and with his daughter, are incommensurable: to violate either involves an evil which cannot be remedied. To choose either would involve acting and feeling in a way which shows 'that this is an act deeply repellent to him and to his character' so that afterwards he would feel inevitable remorse, acknowledging the evil he has reluctantly done.[27] It is because Agamemnon's attitude changes after the decision is made that the Chorus condemns him, not because of the choice itself. Agamemnon tries then to see the decision as implying a common standard for the cases so that the evil involved in choosing either should be removed. If he chooses what is best, then surely there is no room for remorse, and the chosen alternative should be pursued with passion. 'For it is right and holy' he says in Nussbaum's translation, 'that I should desire with exceedingly impassioned passion the sacrifice staying the winds, the maiden's blood.'[28] It is characteristic, Nussbaum claims, of the tragedy's presentation of human possibilities, in relation to a conception of learning I shall come to shortly, that it should show us both the way of living in terms of incommensurable values vulnerable to contingency which she has called Aristotelian, and ways determined by a desire to avoid the remorse and pain such a view may involve.

> The impulse to create a solution to the problem of conflict is not foreign to tragedy . . . It is present within tragedy as a human possibility . . . Like any works that truly explore the human 'appearances', these tragedies show us, alongside the 'tragic view', the origin of the denial of that view.[29]

The *Antigone* of Sophocles finds in Creon and Antigone such lives devoted to the avoidance of conflict. Creon, as ruler of Thebes, has a single measure, the well-being of the city, in terms of which everything is to be judged. For him, Polynices is merely a traitor, rather than being also the dead son of his sister whom he has an obligation to see properly buried. 'He is determined to conceal from deliberative view the claims of both familial and affective ties . . . insofar as they clash with civic interest.'[30] For Creon, there can be no irreconcilable conflicts 'because there is only a single supreme good, and all other values are functions of that good'.[31] Antigone too displays a ruthless adherence to a single value, that of piety to the familial dead. Both Creon and Antigone are shown as ultimately forced to recognize the falseness of their strategies through the shock of suffering. (I shall note the connection of this with the conception of learning later.) Creon's son dies as a result of his treatment of Antigone and he is compelled by his grief to recognize the incommensurability of his relation to his son with that other value, the well-being of the city, which he had tried to make the supreme measure. His grief shows 'how impoverished [*anolba*] [his] deliberations were'.[32] Antigone in her turn is compelled to recognize the value of the city by seeing that, in dying, she deprives her family of a guardian for their tombs and memory, save for the city and its gods.

If *Agamemnon* and *Antigone* in their different ways explore the vulnerabilty

94

of human values to conflict created by external circumstances, Euripides' *Hecuba* shows us the vulnerability of ethical character itself. Hecuba, enslaved after the fall of Troy, is shown secure in her nobility, believing 'A good person will be stably disposed to choose noble actions and to avoid shameful ones. No matter what happens in the world, this character will escape defilement or corruption.'[33] But all this changes when she discovers her son has been murdered by the guest-friend, Polymestor, with whom he has been entrusted. Abandoning her former noble values, she organizes her life now in terms of revenge, killing Polymestor's child and blinding him on an occasion when he is her guest. Although other commentators have found this sudden alteration in Hecuba a defect in the play, Nussbaum argues for its inner logic. Hecuba's nobility involves an adherence to social and relational values and to an 'anthropocentric' view of these values, that 'ethical commitments are human things, backed by nothing harder or more stable . . . than our agreements . . . Deep human agreements (or practices) concerning value are the ultimate authority for moral norms.'[34] But such agreements can disappear, or a situation may be created in which it can present itself as an undecidable issue whether they ever existed. Then the main component of all such values, trust in others' agreement with you and in their consequent feeling and conduct, becomes impossible. 'In certain externally caused conditions any normal, reasonable person will come to be sceptical and suspicious.' But if I become sceptical and suspicious, 'I am . . . no longer a noble person; perhaps no longer a person at all.'[35] I am no longer noble since I am no longer characterized by the virtues which depend on trust: they have become an irrelevance since now I trust no one. What they are transmuted to in Hecuba's case I shall mention in a moment. But, further, if such trust in others' agreement is necessary for engaging in living speech with others, then perhaps I am no longer capable of real speech any more, and so perhaps am no longer really human. Polymestor's murder of Hecuba's child is, Nussbaum suggests, the violation of this fundamental trust exemplifed in the disregard for the tie of guest-friendship, 'the most binding tie that exists by nomos, the tie that most fundamentally indicates one human's openness to another, his willingness to join with that other in a common moral world'.[36] Polymestor's crime is at the same time a 'worst case' because of the child's defenceless simplicity and because of the future of Priam's line and of the city which depended on him. Hecuba sees here that what appeared most firm and most valued can be set aside, raising the question for her of whether that trust and value ever existed. Such generalized suspicion undermines the possibility of social and relational values, and Hecuba now organizes her life around the value of revenge which requires no trust or dependence on others. Such organization, like the very different ones of Creon and Antigone, is motivated by the desire for an absence of vulnerability, whilst it seeks to treat Polymestor as he has Hecuba. In this way, she acts in terms of what she now sees to be the truth: there never had been the trust which would have supported noble values. Her life has been lived in illusion in which others have expoited her simplicity. The value of revenge gives a single focus for the organization of her life and one whose activity seems to depend solely on herself. The social virtues which characterized her become stripped of their social reference. Courage becomes 'a kind of brazen daring', prudence 'a solitary cunning which has no respect for any decency and trusts no man's respect for hers', justice becomes a means of 'personal punishment and personal safety . . . wisdom is simply . . . clever plotting'.[37] Hecuba's character remains as this desocialized husk: her fate is to become a dog, that creature, for the Greeks, most impervious to *nomos*.

Tragedy for Aristotle is 'a mimesis of pitiable and fearful things'[38] and 'accomplishes its characteristic effect through these emotions'.[39] The emotions of pity and fear determine plot, the sort of hero, and the structure of the events of the story. A tragedy shows us the undeserved fall from good fortune to bad of a good (but not perfect) human being through a sequence of events taking place in the way we understand them to take place in our world and so without the use of supernatural agencies or amazing coincidences. Poetry, Aristotle says, deals with 'things such as might happen' and so with general human possibilities. The hero is 'like us' and being involved in what we recognize as a reasonable course of events, 'we see what happens to the hero as . . . general human possibilities, possibilities for us'.[40] Experiencing them as possibilities for us means being emotionally involved: I am not a mere observer of events but rather what is taking place here concerns me, shows what can happen to me. Pity and fear thus become the appropriate form of response in terms of which the audience really sees what is before it. Aristotle emphasizes that poetry is more 'philosophical' than history, and, Nussbaum says, this seems to imply that it speaks to the human desire to understand which Aristotle elsewhere has claimed is universal in humans. Poetry is a form of mimesis, and Aristotle claims that the pleasure we take in mimesis is one of coming to understand, of recognition that 'this is that'. Through the experience of tragedy we recognize certain human possibilities which reveal to us our most deeply held values and we recognize them through the experience of the emotions of pity and fear. These 'emotions can be genuine sources of understanding'.[41]

Through our response to the play, through our pity and fear, we attain a 'self-understanding concerning the attachments and values that support the responses'.[42] This is the significance of catharsis. In a highly suggestive account, Nussbaum points to the primary meaning of the group of words containing *katharsis* as 'clarification', of which the medical usage in the sense of purgation is a special case, referring to the removal from the body of internal obstacles, thus 'clearing it up'. So in the *Poetics* she reads catharsis as a cognitive clarification produced by the influence of pity and fear. This process has two aspects we have met before. First, through our emotional response we recognize the nature of our values and so acknowledge the significance of contingency for our desire to live well, whilst being shown at the same time our own desire for a simpler, less vulnerable form of existing. Emotions, although they can distort judgement, can also lead us to a recognition of our true values, ones which we may have disguised from ourselves through rationalization. Second, the emotions of pity and fear we feel are not simply valuable as a means to an intellectual recognition of where our values truly lie. These responses are valuable in themselves as 'elements in an appropriate practical perception of our situation'.[43] That is, human excellence involves the possession of the right emotions and their activity is itself part of human good living. Tragedy provides us with an occasion for both self-recognition and good living, the one via the other. And Nussbaum would say the same of the novels she discusses. In this way, such plays and novels are 'not just irreplaceable fine representations of moral achievement, they are moral achievements on behalf of our community'.[44] Attending to the play involves itself the exercise of the social virtues and their characteristic form of thought. We have seen that this thought involves the rejection of the primacy of rule in favour of perception of the individual situation. The world of change submits us to ever new situations to which we must respond in new ways; which are the relevant features of a situation is something we must always judge; and we are often responding to particular individuals in situations which are not even in principle repeatable since it may be just this moment in our shared history which may be morally relevant. This perception of the particular is both intellectual and emotional: to see the situation in its morally relevant aspects is to feel in a certain way towards it. Similarly with our attention to the play. It is up to us to perceive what is there, and to do this we must exercise an attention which is open to the new and unexpected in its bearing on how we read what we have already seen. 'We reflect on an incident, not by subsuming it under a general rule, but by finding images and connections that will permit us to see it more truly, describe it more richly.'[45] Thus, for example, the apparent optimism of the Chorus's famous ode in *Antigone*, which begins 'There are many *deina* [strange, terrible] things', celebrating man's triumph over contingencies, is undermined by the way its images connect up with others in the play so that 'the statement of human triumphs through reason turns out to be also a compressed document of reason's limitations, transgressions and conflicts'.[46] Thus, although 'This thing [the human] crosses the gray sea in the winter stormwind, making its path along the troughs of the swelling waves', such ships can be dashed by storms (line 163), and the city itself is imaged as a ship and so is liable to upset and destruction, here by the simplicities of Creon's and Antigone's views of life which do not themselves engage in this form of contextual reading. This form of reading demanded by the play is itself an exemplification of the sort of moral reading and attention which our relational attachments continually demand of us: to read the present in relation to the past, whilst recognizing that the present may alter our view of the past, and that the future may alter either or both. Such perception is always particular, involves feeling, and is open to revision. We search for and see relevant aspects of our situation because we care about others and the world: 'good response involves not only intellectual appreciation but where appropriate emotional reaction'.[47]

Attending to the tragedy exercises our capacity for moral perception and involves our central values expressed in our emotional reaction. But it does so in a situation where we are not individually involved, and so provides us with the learning which can take place in relation to a mimesis, a recognition. We come to a recognition of our deepest values, and of our attendant desire to deny them through the attraction of safety and invulnerability, to a self-knowledge through the experience of emotion. '*Pathei mathos*', learning by suffering, has its sense both within the tragic plot and within the audience's relation to it.

Yet what we recognize here is at odds with what Iris Murdoch's experience of tragedy would propose. For her, the experience of tragedy is, at its best, the sharing of the position of the saint, from whose vantage point the orientation to the Good overcomes the power of death and destruction in relation to the value of life. For Nussbaum, however, the experience of tragedy shows us just that power, and convinces us, through our emotional reactions, that our values are indeed founded on the very fragility and neediness of life: what we most value can indeed be destroyed by contingent events in such a way that the best of humans can fail to live well. Nussbaum suspects that Murdoch's vision, like Plato's, is motivated by a desire to eliminate the suffering attendant of the Aristotelian view. But although this may be true of Bradley Pearson's understanding, it is possible that this is shown us as defective, that the 'saint' passes beyond such motivation in an embrace of the pointlessness, the contingency, of the world and life. Nevertheless even then, it would remain true that for Nussbaum, this would still maintain a position within which the necessity of suffering for the value which life has is denied, and I think this would mean for her that within such a view the individual in her mortality is not the object of love. She is loved only by way of love of the transcendent Good so that one's love of her is removed from its essential relation to suffering in respect of her pain and the prospect of her loss.

The experience of tragedy is thus appealed to within a broadly shared conception of an 'empirical' and 'practical' inquiry into the truth of the human good but in support of opposed views. There seems no reason to reject either of them in terms of the requirements of such an inquiry, whilst in relation to the human good the demand that such an inquiry should be both 'empirical' and 'practical' in the given senses seems plausible. Surely it should result in something we can recognize as making sense of our lives and in terms of which we can at least try to live. Yet it is not clear why the result of this inquiry should be regarded as the 'truth' about human life in Murdoch's and Nussbaum's sense. It is likely, and their disagreement suggests it is actual, that no such agreed result will be forthcoming. Even if it were, this would constitute a merely empirical result which, as Kant observed in relation to Hume's 'naturalism', could not claim the universal validity which an appeal to 'truth' seemingly involves (and does involve for both Murdoch and Nussbaum. I shall query this assumption in Chapter 8). The validity of such a result would be conditional on the agreement of the parties concerned and could therefore be rejected if they later, or some other inquirer who complied with the demands of the methodology, failed to agree. It is because of the weakness of such an appeal to agreement, if what is at issue is 'truth' in the desired sense, that Aristotle needs the metaphysical underpinning for his method in ethics I mentioned earlier. But perhaps the desired universal validity may be derived by attending to what Murdoch's and Nussbaum's inquiries fail to address, namely their fundamental character, and indeed that of inquiry itself. Self-recognition and its practical import are only possible for a *linguistic* being, for beings who can 'make sense' of their lives and raise the question of how to live. Perhaps if we understand our nature as such linguistic beings we can see what such self-recognition and its practical import must be and address the role which literature, as a distinctive form of language use, can play there. These issues are raised in the work of Richard Rorty and Stanley Cavell.

7

RICHARD RORTY
Philosophy as literature

Rorty's 'pragmatism' is directed towards the 'dissolution of the traditional problematic about truth'.[1] This traditional problematic is provoked, according to Rorty, by sceptical worries, the need to ask and try to answer questions like 'Why believe what I take to be true?' and 'Why do what I take to be right?'[2] In order to answer such questions we have to appeal to 'something *more* than the ordinary, retail, detailed, concrete reasons which have brought one to one's present view'. This 'something' must transcend the actual procedures for justifying beliefs and actions of any community since it is what will determine whether and to what extent their procedures are capable of producing true beliefs or right actions. This 'common ground' of all communities has sometimes been located in the realm of Being as opposed to that of Becoming, as with Plato's Forms, sometimes within ourselves, as with the seventeenth-century idea that examination of our minds could show us the method for discovering truth, and more recently in the nature of language itself.[3] This urge to transcendence leads to the notion of truth as correspondence to 'the way things really are' where this relates to the 'common ground' and how things appear in its light, and to the idea of procedures of justification which are in accordance with reality and not just a historical community's ways of doing what it calls 'justifying'. We thus get the development of the philosophical disciplines of ontology, as the specification of the nature and fundamental structure of reality, and epistemology, as showing how we are to get in touch with reality as so understood.[4] The attempt to resolve sceptical questions leads to the view that the universe has an 'intrinsic nature', either, as it were, speaking its own language (which we can perhaps learn) or having been made in accordance with a language, the world as God or as made by God.[5] In order to think or act correctly we must subordinate ourselves to something non-human, to 'the Intrinsic Nature of Reality'.[6]

What are the possibilities for criticism of this 'transcendent problematic'? We can't say it is false and oppose it with some further account claiming to be the truth since this would simply repeat it. We can't say that we have discovered there is no truth, since this would itself be a claim to truth.[7] This is the general problem of self-reference which all attempts to criticize this problematic face, 'the problem of how to distance one's predecessors without doing exactly what one has repudiated them for doing'.[8] Nor can we say the transcendental problematic is 'confused'. Such an idea presupposes that there is 'our language' which philosophers become confused about, that there is, that is, 'the truth' about our language which can show what is confused and what is not. Such a move is complicit, again, with what it seems to criticize. Clarity, Rorty says, is familiarity rather than a property whose presence or absence can be demonstrated. Those who develop a transcendent problematic find its necessity clear enough.[9]

Nor does Rorty take the tempting line of some post-Nietzscheans (Derrida in some writings, for example) that the transcendent notions of 'the truth' and 'reality as it is in itself' are illusory since they are constituted in language and the nature of linguistic meaning, being dependent on context where context cannot be made determinate, precludes the intelligibility of such notions of finality. He doesn't because, again, he regards such a view as claiming itself to have arrived at 'the truth' about language, to be arguing in terms of the 'essence' of language that the notion of 'essence' is illusory – a self-defeating move.

Rorty's approach, rather, is to address the transcendental problematic as a human phenomenon which answers to human desire and aspiration. The human need for transcendence is a response to the desire to pass beyond the possibility of questioning and the demand for justification, to become, as Rorty puts it, 'a properly programmed machine', to attain a position from which our view on life and the world would be beyond the possibility of criticism from any other viewpoint since it would transcend all viewpoints. This (very human) desire is the desire not to be human, but to be God.[10] In practice, this is a submission of ourselves as human to the non-human. Rorty's reason for rejecting the transcendental problematic, therefore, is that it preserves 'an image of the relation between people and non-people that might be called "authoritarian" – the image of human beings being subject to a judgement other than that of a consensus of other human beings'.[11] This is an 'unnecessary and dangerous' view because 'the maturation of [Western humanity] has consisted in the gradual realization that, if we can rely on one another, we need not rely on anything else'.[12] One cannot present arguments against the transcendental problematic as these would have to claim it was false or confused in some way. Rather, as it is the expression of a human desire, it is opposed from the viewpoint of another desire, that of being self-reliant and not subservient to any non-human standard. Rorty's proposal is that we should drop the language of 'the truth', of the intrinsic nature of the world and the human, as expressive of a desire which we, who see ourselves as self-reliant human beings, have no use for.

There are, of course, considerations which Rorty brings to bear against the transcendent standpoint. In particular, that we have no way of formulating an independent test of accuracy for whether our account of the world corresponds to an 'antecedently determinate reality' or is closer to it than proposed alternatives, and no way of deciding which description of an object gets at what is intrinsic, essential to it. All descriptions are part of human practices which serve or constitute human purposes and there is no way of determining that descriptions produced in terms of certain of these practices are in accordance with reality as it is and others not. In practice, the appeal to the transcendent viewpoint has been a way of privileging a certain historical vocabulary, the appeal to truth being a product, as it were, of a Nietzschean will to power. Hence, Rorty says that the best argument against the transcendent problematic is that 'It has become as transparent a device as the postulation of deities who turn out, by a happy coincidence, to have chosen *us* as their people.'[13] It requires the 'absurdity of thinking that the vocabulary used by present science, morality, or whatever has some privileged attachment to reality which makes it *more* than just a further set of descriptions'.[14] Nevertheless, this 'absurdity' is only seen and felt by someone who has rejected the desire for transcendence in the name of human self-reliance. It is always open to the believer to maintain the belief that there is the truth and that the present represents progress since it is the result of the revelation of the falsity or limited vision of past positions.

What, then, would constitute the self-image of those content to 'rely on one another'? It would be the replacement of our self-image as dependent on a non-human otherness by one which shows us as dependent on human communication, conversation, argument and debate alone. We are answerable solely to human discussion for the justification of our beliefs, actions, our lives. Concretely, for Rorty this new self-image is developed largely through a reinterpretation of the terms central to the transcendent standpoint, from an authoritarian to a self-reliant sense. 'Objectivity' as 'accurate representation' becomes replaced by objectivity as conformity to the norms of justification for assertions and actions of our current linguistic practices. 'Knowledge' as 'congruence of mind and reality' is replaced by knowledge as the right, by current standards, to believe. 'Truth' as 'correspondence with reality' is replaced by truth as what comes to be believed in the course of free and open encounters, with the proviso that, of course, someone may come up with a better idea in the future.[15] The results of all inquiry are thus replaceable; all inquiry is interpretation which can itself be recontextualized.[16] We must, therefore, be actively engaged in the process of recontextualizing, constantly seeking the new viewpoint.[17] Epistemological and ontological questions like 'What is the nature of reality in itself?' and 'How do we get in contact with such reality?' are therefore to be replaced by ethico-political questions such as 'Are our encounters sufficiently open?' 'Are we open to new ideas from outsiders?'[18] The sceptical anxiety which leads to the 'necessity' of the transcendent position, the fear that what it is rational to believe according to our norms of justification may not be true, is replaced by hope and expectation, that someone may come along with a better idea, an improved belief since new evidence, new hypotheses or a new vocabulary may be produced.[19]

Rorty's reformulations are meant to show how things appear when we drop the transcendent notions of 'reality' and 'truth'. He suggests that rejection of the metaphysical idea of reality means that we have no contact with a non-human reality.[20] Rather, 'knowledge' is of propositions, and justification is a relation of such propositions to others. Now, propositions are uses of vocabularies and vocabularies change with the creation of new ones, thereby altering the stock of available propositions. Hence, any propositions which constitute 'knowledge' at present by appeal to other propositions only constitute a set of descriptions which the future may and almost certainly will replace. At any rate, they can only be held as potentially revisable.[21] We must, therefore, always be open to such change and we can only do this if we actively subject them to the conditions for change. Exposure to constant discussion, openness to other, alien viewpoints is required.

It has been pointed out[22] that these supposed consequences of the rejection of the metaphysical conception of reality are actually complicit with it. The idea that all we ever encounter are sets of descriptions always replaceable by others is a vestige of the metaphysical position within which reality is always beyond the range of human capacities so that all we can ever have are human descriptions of how it appears. But this is to distort the non-metaphysical language such a position must appeal to for its plausibility (or attraction in Rorty's view). If I describe my desk to you what I am describing is not a further set of descriptions. And if what I say is true, then it doesn't need revising, although, of course, I might tell you other things about it. The possibility of saying other things, or doing other things (writing a poem about the desk, say) doesn't revise what originally was true, does not show that this was a matter of 'descriptions' which were revisable. It is as if Rorty thought that without the metaphysical notion of reality for our thought to be 'about' we could no longer speak of knowledge, truth and reality but only of (revisable) claims to justification and the (revisable) descriptions which such justification consists in, although it is difficult then to see what 'justification' could mean. We shall see shortly the consequences of Rorty's reformulations for morality and how they too seem to be complicit with the metaphysical picture he ostensibly rejects.

This change in self-image cannot be produced by argument according to Rorty since argument presupposes a shared vocabulary whereas the change is constituted by the replacement of one vocabulary by another. Rather, the change is not proposed as a better way of doing the same things (satisfying our desire to put a stop to questioning) but as part of the proposal that we should stop doing those things and do something else.[23] The appeal is to 'utility' in a broad sense: do we now see that being self-reliant is what we want so that having such a self-image will satisfy us? We may come to realize that the self-image is the one we want through our being taken by its redescriptions of things (science, morality, politics, and so on); these may effect a change in the way we see things through showing us what, perhaps to our surprise, we find we want.

In this sense, Rorty sees his pragmatism as contributing to 'a world historical change in humanity's self-image'.[24] It is the formulation of a new vocabulary, old words in new meanings and neologisms, to do a new job, to form the self-image of a non-subservient humanity. In terms of this self-image, the development of new vocabularies (the replacement of Aristotelian by Newtonian science, for example) is not a matter of bringing hidden secrets to light but rather of showing us things in a new light which satisfies what we find we want (and this, of course, is not the revelation of a hitherto hidden desire but its creation). Such a change takes place by the uttering of 'meaningless' sentences, ones which don't fit existing linguistic practices, which, if taken up, modify those practices or create new ones.[25] In this creative use of language, success occurs because it creates it, not because that use satisfies pre-existing standards. And this, in terms of Rorty's new self-image, he calls 'literature'. 'By "literature" . . . I shall mean the areas of culture which, quite self-consciously, forego agreement on an encompassing critical vocabulary, and thus forego argumentation.'[26] This captures something which writers and readers have often insisted on in relation to what is conventionally called 'literature', namely, that new kinds of poem or novel are introduced without argument. They don't succeed because there are good reasons why poems or novels should be written like this but because they create their own 'taste'. And in this sense, Rorty's own writings aim at this 'literary' condition, the creation of a new vocabulary to satisfy a desire which it will in some part create.

We've seen reason to suspect that Rorty's reformulations of the notions of 'reality', 'truth' and so forth involve suggestions which seem to proceed from a failure to break free from the metaphysical conceptions he opposes. They distort what we can understand by 'inquiry'. And this raises the question of whether Rorty thinks that the philosophical provision of his pragmatist 'self-image' has any implications for the forms of thought and life we may live if we reject the transcendent notions of the traditional problematic. There is an ambiguity in Rorty's response to this question. He presents his 'pragmatism' as consisting '*simply* in the dissolution of the traditional problematic about truth, as opposed to a constructive "pragmatist theory of truth"'.[27] In this sense, it represents just the rejection of the necessity of responding to the sceptical questions which prompt the development of the traditional problematic. In this vein, he says, for example, 'The absence of an intrinsic human nature, and thus of inbuilt moral obligations, seems to us pragmatists compatible with any and every decision about what sort of life to lead, or what sort of politics to pursue.'[28] This might seem clear, since it is impossible for Rorty to claim that the philosophical position that there are no transcendent grounds provides a ground for some preferred modes of life. We won't change our practices, he says, if we adopt philosophically his position.[29] Social practices do not, according to that position, have philosophical presuppositions, and the philosophical propositions said to be foundational are to be regarded rather as rhetorical ornaments of practice.[30] This means, presumably, that these propositions are to be seen as a way of affirming participants' adherence to certain practices, emphasizing their commitment to them and their rejection (ungrounded) of other forms of life. To undermine the claim of these propositions to ground these practices leaves the latter where they were with the possibility, for those who want it, of another form of self-image in terms of Rorty's pragmatist notions. As Rorty himself recognizes, the scientist will go on conducting his experiments in the same way whether he talks of himself as reading nature's own language or detecting God's plan or not. Indeed, as Rorty recognizes, the transcendent vocabulary has been brought into play as a rhetorical device in relation to the liberal form of life he himself will espouse.

However, something rather more radical is suggested when he sees his new self-image as 'the end of essentialism and logocentrism' and characterizes the latter as

> merely the latest stage in a gradual and continuous shift in human beings' sense of their relation to the rest of the universe – a change which led from worshipping God to worshipping sages to worshipping empirical scientific inquirers. With luck, this process will end by leaving us unable to *worship* anything. But the resulting inability to love one thing with all one's heart, soul, and mind, will not entail the inability to rejoice in a lot of different things ... no high altars ... [but] lots of cultural options but no privileged central discipline or practice.[31]

But this treats rejecting a philosophical attempt to ground our life and its practices in a transcendent ground in response to sceptical questions as if this constituted rejecting a life which 'loves one thing with all one's heart, soul and mind', whereas on its own ground this must surely remain one of the ungrounded cultural options. There seems to be an oscillation here between a philosophical sense of 'self-reliance' (the rejection of a philosophical attempt to ground our practices by reference to a transcendent ground) and a sense of 'self-reliance' which refers us to certain concrete forms of individual and social life in opposition to others (for example, religious and traditional ones). But the rejection of the necessity for grounding means that the latter do not depend on a philosophical belief in a transcendent ground. They are, on Rorty's own terms, as 'justified' as the secular and progressive forms of life he prefers since there is no transcendent ground they must satisfy.

This ambiguity perhaps suggests that Rorty is not free of the urge to justify his preferred values instead of leaving them as ungrounded. He explicitly rejects what he takes to be a Heideggerian and Derridean attitude to the traditional problematic, that the concrete forms of life we have inherited indeed presuppose the metaphysical picture, so that when we are forced to rethink what Derrida calls the 'universal problematic' this has direct consequences for what we can now think ethically, politically, religiously, and whether there will now be anything to be called by these names. Rejecting this as remaining complicit with the idea of grounding, Rorty's self-image seemingly can have no implications for the way we may live.

This issue of the relation of the 'pragmatist' self-image to non-philosophical forms of life arises clearly in his conception of an ideal society and of forms of individual life appropriate to such a society. Here we can see that Rorty's reformulations embody certain concrete ethical and political proposals. A society with such a self-image, he says, would be one without the ambition of transcendence.[32] This would be a society oriented to intersubjective agreement, and since linguistic practices can change, to novelty. It would be a democratic, progressive and pluralist community. In order that its linguistic practices should remain open to the future, it would pride itself on encouraging debate amongst its members through its 'tolerance for a plurality of subcultures and its willingness to listen to neighboring cultures'.[33] It would not think of humanity as moving towards a goal already determined, but think of progress as the possibility for us to become more interesting people. It would be a community characterized by tolerance, free inquiry and the quest for undistorted communication, in which individual moral progress is seen as self-creation in the exploration of possible ways of being. Since there is no longer any ground for claiming that some one goal exists for all, it would separate the individual's project of self-creation from the maintenance of a free community within which that project has the widest possibility. Solidarity would thus be emphasized through the values of tolerance, freedom and undistorted communication and the institutions which embody them, whilst individuals would be left to their own self-creative devices compatible with the same freedom for all. An 'ideal liberal society is one which has no purpose except freedom, no goal except a willingness to see how such encounters go and to abide by the outcome'.[34]

Members of such a society would see themselves as contingent through and through, without a ground for their forms of life.[35] They would exhibit no aspiration after transcendence. But intellectuals, those presumably who understand themselves explicitly as contingent in terms of the pragmatist self-image, would be 'ironists'. For ironists, the contingency and groundlessness of their vocabulary means that they are 'never quite able to take themselves seriously because always aware that the terms in which they describe themselves are subject to change'.[36] This 'doubt' about whatever values the ironist currently subscribes to means that she 'spends her time worrying about the possibility that she has been initiated into the wrong

106

tribe, taught to play the wrong language game'. She worries that contingent circumstances have 'given her the wrong language, and so turned her into the wrong kind of human being'.[37] This is, of course, strange, since such doubt seems to hanker after some justification beyond the contingent values she possesses: she appears to be nostalgic for a transcendent standpoint she ostensibly rejects which would give a sense to 'right' and 'wrong' in terms other than those of any particular values she may espouse. This suggests that the diagnosis of her situation as a lack of seriousness is nearer the mark.

Rorty suggests that if we recognize that there is no 'truth' in the transcendent sense to underpin our values, we must engage in a life of constant experimentation. It seems, as D. Z. Phillips remarks, as if he implies that in 'disposing of metaphysical absolutes . . . no place remains for ordinary absolutes in the realm of values'.[38] But to reject the necessity for a transcendent ground does not mean that one cannot be committed to what one inherits as a matter of historical contingency or what one contingently discovers for oneself. Indeed, the possibility of intellectual, moral and religious practices involves the idea of people being committed to them in a way which precludes the kind of experimentalism Rorty speaks of here. As Phillips goes on to remark,

> If people are committed to a point of view, they may or may not be prepared to talk to those who disagree with them. They will not be prepared to give an open-ended commitment to converse no matter what the topic in the conversation may be and to regard as 'agreement' whatever the outcome may be. Such a reluctance would not be, as Rorty thinks, a failure to be realistic about the times in which they live. Rather, their reservation is a qualifying mark of seriousness in *any* conversation.[39]

The liberal ironist is portrayed as constantly sampling forms of life, a relation to them which would indicate an alienation or dilettantism precluding seriousness and so the possibility of any meaningful engagement with them. It is as if Rorty thinks that any such commitment must depend on believing in a transcendent ground for one's practices so that if one rejects such a philosophical view the only alternative is to be uncommitted, open to suggestions. But this indicates, rather, that Rorty's position here, as we have seen elsewhere, is still complicit with the transcendent problematic it explicitly rejects.

The removal of the notion of 'essence' means for Rorty that the liberal ironist has no use for absolute distinctions between literature, philosophy, sociology, ethnography, and so forth.[40] Rather, she treats writers as presenters of certain values and the sorts of beliefs and desires which go with them. Since she is engaged in an explicit project of self-creation, she reads such authors in order to discover if she wishes to re-create herself in their image.

(Rorty mentions here Nietzsche, Kierkegaard, Proust, Trilling, Blake, Freud, D. H. Lawrence and Orwell.) She discovers this by experimenting with the vocabularies these writers create, redescribing herself, her situation, her past, in their terms and comparing the results with those produced by alternative perspectives. 'We ironists hope, by this continual redescription, to make the best selves for ourselves that we can.'[41] Again, it is difficult to know what 'best' can mean here since it cannot be understood in terms of any of the perspectives at issue. This purported project appears to be aspiring after a position beyond the contingent perspectives which, ostensibly, she believes are all there are. This doubt about herself 'can be resolved or assuaged only by enlarging our acquaintance' so that she experiences a variety of perspectives, and the easiest way of doing this is reading books. 'Ironists are afraid that they will get stuck in the vocabulary in which they were brought up if they only know the people in their own neighborhood' so they read about strange people (Alcibiades, Julien Sorel), strange families (the Karamazovs, the Casaubons), strange communities (the Teutonic Knights, the Nuer, the mandarins of the Sung).[42] Since such doubts seem only intelligible as a vestigial attachment to a position beyond contingent values, it is not surprising that it is difficult to see how doing this could 'assuage' them – whatever books I read, there are always more, and even if there weren't, I could always suppose that a 'better' perspective lay just out of sight.

In terms of this conception, however, books may either serve the ironist's need for explicit self-creation, or serve both her and non-intellectuals' need for the maintenance and expansion of the realm of freedom. The latter need is addressed, first, by books which help us to see the effects of social practices and institutions on others and which either alert us to cruelties they produce which we may have averted our eyes from or show us new forms of cruelty we had not imagined. Books about slavery, poverty, prejudice: Rorty cites *The Condition of the Working Class in England*, and novels such as *Uncle Tom's Cabin*, *Les Misérables* and *The Well of Loneliness*. The need is addressed, second, by books which help us see the effects of our private self-creation on others, which show us the blindness of a certain kind of persons to the pain and humiliation they inflict on others. Through identifying with Casaubon in *Middlemarch* or Mrs Jellyby in *Bleak House* we may come to recognize the pain we inflict on others through our own attempts at self-creation.[43]

The liberal ironist's experimentation is a way of responding to the task which faces individuals in making what is given them contingently into their own life. This need is to take over what chance has given us in an individual way and so master contingency. Rorty sees that there are many forms of such adaptation,[44] and since for him there is no 'truth' already written into human nature or the cosmos, there can be no philosophical arbitration between them. But elsewhere he is inclined to weight the scales. In 'Freud and Moral Reflection', for example, he suggests that this attempt to make oneself out of the givens of chance can take one of two antithetical forms, producing either the ascetic or the aesthetic life. Ascetically, he says, the attempt is to 'peel away everything that is accidental, to will one thing, to intensify, to become a simpler and more transparent being' whereas aesthetically the desire is 'to enlarge oneself . . . to embrace more and more possibilities, to be constantly learning, to give oneself over entirely to curiosity, to end by having envisaged all the possibilities of past and future'.[45] Presumably the last clause refers to an aspiration for the impossible suggested by the trajectory of the aesthete's life. But Rorty isn't prepared simply to describe these two possibilities and consider what concretely they might involve. Rather, he suggests that the ascetic attitude presupposes a belief in 'the true self' so that living such a life involves the presupposition that one is revealing something which is, in some sense, already there. But this is to suggest that this attitude to life involves a philosophical presupposition, something which Rorty has been at pains to deny elsewhere in relation to human practices. Why shouldn't we rather say that the individual who comes 'to terms with the blind impress which chance has given her' by 'willing one thing' (however that may be understood in different religious and ethical traditions) is *making* her self, bringing together in a unifying way the disparate aspects of her talents, activities and relationships?

We have seen that for Rorty the liberal ironist is someone who explicitly recognizes the contingency of human life, that there is no 'truth' written into human life or the world to which one could appeal to guide one's life. She is an intellectual, a philosophically inclined individual. Rorty suggests, however, that in conveying this vision the novel has an advantage over philosophical approaches. Indeed, the very nature of philosophical reflection is likely to lead the writer into a temptation to betray her insight. Ironist theory, the attempt to philosophically undermine the traditional philosophical problematic, such as we find in Nietzsche, Heidegger and Derrida, is faced by the problem of how to undermine the claims of 'truth' without appearing to claim for itself a timeless authority, to be telling us 'the truth'. Ironist theory has to take a narrative form: it cannot claim to relate to a timeless truth that can be demonstrated or argued for, and so can only establish a relation to the past. Yet how is the theorist to avoid the obvious charge of claiming to tell 'the truth' about the past and so claiming to occupy a position of timeless authority? Only, Rorty suggests, by claiming to stand at a point where the possibilities of the past are shown to be exhausted by the past itself and the thinker becomes a prophet for a new age. The 'ironist theorist cannot imagine any successors, for he is the prophet of a new age, one in which no terms used in the past will have application'.[46] It is the past history of 'truth' which, for example, in Nietzsche's 'How the True World became a Fable', overcomes itself, running through the possibilities which, in their self-overcoming, allow the glimpse of a new age and a new language rid of its attachments to the ideas of 'truth', 'essence' and so forth. This is why the narratives of the ironist theorist detail, as Rorty says of Nietzsche's, 'not a chance collection but a dialectic progression, one which serves to describe the life of somebody who is not Friedrich Nietzsche but somebody much bigger . . . "Europe". In the life of Europe, unlike that of Nietzsche, chance does not intrude.'[47] The story the theorist tells must have a necessary structure, one in which the pursuit of truth undoes itself, resulting in the situation in which the theorist announces the new dawn. So the theorist must appeal to the 'somebody much larger' since the history he tells has got to have its own impetus, a 'life' of its own. Nietzsche's history of truth and Heidegger's History of Being are examples of this tendency. The theorist avoids claiming to speak 'the truth' by recording what the history of truth or Being sees itself as having done, creating a situation in which the transcendent notions no longer apply and thus making possible a new age and a new language.

This kind of narrative (taken at face value; Rorty will go on to suggest another way of reading it) may appear to defeat its own object. The authority which the traditional philosopher claimed through access to the non-human standard of truth is now shifted to the 'larger somebody' of history, Being, or whatever, whilst the thinker becomes, as it were, the medium through whom the end of a particular history announces itself and the new age, liberated from 'truth' and 'essence', appears. But it does so only through the 'truth' and 'essence' of a history which announces its own necessary unfolding. The ironist theorist is tempted to demonstrate the *necessity* of the recognition of our finitude, our contingency, now, and in succumbing to that temptation, he betrays what he wishes to convey.

The ironist novelist, however, has no such motivations which the theorist inherits from his philosophical training. The ironist novelist, of whom Rorty takes Proust to be exemplary, debunks 'truth' through showing individuals claiming such authority as contingent individuals. Proust

> managed to debunk authority without setting up as authority, to debunk the ambitions of the powerful without sharing them. He finitized authority figures not by detecting what they 'really' were but by watching them become different than they had been, and by seeing how they looked when redescribed in terms offered by still other authority figures, whom he played off against the first.[48]

Proust recognizes contingency and shows the comedy of individuals claiming to be something more than particular human beings. The ironist novel shows us contingency, and gets us as the human readers we are to recognize ourselves, without the temptations to essentialize and assume authority which theorizing brings with itself. It can do so because novels are about people, who are, unlike ideas or forces of 'History', obviously situated in time and place and subject to chance. In so far as the people in a novel involve themselves with such ideas or forces, they remain individuals whose claims to speak for a non-human authority appear in comic contrast to the play of perspectives which constitutes the novel's form. Novels in this way 'are a safer medium than theory for expressing one's recognition of the relativity and contingency of authority figures'.[49]

This leads Rorty to a radical rereading of ironist theory. The histories of Truth, Being and so forth are as much mythologies as 'truth' and 'essence' have been. But we can read them as (misleading) accounts of the self-creation of their authors, of ways in which individuals finding themselves with philosophical interests situated in a tradition of philosophical writing 'come to terms with the blind impress which chance has given' them. They liberate themselves from contingency by making something individual out of what they have been given. What such authors say has no general significance (as they believe) but how they do this, the way they take the given materials and make of them something new and individual, can be an example to us, both generally, in so far as we are all faced by this task, and in particular for those of us who share their interests and traditions of philosophy.

> When Nietzsche and Heidegger stick to celebrating their personal canons, stick to the little things which meant most to them, they are as magnificent as Proust. They are figures whom the rest of us can use as examples and as material in our own attempts to create a new self by writing a bildungsroman about our old self.[50]

If neither of these thinkers can plausibly be understood as understanding himself simply as creating an individual self out of the philosophical interests and materials they found themselves with, Rorty sees Derrida, at least in his later manifestations, as seeing his practice in this light. The earlier Derrida had indeed been tempted in the direction of ironist theorizing. He located himself at the moment when language invaded the 'universal problematic' showing us that the notions of metaphysical finality were at odds with the differential nature of language. Derrida's preferred 'notions' of 'trace', *différance* and so forth, then claim an adequacy in speaking of language which the traditional notions of 'sign' and 'signified' lack. But such theorizing in claiming to reveal what language 'really is' contradicts its own anti-metaphysical ambitions. The later Derrida, for Rorty, abandons theory and 'privatizes his philosophical thinking'. 'He simply drops theory – the attempt to see his predecessors steadily and whole – in favor of fantasizing about these predecessors, playing with them, giving free rein to the trains of associations they produce.'[51] Treating the traditional problematic in this way is the only strategy for avoiding the problem of ironist theorizing, that of remaining complicit with what one wishes to abandon, the claim to speak 'the truth'. Derrida is true to his contingency, *shows* it to us, precisely in declining to argue with the tradition or to tell the truth about it, and playing with it, using it to make something individual and unique. There is nothing to be learnt from these fantasies in the way of a teaching, but they can nevertheless be exemplary, 'suggestions of the sort of thing one might do, a sort of thing rarely done before'.[52] They show us self-making, the taking of the contingent givens of particular individuals' interests and talents in their historical situation and the impressing upon them of an individual voice. And they do so in relation to the givens of the traditional problematic of truth. In exemplifying the task the contingent human being faces in the context of someone with philosophical interests and a training in the discipline which in one way or another occludes a clear recognition of our contingency, these fantasies liberate us from the fantasies of philosophy and ironist theorizing. 'He has played all the authority figures, and all the descriptions of himself which these figures might be imagined as giving, off against each other, with the result that the very notion of "authority" loses application in reference to his work.'[53]

The ironist novel doesn't argue that we are really finite contingent beings in a world without its own truth: rather, it shows us human beings in their contingent particularity living in such a world and invites our self-recognition. It displays 'a diversity of viewpoints, a plurality of descriptions of the same events' and it shows the comedy of believing 'that one human being is more in touch with something nonhuman than another human being'.[54] The traditional philosopher in order to justify privileging one viewpoint must appeal to a non-human standard for the variety of perspectives, whilst the ironist theorist appeals to the hidden impetus of History or Being to justify privileging his own position. But if we abandon belief in both a transcendent viewpoint and the 'greater Somebody', we are left with the multiple perspectives of individual human beings in their agreements and disagreements, in their honesty and self-deception, their sympathies and their cruelties, and this moral scene is something the novelist's art is peculiarly able to show. The arts have in the past provided the appropriate form of moral justification for a group's institutions and practices by showing human life in terms of its values, by 'apotheosizing its heroes, diabolizing its enemies, mounting dialogues among its members, and refocussing its attention'.[55] The ironist novel, however, shows us the moral scene of a plurality of viewpoints in which society's shared values concern the maintenance of communal solidarity as a framework within which individuals can pursue their private projects of self-creation, the moral scene of liberal society. Within such a society, the role of philosophy as 'rhetorical ornament' is played by Rorty's reformulation of the human self-image, whilst the novel and the arts can not only provide that society's self-image, but can alert us to the cruelties which institutions and the pursuit of private self-creation can inflict and propose new forms which self-creation can take.

Rorty has argued that the transcendent notions of 'reality' and 'truth' are generated in order to answer sceptical questions. Appeal must be made beyond any historical community's forms of thought and life if sceptical questions directed at those forms themselves are to be answered. Rorty proposes we drop these transcendent notions and replace them with 'pragmatist' ones. But to see our practices and life in terms of the latter has unfortunate consequences. According to Rorty's vision, what we encounter in the world always has the character of revisable descriptions. Any claim that a proposition is 'true' can only mean it is related to other propositions which 'justify' it temporarily, awaiting further interpretation or recontextualization, so that it is always intelligible to raise further questions about any proposition whatever. Whereas the transcendent position wishes to put a stop to questioning, Rorty asserts the infinite possibility of questioning. Similarly, in relation to the liberal ironist who sees life in pragmatist terms, any present values she may espouse are only held temporarily, awaiting further moves in her self-creation. Whereas the transcendent standpoint wishes to assert a way of life as true for all, Rorty wishes to portray life as non-ending interpretation. I have suggested that both moves are complicit with the transcendent position, implicitly assuming we could only speak of 'truth' and 'justification' in a non-revisable form if we subscribed to it. We are left then in the strange position of inhabiting our world in a condition of permanent revisability and our lives in a state of a permanent lack of seriousness. The hidden complicity of Rorty with the transcendent position lies in their both interpreting our relation to the world and our lives in terms of 'knowing', the latter asserting that this must be brought to a final state, the former that it cannot be and so must consist in unending interpretation. It is this assumption, of course, which makes possible sceptical questioning.

Rorty sees Wittgenstein as a fellow traveller on the pragmatist road. Stanley Cavell, however, sees Wittgenstein's work as standing in a quite different relation to scepticism. For Cavell, Wittgenstein tries to get us to recognize that our fundamental relation to the world and to each other is not that of 'knowing', however interpreted, and only if we are already in the world and with each other in another, more fundamental way, can we understand what it is to raise questions, claim knowledge and assert truth. 'The basic form of our game must be one in which there is no such thing as doubt.'[56] I turn now to Cavell's treatment of this issue and to the relation he sees between the impulse to scepticism in philosophy and literature.

8

STANLEY CAVELL

Language, therapy and perfectionism

> modern scepticism [is] philosophy's expression or interpretation of the thing known to literature (among other places) in melodrama and in tragedy. (By the thing known in melodrama and in tragedy I mean, roughly, the dependence of the human self on society for its definition, but at the same time its transcendence of that definition, its infinite insecurity in maintaining its existence ... in determining and maintaining what belongs to it. 'It'.)[1]

Stanley Cavell sees in Wittgenstein's thought a 'new form of criticism', not 'trying to argue a given statement false or wrong, but ... showing that the person making an assertion does not really know what he means, has not really said what he wished'.[2] This mode of criticism does not claim that the words the sceptic uses don't mean anything (how could he, another competent language speaker, be so wrong about that?) but rather that *he* doesn't: 'the point of saying them is lost' so that 'we no longer know what *we* mean'.[3] It is not that what the sceptic says is mistaken: rather, he appears to be making a claim in a situation where no claim (claiming being a human activity with its own conditions) can be made. He fails to *say* anything, not fails to say *anything*. How, then, does scepticism arise?

A language user speaks and thinks, and *what* she speaks and thinks she *speaks* and *thinks*: she asserts, remarks, speculates, hypothesizes, etc. But 'not just *anything* people will do will *be* asserting, calling, etc.';[4] 'to say (or think) something is the case *you must say or think it* and "saying that" (or "thinking that") has its conditions'. Now, the sceptic suspects there is something questionable about our knowledge in its totality, a suspicion which is a manifestation of the desire Cavell ultimately wishes to reveal. But, the sceptic must allow his questions to arise naturally; otherwise what he says will not have the alarming consequences for our non-philosophical lives he suggests. But the oddity we experience in his questioning, which the sceptic takes for illumination, is produced by his unknowingly abandoning the conditions for his asserting, stating, questioning, etc., that is, for doing something with his words. So he asks how we can know someone is really in pain in a situation where the question 'why do you think this expression of pain gives a false picture of it?' has no answer.[5] Or, in order to raise the question of whether we really do know there is a fire (table, chair, etc.) here, he must first claim that we do think we 'know' it in a situation where 'how does he know it?' has no answer, or not the right kind of answer, where the 'reasons' that are given (he just looked at it, he must glance at it a hundred times a day, etc.) are inoperative as reasons, incapable of removing doubt.[6] In order to express his 'sense that . . . something is, or may be, amiss with knowledge as a whole'[7] the philosopher is forced to address a 'non-claim' context, where the conditions for claiming to know, removing doubt, questioning, are inoperative, whilst attempting to construe such a context as involving our making claims to knowledge and so open to questions of justification and so doubt, treating it as if it were a situation in which these notions made sense. A characteristic unnoticed shift occurs in the sceptic's text: 'to ask us to imagine a situation in which we are seated before the fire is not to ask us to imagine that we have *claimed* (*to know or believe*) that we are seated before the fire'[8] (my emphasis). Yet the philosopher must then treat the former situation (imagine we are seated before a fire) as if it were the latter (imagine we are claiming to be seated before the fire) without recognizing the difference in the conditions for these two imaginings (for example, if you imagine claiming to be seated before the fire, what are you imagining is suspicious about your situation?). Once this shift has taken place, it seems possible to ask what justifies this claim to know. And our natural response is to answer in the way we would if we really were entering a claim: 'Well, I can see it, feel the heat' and so on. But these cannot act as reasons here, as removing a doubt, since obviously if the claim to know there is a fire here is in question, it can't be answered by appealing to my seeing or feeling *it*. We appear to have an unjustifiable claim made about what is in the external world, 'outside me', on the basis of what is 'in me', my 'senses'. What has happened here, however, is that a situation in which the conditions for 'claiming to know', and so for 'doubting' and 'removing doubt by giving reasons', are lacking is nevertheless construed as involving a claim to know. This construal thus expresses a desire to know beyond the conditions under which we as humans make claims to know, raise doubts, have them removed, and so on, a desire which is, of course, unsatisfiable. Anything we may offer as a 'reason' must be inadequate, but only because the conditions for 'giving a reason' are themselves absent. And the same thing happens when we try to raise the question 'how do you know she is in pain?' in a situation where there are no conditions for this being a case of 'doubt'. We respond in the way we should to remove a real doubt, by appealing, for example, to what she says and does. Yet these can't operate here as reasons, since there is nothing specified as amiss with the situation: all her sayings and doings are, as it were, part of the scenario which is in question. We suddenly appear to have an insuperable barrier between her 'feeling' and anything I might be aware of, her 'behaviour', just as in the previous case we appear to have an unbridgeable gap between my 'senses' and 'what is really out there'. But what really finds expression in these sceptical developments is a desire to escape 'the human conditions of knowledge and action' and so, as we shall see, to escape our responsibility for what we say.[9] We 'want to know the world as we imagine God knows it'.[10] The philosopher's notions of 'the senses' and 'the feeling itself' are thus 'inventions', ideas of what things must be like in order to match what he has the illusion of meaning – made to order with his ideas of 'the object in itself' or of 'behaviour', which are inventions too. Feeling 'being sealed off from the world' the philosopher is left only with his ability 'to sense'. 'The senses' he is left with are as 'a matter of construction *opposed* to the revelation of things as they are'.[11] And feeling others as sealed off from himself, he is left only with 'behaviour' as opposed to the 'feeling itself'. These are inventions produced out of a desire to speak or think beyond our humanity, beyond the conditions for our meaning anything by our words: yet the philosopher is, of course, another human being speaking to human beings. In order to question our knowledge in its totality, he must start out from normal cases where the conditions for claiming and questioning are satisfied, otherwise what he addresses will not be our knowledge. So he must affirm allegiance to those conditions. But then he wishes to understand himself and be understood as questioning and claiming to know where those conditions no longer apply, and so fails to do anything with his words, words which, in other circumstances, could constitute a claim, but one which would not do what the sceptic intends.

The sceptic does not really 'question' or 'claim', that is, do what counts as 'questioning' or 'claiming'. So

> the reason that no basis is satisfactory, is not that there isn't one where there ought to be, but that there is no claim which can provide the relevance of a basis. The reason we cannot say what the thing is in itself is not that there is something we do not in fact know, but that we have deprived ourselves of the conditions for saying anything in particular.[12]

> Wittgenstein's ... implied claim [is] ... that all our knowledge, everything we assert or question (or doubt or wonder about ...) is governed not merely by what we understand as 'evidence' or 'truth conditions' but by criteria ... Without the control of criteria in *applying* concepts, we would not know what counts as evidence for any claim, nor for what claims evidence is needed [my emphasis].[13]

Criteria show 'what kind of object anything is'[14] by establishing the position of that concept in relation to the concepts of its application, use, *our* use of it. It is, for example, part of the grammar of 'colour' and of 'meaning' that *that* is what we call 'to point to the meaning' and *that* 'to point to the colour', *that* 'to raise a question about meaning', *that* 'to answer a question about meaning' and so on. If you don't know that, namely, what we do with the word, you haven't got the concepts of a colour and of a meaning, you don't know what (kind of objects) colours and meanings are.[15]

Criteria tell us, remind us, what counts as something by locating its concept within human practices. But this means then that this counting is something which *counts*, that is, is valued: 'what can comprehensibly be said is what is found to be worth saying . . . So that what can be communicated, say, a fact, depends upon agreement in valuing, rather than the other way around.'[16] Having criteria and so being able to communicate thus involves sharing forms of life, paths of interest and concern (laughing at what we laugh at, noticing what we notice, comforting what we comfort, finding alike or remarkable or ordinary what we do, feeling pain at what we feel pain at, and so forth).[17] Learning language is thus initiation into these forms of life in which the intiate must be able to follow us, in however rudimentary a way, naturally,[18] so that 'our ability to communicate with him depends upon his "natural reactions" to our directions and our gestures'.[19] But this is equally true of initiates: their capacity to communicate rests on their sharing with others ways of applying, using, their words. Intelligibility involves 'pervasive and systematic agreements' which are shown in agreements in judgements, in the assertions and claims we make. This 'agreement' is not one we come to, decide upon, but is prior to anything we could call a decision. It is a matter, as Cavell puts it, of 'being in harmony, like pitches or tones . . . naturally attuned'.[20] But such attunement may therefore be absent.

> When our attunements are dissonant, I cannot get below them to firmer ground . . . not only does he not receive me, because his natural reactions are not mine, but my own understanding is found to go no further than my own natural reactions bear it . . . the anxiety lies not just in the fact that my understanding has limits, but that I must draw them, on apparently no more ground than my own.[21]

It is this which makes the sceptical move itself a natural human response. When my reasons give out, I am thrown back upon myself, in the absence of any appeal to an authority, and the same, of course, goes for the other. This very fragility of intelligibility prompts the desire for access to a supra-human position within which the human being would attain a barrier against the possibility of a collapse of meaning. Dogmatic metaphysics and scepticism appear as two sides of the manifestation of this desire. The one claims access to a non-human position and thus an authority which no human being could have, granted through access to the logos, the ideas in the mind of God, to absolute Spirit, etc. The other, recognizing the impossibility of such access for a human being, nevertheless experiences this impossibility as a lack and so declares our knowledge fatally undermined. Both metaphysics and scepticism are expressions of the desire to transcend the conditions for human intelligibility, aspiring after an impossible safety. Scepticism, disappointed in its recognition of the impossibility, whilst maintaining the desire, thus declares we must deny that we know there is an external world and that there are other people.

However, the appeal to criteria, to the embeddedness of our concepts of the world and of others within human practices cannot refute scepticism, since the sceptic attempts to withdraw from precisely those human practices themselves. The appeal to criteria tries to show that the sceptic has failed to say anything, has failed to 'make a claim', 'express a doubt', and so naturally has failed to find adequate jusitification. But since the sceptic wishes to suspend commitment to any such human practices, hankering after a non-human certainty, such a reminder will not refute him. What is needed, rather, is a recovery from fantasy, from a desire for the impossible. And, Cavell says, such desire is itself thoroughly human and reveals itself in other, non-intellectualized forms in human life, in those forms tragedy concerns itself with, for example.

Nevertheless, the thesis of scepticism contains a truth if heard in the right way. That thesis is that we do not know there is an external world or that there are other people. And this is true, in the sense 'that the human creature's basis in the world as a whole, its relation to the world as such, is not that of knowing, anyway not what we think of as knowing'.[22] Claims to knowledge can occur only within ongoing human practices which involve a relation between people and between people and their environment which is prior to 'what we think of as knowing'.[23] These relations are not matters of choice, but underlie anything we could call choice, even the choice of trying to deny them.

> Whether or not we acknowledge others is not a matter of choice, any more than accepting the presence of the world is a matter of choosing to see or not to see it . . . avoidance of the presence of others is not blindness or deafness to their claim upon us; it is as conclusive an acknowledgement that they are present as murdering them would be.[24]

What Cavell is indicating here is the basis of responses to the environment and to each other which is presupposed for the formation of concepts in terms of which propositions can be expressed and so claims to truth made. Such responses are non-propositional, don't presuppose beliefs but rather are the condition for our having beliefs at all. Thus, for example, Wittgenstein writes: 'We react to the cause. We instinctively get rid of the cause if we don't want the effect. We instinctively look from what has been hit to what has hit it (I am assuming that we do this)' and 'A sound seems to come from over here, even before I have investigated its (physical) source.'[25] That is, it is not that we react in these ways to what we judge to be the cause, but rather, we react instinctively towards certain things in these ways, and this makes it possible for us to form a concept of 'cause' at all. Wittgenstein refers to such a form of reaction as a 'prototype of a way of thinking and not the result of thought'.[26] Language is a development of such reactions; its learning presupposes that we share them and a common way of taking words which extend them.

> Being sure that someone is in pain, doubting whether he is, and so on, are so many natural, instinctive kinds of behaviour towards other human beings, and our language is merely an auxiliary to, and further extension of, this relation. Our language game is an extension of primitive behaviour (for our language game is behaviour).[27]

These primitive reactions are involved in the formation of the concept of pain, for example, and determine the situations in which doubt can be expressed and the kinds of thing which count as evidence within the language game involving the concept. That a doubt can be raised and someone's behaviour presented as evidence to remove it is possible only because in certain circumstances we react without belief towards someone as in pain. 'My attitude towards him is an attitude towards a soul. I am not of the opinion he has a soul.'[28] For unless I responded towards him naturally in various ways simply as one human being to another I couldn't develop the concepts which would enable me to have any opinion about him whatever. Now, the sceptic claims that our various kinds of judgement presuppose certain fundamental kinds of belief: that there are other human beings, that there is an external world, that the past is evidence for the future, and so on. If these were judgements, they would require evidence of the appropriate kind. But, as the sceptic insists, if we question them we must question anything which could be offered in the way of evidence. But if nothing counts as evidence, the notion of evidence cannot apply and so they cannot be regarded as propositions at all. They point rather to the instinctive modes of reaction which underlie language games and which language games are a development of. When Cavell says 'The world is to be *accepted*; as the presentness of other minds is not to be known, but acknowledged'[29] he is emphasizing the instinctive reactions to the world and to each other which underlie concept formation and therefore the possibility of claims to and questions about knowledge. To conceive these relations as involving claims to knowledge themselves, as both scepticism and metaphysics do, is to fatally intellectualize the way we are in the world and with other people. But in this sense, acknowledgement of others and acceptance of the world cannot function to privilege particular forms of thought and life or relations to others or the world. Acknowledgement in this sense is presupposed, for example, in care and compassion for others or in indifference and cruelty to them, in an ethic of love or that of the Nietzschean superman, since they all involve a relating of one human being to another. But the problem with Cavell's development of his position, to which I will now turn, seems to me that he does want to utilize these notions to support a particular ethical stance.

If scepticism about the external world sees me as confined within my experiences cut off from the world, that about other minds envisages others as cut off from me and me from them, as if I could not be known by them nor they by me. But the search for criteria on the basis of which we say what we say is, according to Cavell, a claim to community, to an attunement with one another. But, since there is nothing more than such attunement underlying intelligibility, reason, it may prove in specific cases to be absent. That I make sense, and so am intelligible not just to others but to myself, is thus always subject to breakdown, in which I am separated from others and, as we shall see, from myself. Scepticism about other minds, as it were, reads the general situation as one of such absolute collapse of community, or as if it has always been an illusion. Whereas in its intellectual form this may be treated by showing that the sceptic does not mean what he says, that he has violated the conditions for questioning and asserting which the setting up of his problem already implicates him within, nevertheless other minds scepticism proceeds from an all too human desire. The sceptic of the external world envisages a non-human totality of knowledge in terms of which we are always inadequate. But the totality of community in terms of which other minds scepticism feels the absolute inadequacy of my relation to others seems only too humanly desirable: 'the ideal of knowledge implied by scepticism with respect to other minds – of unlimited genuineness and effectiveness in the acknowledgement of oneself and others – haunts our ordinary days, as if it were the substance of our hopes'.[30] But why is this?

The 'condition under which we can think and communicate' is our sharing criterion; but criteria are the expressions of 'our attunement with one another'.[31] Hence, my claims to intelligibility are at the same time, Cavell argues, claims to community, to a sharing with others in our fundamental attunements, and this is, as we have noted, always subject to failure: 'I have nothing more to go on than my conviction, my sense that I make sense. It may prove to be the case that I am wrong, that my conviction isolates me, from all others, from myself.'[32]

This last phrase indicates that I am myself at issue in this question of intelligibility. 'We are subject to expression and comprehension, victims of meaning';[33] 'there is no assignable end to the depth of us to which language reaches'.[34] The other minds sceptic asks how he can know that there are others: that is, other 'I's. But the 'I' is subject to meaning, to a claim to intelligibility: so the existence of the 'I' is dependent on others rather than the other way about. Whether I am, as this human being who qua human is subject to intelligibility, is rather the question: 'that I am not alone in the world has turned out to require that I allow myself to be known (I have called this requirement subjecting myself to intelligibility, or say, legibility)'.[35]

Whether I am remains a matter of proof, one which takes place in the claim to intelligibility and community addressed towards others, and this question remains, 'since the process is never over while we live'.[36] We are thus subject to the 'demand that we accept the claim of others as the price of knowing or having one's existence':[37] 'against annihilation, ceasing to exist as the one I am, there is no safeguard, none suppliable by the individual . . . its safeguard is the recognition of and by others',[38] but one which must be constantly sought and renewed and so can never be final. Hence, the ideal of, as it were, 'absolute community' as the 'substance of our hopes' is an expression of the desire of the 'I' for its own identity, its own existence as an 'I', where the desire wishes to immure itself against the possibility of failure. An impossible dream whose enactment, as we shall see, is the stuff of tragedy.

This process of proving one's own existence involves, on the one hand, what Cavell calls 'separateness': 'the fact of having one life – not one rather than two, but this one rather than any other. I cannot confirm it alone.'[39] The fact that I have this life to lead and not another, situated historically and socially as I find myself to be with the capacities I find myself with, means that I have to go on myself, take responsibility for my intelligibility. I have to make my own claims to intelligibility, and thus run the risk of rejection, of finding my separateness is alienation. On the other hand, the process involves community, since language, the very medium in which I exist as a 'victim of meaning', is inherited. Thus the issue of 'proving my existence' is a matter of taking responsibility for what I inherit:

> language is an inheritance. Words are before I am; they are common
> . . . the question whether I am saying them or quoting them – saying
> them first-hand or secondhand, as it were – which means whether I
> am thinking or imitating, is the same as the question whether I do or
> do not exist as a human being and is a matter demanding proof.[40]

The issue is whether I exist as a human being or as a simulacrum, an imitation of one. The sceptic, one might say, isn't sufficiently sceptical about himself.

I cannot live, Cavell claims, material object scepticism, for 'there is an alternative to its conclusion that I am bound, as a normal human being to take'.[41] Leaving the study, as Hume said, compels my recognition of the world, and thus, for Cavell, the acknowledgement of my participation in human forms of life in terms of which there is a 'world' at all. But 'I [can] live scepticism with respect to others [for] there is no such alternative'[42] and the 'reason is that there is no human alternative to the possibility of tragedy'.[43] The human condition is one of separateness, the necessity that I, and all I's, take their existence upon themselves, the task of proving their existence as human beings, which requires exposure to others, in acknowledging and being acknowledged by them in the claim to intelligibility and so to community with them. Tragedy arises from a failure to acknowledge others and be acknowledged by them which results in a loss of selfhood whilst being motivated by the desire to secure that selfhood against the possibility of loss. The possibility of such failure of acknowledgement is intrinsic, for such acknowledgement is always to be carried out, to be done, and so at the constant risk of collapse, whether through my fear of exposure, my refusal to confess in action my dependence on others for my existence as an 'I', or the refusal of others to acknowledge me, or the breakdown of the 'attunement' involved in intelligibility.

I think we can see in this course of reasoning a move from a notion of acknowledgement as an instinctive relation to other human beings, a matter of 'primitive reactions', to one which is implicitly ethical. Acknowledgement has now become something which one can do or fail to do, whereas in the original sense it is as much in evidence in neglect and avoidance as in recognition of another's claims. It becomes a claim to community over and beyond the instinctive reactions which underlie language games and which are involved in a common way of taking words. Cavell argues that as a linguistic being, I have to continually prove my existence by claiming community with others in participating in shared practices and this requires I acknowledge them as those upon whom my existence depends. But what is the nature of this 'acknowledgement'? In proposing that the only safeguard against my 'ceasing to exist as the one I am' is 'the recognition of and by others', there seems to be the suggestion that when, say, I make a claim about the world or a moral judgement, I do so *as* a claim to community, as though the intelligibility of what I say or think depends on the agreement of others in its intelligibility, with the implication that there is a requirement on me to enter into and maintain a relation with others within which such agreement could be sought, a relation which would involve recognition of certain concrete values. I must relate to them in a certain open manner, prepared to enter into free discussion and prepared to revise my claim to make sense. Of course, their agreement may not be forthcoming: perhaps the thought is beyond them. But my claiming it as intelligible involves the projected agreement of others and so the requirement that I seek it. The question is whether Cavell is here trying to justify certain concrete values on the basis of his reflections on language. This suspicion may be supported by two further developments of Cavell's thought, his conception of moral 'perfectionism' and his claim that Shakespeare's work is 'in competition' with religion.

Understanding ourselves as linguistic beings whose existence as such is always at issue, shows, Cavell appears to argue, that we must engage in a constant, unending appeal to intelligibility and so to community, within which our own existence and that of others is held continually in process. That we are linguistic beings means we face the demand to speak for ourselves, express ourselves, as Cavell puts it, which is at the same time an appeal to intelligible community with others, whilst equally it means the demand to grant this expression to others: 'the demand of one's human nature for expression demands the granting of this human demand to others'.[44] To express oneself means to express one's *self*, to find oneself through finding one's own voice. It is becoming intelligible to oneself in an unending process: '"having" a self is a process of moving to, and from, nexts . . . the self is always attained, as well as to be attained'.[45] This is what Cavell calls 'perfectionism'. It is living the life of the self as constant becoming, of always having to keep one's voice from becoming mechanical, routine, dead. It needs, therefore, another, relation to whom reveals our own conformity and prompts us to live again in the language we share with him or her. Texts and individuals, contemporary or historical, can, since they are equally constituted as linguistic, play this role. 'Whenever another represents for us our rejected self, our beyond, causes that aversion to ourselves in our conformity that will constitute our becoming, as it were, ashamed of our shame', there we enter into our true human nature.[46] We find, in relation to the other, a living voice, a living relation, for the time being, a redemption from conformity: 'the draw toward the further self is a draw toward one's freedom, not from the chains forged by society but from the violence shaped by the lack, or the falseness, in the social . . . society's partaking of the state of nature'.[47] The self is never complete but

> is open to the further self, in oneself and in others, which means holding oneself in knowledge of the need for change . . . which . . . means expecting oneself to be, making oneself, intelligible as an inhabitant now also of a further realm . . . the realm of the human – and to show oneself prepared to recognize others as belonging there.[48]

We must each take over our inherited language and come to speak for ourselves, come to express ourselves in the lives we lead, maintain ourselves in the living language. We can never be finished in this, and in order that we should maintain ourselves in constant becoming, we must relate constantly to what is other to us, relation to which or to whom can prompt our living reaction and so disturb our tendency to conformity and habit.

Texts can play this role of the other. Cavell says of Emerson: 'The writing must illustrate thinking so that the incentive will consist in recognizing that we are not engaged in it, not doing something we nevertheless recognize an instinct for'[49] which reveals us to ourselves: 'what goes on inside us now is merely obedience to the law and the voices of others – conformity. No thought is our own.'[50] In such a text, its thoughts are neither mine (since they must disturb my conformity) nor not mine (since otherwise they wouldn't attract). They appear as 'my rejected – say repressed – thoughts, they represent my further, next, unattained but attainable self'.[51] I appear to discover myself in them, through them, as if revealing what I have repressed of myself. And it is only in this process of discovering oneself that one's life is maintained as becoming, a discovery that requires articulation, or is articulation, to oneself and so in a claim to intelligibility to others. Clearly, too, texts and individuals may cease to play this role, to be replaced, endlessly, by others who can seduce us 'from our seductions (conformities, heteronomies)'.[52]

Now it seems clear from this that Cavell thinks our possessing language implies a particular kind of appropriate existence, namely that of a self which must always be attained, be as becoming, and so one which must maintain itself as open to the overthrow of its current form of life. But if this openness is a matter of allowing the 'self' to find expression, then it would seem to rule out the unconditional commitment of that self, and therefore to rule out certain kinds of moral and religious life. This suspicion is reinforced by Cavell's treatment of the historical connection he sees between the rise of modern philosophical scepticism and Shakespeare.

Shakespearian theatre, he claims, is 'in competition with religion as if declaring itself religion's successor'.[53] Scepticism in relation to the external world and the existence of others emerges historically for Cavell at the same time as Shakespearian drama. What begins to become apparent in the threat of scepticism is, Cavell thinks, the 'death of God', God being understood here as the transcendent ground for our practices. With the 'attenuation or displacement of God', language, and so intelligibility, appear for the first time to be groundless.[54] The intellectual response to the fear this generates is scepticism and its attempted intellectual resolution. The relation to the external world and to others now devolves for its certainty upon the senses and reason of the individual. This marks the moment when the individual experiences being cut off from the world and from others, whilst finding in terms of his own capacities defined by this very divorce (the notions of the 'senses' and of 'behaviour' Cavell has referred to as 'inventions') no persuasive means of removing the gap.

Philosophy and literature in the modern period, for Cavell, both respond to the 'death of God', to the unbelievability of a conception of a transcendent ground which has underwritten our forms of knowledge and life. This precipitates, of course, attempts at rectification in philosophy, in the provision of foundations provided within the terms of human reason and experience. These attempts are accompanied by their attendant forms of scepticism which they cannot adequately dismiss. It precipitates too, according to Cavell, Shakespeare's diagnosis of this situation and his theatrical form of its redemption. Shakespeare's plays, that is, concern themselves with the situation in which individuals, deprived of a transcendent ground, refuse to acknowledge the consequences, that we are shown to be linguistic beings whose existence depends on recognition of and by others, whilst providing, in the theatrical experience itself, a redemption from this denial. 'In Shakespeare's measures of the withdrawal of the world we are offered a picture of

the privatization of the world, a picture of the repudiation of assured significance, repudiation of the capacity to improvise common significance, of the
capacity of individual human passion and encounter to bear cosmic
insignia.'[55] In the experience of Shakespearian drama we realize our dependence for our existence as linguistic beings on the acknowledgement of and
by others, for the theatrical experience both shows us this and involves us
ourselves in such acknowledgement.

Cavell's position here seems to be that life, having been grounded in a
belief in a transcendent ground, must be rethought when that ground
becomes unbelievable, so that its dependence purely on human communication is accepted. Shakespeare shows us the resistance to this and provides a
remedy for it. But the philosophical revelation of the roots of the sceptical
impulse and the reason for the failure of metaphysical attempts to respond to
it awaited the twentieth-century turn to language in philosophy, the articulation of our nature as linguistic beings whose relation to the world and to
others is not a matter of knowledge but is possible only through community
in language, a community which is always to be maintained and which is
always therefore at issue. The search for the good of the human being,
underwritten by an appeal to an 'empirical' and 'practical' inquiry, which we
found in Murdoch and Nussbaum, shows itself here as one more form of a
reference to a foundation, one to be found in ourselves, and so reveals itself
as a further manifestation of the modern malaise, an attempt to substitute a
human ground for a transcendent one. What must be given up, in the revelation of the groundlessness of our lives, is the conception of the good, of a
determinate mode of life which claims universal validity for humanity in
general. Rather, as linguistic beings, we must engage in constant self-
creation, the process of always bringing forth our repressed selves, at the
same time as this process involves us in an unending appeal to recognition of
and by others. Thus, Cavell's notion of acknowledgement appears as part of
the articulation of the form of human life required of us when we realize the
linguistic constitution of our lives, that there is nothing to appeal to in justification except recognition by others. It has become an ethically loaded term
rather than, as originally, one which drew our attention to the 'primitive
reactions' which underlie our concepts and constitute the common way of
taking our words. The characteristics of perfectionism, openness to change,
holding one's current values conditionally as part of the process of self-
becoming, seeking to hear in the voices of others that of one's own repressed
self, express a particular attitude to life which excludes others. In particular,
it seems to exclude the absolute commitment to a way of life, morally or
religiously understood, of seeing that as the good, as if such commitment
involved belief in a philosophically untenable transcendent ground.

Let me then move on to consider the relation of Shakespearian tragedy to
the impulse towards philosophical scepticism. 'The human form of life is
the life of language.'[56] Intelligibility involves going on for oneself within

communally shared forms of language. This involves the always present contingent possibility of a failure of community, in which one becomes unintelligible to others and to oneself. Such unintelligibility represents the loss of one's existence as a human (linguistic) being. This is an irreducible condition of being human. 'But [the power of scepticism] is a power that all who possess language possess and may desire: to dissociate oneself from the community in whose agreement, natural attunement, words exist.'[57] The desire for excommunication is thus a consequence of one's desire that one's existence qua human not be subject to conditions of communal rapport over which one has no control, of the desire for one's unconditioned existence. This desire for a relation to a transcendent ground beyond the interplay of human communication is common both to the sceptic, who believes it cannot be satisfied, and the metaphysician, who believes it can. But to imagine oneself as unconditioned is to imagine oneself cut off from all others and from the world: hence the sceptical problems which arise when this desire manifests itself in intellectual form. But this desire, and the fear of non-existence which provokes it and the consequent disgust at one's contamination by others and the world,[58] are recognized as such in literature, which too, as we shall see, provides an appropriate form of redemption. There the finitude, the essentially conditioned nature, of the human isn't conceived, as it is within traditional philosophy, as an intellectual lack, to be resolved or despaired of in argument, but rather as the conditionality of our existence as linguistic beings whose denial is the manifestation of an impossible desire. The 'death of God' creates a situation in which the desire for a transcendent ground searches in philosophy for a replacement, in the nature of the human mind. But deprived of its traditional object, it can also be seen as itself a human phenomenon, seen, as it were, from the side of human finitude. If there is nothing to appeal to save human communication, then the desire appears as the aspiration after an existence unconditioned by the recognition of and by others, and so as a rejection of the human condition. The desire appears as a form of self-hatred which recognizes obscurely the impossibility of its object. To treat this desire is to bring the self back into harmony with itself through bringing it into harmony with others so that it is content to let recognition of and by others be the only basis for its life.

The specific plays of Shakespeare Cavell considers can be seen to explore the various manifestations which the desire to be unconditioned and the fear of non-existence which underlie it may take, and the possible forms of redemption there may be. *King Lear* explores the nature and consequences of the 'terror of being loved, of needing love',[59] that is, of needing the involvement with others for one's own existence. Lear both obscurely recognizes this need, and at the same time desires to deny it, to preserve himself in an illusion of the unconditioned. Hence the significance of the abdication scene: he desires to buy the public appearance of the expression of love, but is threatened by the expression of real love contained in Cordelia's perplexed response to his demands. *Othello* explores the nature and consequences of 'The refusal of imperfection'.[60] Othello's obsession with 'purity', his own and Desdemona's, is the appearance of his desire to exist in perfect independence of others, and to find at the same time this reflected in another. In this way, the need for the other is obscurely recognized and denied at the same time. The reflection he desires is one between perfect autonomies, and thus between fictions: hence Othello's theatricality, the sense that he is always playing the role of the hero of a romance. The denial of the need for the other finds its manifestation in Othello's horror at human sexuality 'in himself and others . . . human sexuality is the field in which the fantasy of finitude, of its acceptance and its repetitious overcoming is worked out'.[61] Human sexuality displays the conditionedness of the human individual, of the need of our individuality for relatedness to others in its definition (as the individual is a man in relation to women and vice versa), and is experienced by Othello, in his desire for purity, his fear of dependence, as impurity, contamination. In his destruction of the impurity, in destroying Desdemona on their marriage bed, he thus destroys himself.

This desire for destruction that attends the fear of dependence, the desire to destroy what one depends on for one's human existence, is central to *A Winter's Tale* which 'paints the portrait of the sceptic as a fanatic', that is, as one who claims the presence of the unconditioned, of the individual as autonomous, and who acts to destroy what would deny this. But this claim at the same time manifests a recognition of what it denies. Its expression in destruction shows it to be a sense of 'the unforgiveability of one's owing, as it were for being the one one is, for so to speak the gift of life, produces a wish to revenge oneself upon existence, on the fact, or facts, of life as such'.[62] Leontes destroys his son, loses his daughter, and turns his wife to stone.[63]

Disgust as the manifestation of one's denied dependence on others is explored in *Coriolanus*, whose 'disgust is . . . directly and emblematically a disgust with language, with the vulgarity of the vulgar tongue'.[64] Coriolanus desires 'to lack nothing, to be complete'[65] yet his necessary implication in language reveals his desire as fantastical and so produces a withdrawal from the very conditions of intelligibility, a move into inexpressibility, and so 'of the sense of oneself as having lost the power of expression'.[66] Such withdrawal takes a different form in *Hamlet*, which explores a 'refusal of participation in the world',[67] 'the refusal to admit himself to life . . . the refusal to partake and be partaken of'.[68] Hamlet declines the creation of his own individuality through participation with others by taking the place of his father and so becoming himself a spectre haunting the world. The desire to take on another's identity is a fear of what is necessary for one's own, participation with others, a willingness 'to partake and be partaken of', and this fear itself is a product of a desire for an impossible individuality.

If we are linguistic beings, then we have to continually preserve that existence through engagement with our shared language. In this sense, 'To exist is to take your existence upon you, to enact it, as if the basis of human existence is theater, even melodrama.'[69] This enactment of one's existence through participation in shared forms of language and activity is what saves the individual from becoming a mere 'simulacrum' of a human being, whilst its refusal 'is to condemn yourself to scepticism – to a denial of the existence, and hence of the value, of the world'.[70] Recovery from the desire for the unconditioned, and thus from the disgust and fear of others and the world, comes through being recalled to our essentially conditioned nature, by being reminded of the sharing with others which is the condition for our own intelligibility and so existence as human. This reminding, in the appropriate form where what we are being reminded of is ourselves and so in terms of our essential concern, is the 'work' of Shakespearian drama.

As Cavell says of *Coriolanus*, 'the play celebrates, or aspires to, the condition of community' for this is what an audience is: 'A performance is nothing without our participation in an audience; and this participation is up to each of us.'[71] Community exists through our sharing in a common form of language as individuals, each taking upon ourselves our responsibility for enacting our own existence through which the shared language is itself maintained in its existence, its life. Without this, we become mere 'imitations' of human beings, and the language becomes dead, the repetition of lifeless sentences. In the event of drama, these necessities become for the audience explicitly lived and so provide a redemption from our own potentiality for a lifeless life.

As we have seen, Cavell argues that as a linguistic being, each of us is faced with the constant task of proving our existence as human, where to 'prove' my existence is to engage in constant self-revelation in an appeal to community with others. In engaging with the play, I thus reveal myself, but in such a way that the community of my situation, as human, rather than the particularity of my individuality, shows itself to me as a member of the audience: the communality of the human condition reveals itself to all as to me, to each individual member. It 'is the work of this theatre to present itself as an instance of the ceremonies and institutions toward which our relation is in doubt, exists in doubt, is unknowable from outside; one whose successful taking, or receiving, our lives, in some sense our immortality, depends on'.[72] The work of Shakespearian tragedy thus implicates us in the very process of avoiding recognition of others through which we fail ourselves to be human, to be 'I's. It thus tests our potential and actual inclination towards a purity, autonomy of the self motivated by our fear of the possibility of a loss of our selfhood through circumstances beyond our control. Thus, for example, Cavell says that we 'do not notice Regan's confusion of identity [of Gloucester with Lear when she says, for apparently no textually based reason, that he is going to Dover] because we share it, and in failing to understand Gloucester's blanked condition (or rather, in insisting upon understanding it from our point of view) we are doing what the characters in the play are seen to do: we avoid him. And so we are implicated in the failures we are witnessing: we share the responsibility for tragedy.'[73] Shake-spearian tragedy is a medium 'which keeps all significance continuously before our senses, so that when it comes over us that we have missed it, this discovery will reveal our ignorance to have been willful, complicitous, a refusal to see'.[74] In responding to the characters in ways we respond to others in everyday life, the inadequacy of these ways is both revealed and revealed as willed, as indicating the nature of our relation to others, as avoidance, and so as motivated by our fear of a loss of selfhood. In order that we should be revealed to ourselves in this way, we must be at once removed from our everyday intercourse with others, whilst the connection is nevertheless maintained. The situation of the audience is one in which, on the one hand, it is 'free of the circumstances and passions of the characters, but that freedom cannot reach the arena in which it could become effective' – we can do nothing in relation to what is happening before us. But, on the other hand, the characters are to be related to as 'men and women; and our liabilities in responding to them are nothing other than our liabilities in responding to any person – rejection, brutality, sentimentality, indifference, the relief and the terror in finding courage, the ironies of human wishes'.[75]

This diagnosis of the audience's situation informs Cavell's account of the nature of the existence of a character on the stage. We are not in, and cannot put ourselves in, the presence of the characters. A character isn't, and can't become, aware of us. We cannot be heard by them, nor can we intervene in what is happening: 'It is not that my space is different from theirs but that I have no space in which I can move.'[76] But we are in, or can put ourselves in, their *present*. We are present at what is happening. And this means, not merely that we are seeing and hearing them, but that we are acknowledging them or failing to do so, relating to them as an I who must prove their existence to an other, an other I. But what form can such acknowledgement take, given that we are not in their presence and so cannot act in relation to them and so participate in the mutual creation of intelligibility and so of each other? It lies in 'making their present ours' which requires 'making their present theirs'. That is, we must repudiate all preconceptions, 'our perceptions altogether', in not bringing to our response to what is happening preconceptions, including prior knowledge of the play, but allowing that response to arise from what happens in the present: 'the time is always now; time is measured solely by what is now happening to them, for what they are doing is all that is happening . . . the time presented is this moment'.[77] To fail to live in this present is to make the character a 'fictitious' creature, a figment of my imagination, caught in the stereotypes and generalities through which I refuse to acknowledge others as others, as those upon community with whom depends my own existence as a human, linguistic being. That is how in everyday life 'we convert the other into a character and make the world a stage for him'. It is the theatricality of our ordinary lives that Shakespearian theatre is meant to overcome by showing the tragedy in failing to overcome it.

Shakespeare's tragedies show us the fear, desire and disgust which characterize the rejection of the human condition involved in the desire for a transcendent ground and which can appear when the belief in such a ground has been fundamentally disturbed, but in such a way that our experience of the plays may serve to redeem us from our own tendencies towards this desire. The plays deliberately involve us in responding to individuals, but in a situation where our own personal purposes, and their attendant emotions, cannot be at issue. Removed from everyday life, I am nevertheless required to respond to what is happening to these people now. In this way, my general relation to others is put into play, and can be revealed through showing my misreadings in the course of the drama's development as due to a wilful refusal to relate to others in terms of the search for a community of intelligibility. My relation to others may be shown to be determined by generalities, stereotypes, or past histories, so that I do not relate to the other *as* other, as the other who is necessary to me for the maintenance of my intelligibility. Only through an openness to the other, in an appeal to a community of intelligibility, do I recognize my dependence on the other. (In the play, this means that my response must be to what is happening in the present, undetermined by preconceptions.) Where this is absent, I make the other a fiction. The experience of theatre, where the silent community of the audience experiences the conditions for a community of intelligibility in the demands the play makes on them for its own intelligibility, redeems us from the theatricality of our own lives.

The plausibility of Cavell's readings of Shakespeare depends on that accorded to the perspective from which they derive. Cavell sees Shakespeare as responding to the loss of the belief in a transcendent ground and as attempting to provide a resolution to the resulting manifestation of the transcendent desire as a hatred of the human condition through a theatrical therapy restoring us to acceptance of ourselves. Our engagement as audience in the Shakespearian revelation of the inevitable tragedy involved in the hatred of the human incorporates us in a process of self-recognition both as beings prone to such self-hatred and as those who live in language, who exist through recognition of and by others. Our condition has no measure other than this recognition. This leads Cavell to an articulation of life in terms of our linguistic constitution. To accept our condition now means giving up the idea of the good, which could only be justified by appeal to a ground, and recognizing that we must live through a constant process of self-revelation, constantly discovering our 'repressed' selves through encounter with other lives, which in its claim to intelligibility makes an appeal to recognition by others. I have suggested that Cavell's perfectionism cannot be derived from his Wittgensteinian beginnings. Cavell rightly indicates that modern scepticism arises through neglecting the conditions necessary for concept formation, the primitive reactions to the world and to each other which are developed and expanded in linguistic behaviour. These reactions are not the product of belief but underlie the possibility of belief. Scepticism and metaphysics, as Cavell indicates, rest on a mistaken intellectualizing of our relations to the world and to other people. To come to possess language is to come to participate in inherited practices with their underlying modes of reaction and the shared reactions involved in a common way of taking words. But since this account would hold for the variety of moral and religious practices, it cannot be used to justify a particular form of life. Cavell seems, in rightly objecting to the philosophical provision of transcendent grounds for our forms of thought and life, to propose a ground in the nature of language itself. But his own reflection on language leads him to a recognition of the groundlessness of those forms. Wittgenstein stresses the differences between forms of language and this might rather be used to show that the constant openness to change involved in Cavell's perfectionism is precluded by, for example, certain kinds of religious and moral commitment. If this openness is a matter of allowing the 'self' to find expression, then it would seem to rule out the unconditional commitment of that self. All that would appear to be intelligible would be a commitment conditional upon my finding it bears the examination of self-expression, keeping my options open for when and if it doesn't, when and if I find it no longer expresses my further self. I will return to these issues in Chapter 9. Despite his Wittgensteinian beginnings, Cavell seems unwilling to recognize that, in showing the groundlessness of our lives, philosophy must give up its inherited claim to arbitrate between conflicting forms of life. These conflicts, too, must be accepted philosophically and left to fight their own battles.

9

A KIERKEGAARDIAN
INTERVENTION

Let me briefly recapitulate the path we have followed. For both Murdoch and
Nussbaum, there is a general question as to how we should live, of the good
life, which is the concern of both philosophy and literature. The question is
empirical, involving a surveying of the ways human beings have determined
the good life, since we do not have access to a metaphysically higher position
than the human, and it is practical, since we must be able to live it. Literature, unlike philosophy, can show us in detail what such a life would be like
and so further the pursuit of truth. Murdoch and Nussbaum, however, don't
agree as to what view of the good life would pass the empirical and practical
test and this raises the question, of course, why we should regard these
opposed views as competing for the accolade of a universally valid 'truth' if
our only access to it is through an appeal to procedures which if adopted by
conscientious, intelligent people have these results. And surely at best we
could only arrive at a form of life which had empirical validity for people
characterized by certain conditions which disposed them to agree with the
offered vision.

It was to avoid similar conclusions of an earlier form of 'naturalism' that
in Kant's third *Critique* God appears as the guarantor of the harmony
between thought and reality, of there being a given order in things which is
also graspable by us. Remove the guarantor, whether God or some other
absolute, which can underpin some particular order as it appears to us, and
you lose the notion of that order as written into the nature of things. Then
you appear to be left simply with the way things appear to us to be in their
historical and cultural variability, where the 'to us' marks the appeal to a
contingent consensus. If, however, the appeal to God, in this sense, or an
absolute, now appears to us as irredeemably flawed, is there still some point
to which appeal can be made, over and beyond such consensus, which would
support some notion of validity beyond the empirical?

The claim of both Cavell and the continental tradition I have outlined is
that once we have abandoned as unintelligible an appeal to a more than
human position, whether religious or metaphysical, we have to give up too
the idea of a concrete form of life which could claim this kind of universal

validity, the 'truth' about life. But this doesn't lead to an abandonment of the inquiry, but rather a transmutation in its form. We are no longer directed towards a universally valid truth as the good of life, but to what it is claimed follows from universal conditions of human life which have been revealed to us through the arguments that have undermined belief in such truth. What has manifested itself to us, at this point in the development of Western thought, is the linguistic character of human life. Appeal to this precludes determination of a 'what' of life, a concrete conception of life which would fulfil us as humans, since the nature of language is such as to make unintelligible notions of finality *tout court*. But this very demonstration indicates to us a 'how' of life as valid universally in the historical situation we find ourselves in, where this apprehension of our linguistic being has forced itself on us, namely that 'how' which is an explicit rejection of finality. What shows itself as binding on us is, for Cavell, 'perfectionism', a constant holding of ourselves open to the 'further self' which draws us to a shame as to our current self and an incitement to change, but one without end. The recognition of the 'further self' is a matter of self-recognition, of recognizing in another what one has 'repressed' in the concreteness of one's attained self, so that the process of unending self-formation has the continuity of self-expression. Literature can here play the role of the 'other', either revealing to us our own fixity and disinclination towards the unending task of self-expression, or through provision of views of life which, temporarily, can play the role of revealing our 'repressed' next self.

But perhaps this appeal to 'self-expression' fails to address the nature of our inheritance of language, fails to be sufficiently historical. For Bataille, Blanchot and Derrida, the language we inherit is one formed in relation to absolutes in which we can no longer believe. It is because of this that our inherited language for Derrida is structured in terms of concepts of presence which determine differences as conceptual oppositions which privilege one of the relata. To understand ourselves as linguistic beings is to understand the fixity of such structures of language as an operation of power against the inherent endless interpretability of what is given us in language which reveals itself in the absence of an absolute. Hence, the task incumbent on us is to intervene into this language, to release these conceptual oppositions into their differential form so as to begin the process of reforming our language, and therefore our ethical, gender, social and political relations, so as to keep the future essentially open, to begin upon the task of making ourselves and our world endlessly anew. Here the appeal is not to self-expression, but to the exigencies of our historical situation, our inheritance of a metaphysically based language, organized in terms of finality (such as conceptions of the human good), but one in which we can, in the understanding of ourselves as linguistic beings, no longer believe. The word 'literature' here gestures towards forms of writing which in their lack of a centre which could ostensibly determine interpretation have offered a silent point of resistance to this metaphysical language, revealing, through history, its various forms of understanding of world and self in an opacity which could free them from their fixity. In modern literature, language itself in its resistance to a final determination of meaning appears, perhaps presaging the dissolution of the aberrance of the literary in new forms of writing (and other media) which would not be constituted in opposition to discourses concerned with 'truth'. To think this opacity would be to think what summons thought, a thinking which must, therefore, evade any attempt to grasp 'it' in thought. Writing which 'addresses' this must, in a sense, fail, its adequacy lying in (the particular manner of) its failure. Such writing must, therefore, take on a form which is true to the necessary incoherence of thinking: Bataille's writing of the 'impossible', Blanchot's of the 'madness of the day', or Derrida's deconstructions are marked by this awareness. The role of the absolute (and so of God) is shown as an evasion of the internal summoning to collapse of any given order of thinking, a 'summons' which is unnameable but which one can be true to in declining the impetus to this evasion. 'God' thus becomes an illicit attempt to name the unnameable, that which precipitates the internal collapse of any attempt to halt the movement of thought. It is what summons us to the constant remaking of the way we think ourselves and the world and which grants validity to that remaking.

In undermining the finality of the question as to the good life, this kind of inquiry nevertheless involves the same kind of claim to validity in asking what our historical position requires of us. This question presupposes that an intellectual inquiry can reveal what is binding on us in relation to how we live, showing alternatives as intellectually inadequate, as failing to understand our situation and what it requires. The inquiry is, as Derrida says, a continuation of the 'universal problematic', but one liberated from notions of finality. But, as Rorty argues, this continuation still seems complicit with claiming 'truth' and, therefore, its own finality. The conceptions of thought as essentially paradoxical and of life lived in terms of this paradoxicality as a constant response to what avoids thought, or of life lived in terms of its linguisticality as the self-creativity of perfectionism, indeed reject the metaphysical ideas of a final state of knowledge or goal in which life would fulfil itself. But they still claim truth for themselves and so access to a point beyond our linguistic practices from which they can be judged. The issue, Rorty argues, is not that of simply rejecting the idea of final states, but of the finality of one's position. In this way, Cavell and the continental theorists remain tied to the metaphysical tradition. Rorty tries to avoid this by declining to have a position: rather, he claims to offer a counter-vision to the metaphysical one, which he supports not by argument (which would imply a shared vocabulary with his opponents) but by persuasive redescription. We may come to realize that these redescriptions speak to how we conceive of ourselves, in terms of self-reliance rather than obedience to a non-human authority. Yet Rorty's vision, couched in terms of the possibility of permanent revolution in relation to our beliefs about the world and constant self-creation in relation to individual life, itself seems complicit with metaphysical ideas. Its rejection of unrevisable claims and absolute commitments seems to presuppose that these would only make sense if one had a transcendent guarantee.

Cavell recognizes that metaphysical thinking arises in response to sceptical questioning. The sceptic wants to raise a question about our knowledge-claims as a whole or about our moral thinking in its entirety: he senses something inadequate in our forms of thinking. The metaphysician responds to this questioning as if it were in place, claiming access to a standard which could settle the sceptic's doubts: the ideas, the logos implicit in the kosmos, the ideas in the mind of God, Spirit and so forth. But Cavell sees that there is something wrong with the sceptic's question: what he says is meaningful (we can think of contexts where we would understand those words) but *he* isn't. He abandons the conditions necessary for his doing something with those words (expressing a doubt, questioning), whilst he must at the same time affirm allegiance to those conditions, since he wants his questioning to relate to our claims to knowledge where those conditions are satisfied. Cavell's move, then, is to return the words to the contexts in which we can understand questioning, doubting, claiming, and so forth, being done with them and which shows that our basic relation to the world and to each other is not a matter of 'knowing'. Now, of course, if the sceptical questions aren't questions, then there can't be any metaphysical answers: the language of the metaphysician needs to be returned too to the contexts where we can understand something being done with them. The 'generality' of the meta-physician's claims and their 'validity' ('universal') both derive from the metaphysician's dreams of access to a position to quell the sceptic's doubts. But since such doubts are confusions, the dreams too are just that. Now, the thinkers we have been concerned with recognize the incomprehensibility of the metaphysical claim to occupy this position and wish to return thinking to its humanity. But instead of recognizing that the incomprehensibility lay in our being unable to understand the sceptic or metaphysician doing anything with their words and so that to return thinking to its humanity is simply a matter of returning these words to the human contexts where we can understand them as expressing doubting, claiming and so on, they respond to the rejection of metaphysics by trying to continue its general ambition. The validity of our forms of thinking is to be referred now, not to a supra-human standard, but to an interpretation of what our historical situation demands. But this is still to respond, as much as in metaphysics, to the possi-bility of sceptical questioning: it is to assume that this general question of validity is intelligible as a question. (Cavell, it has to be said, seems to forget his earlier insistence on returning the sceptic's questions to contexts where they could be understood as questions, fabricating from the form of words 'Do I exist?' a question as abstracted from any living context of questioning as any sceptical one.)

Or to put the matter in another way. Derrida claims the idea of a 'transcendental signified', that which, outside language, can be appealed to in justification of our forms of thought and life, is confused. There is nothing but our language. Cavell, too, argues that the sceptic's and metaphysician's desire for such a justification is for an illusion. There is nothing beyond our ways of speaking which can justify them in the desired way. There is, as it were, nothing to lean on, no metaphysical crutch. Yet both Derrida and Cavell then use *this* as something to appeal to, to show that certain non-philosophical forms of language are misformed, and to determine how we should think now. So there turns out to be a crutch after all. What we should conclude, however, is that there simply is nothing to lean on: there is only the agreement and disagreement of individuals who agree in the language which makes their agreement and disagreement possible. But this shouldn't lead us to a Rortyan change of self-image in terms of permanent revisability of claims about the world and constant self-creation of individual life. With the rejection of the metaphysical or post-metaphysical crutch, we reject the idea that our linguistic practices need grounds, and so we reject too the assumption that only if there is a transcendent ground do the notions of unrevisable claims and absolute commitments make sense. We are linguistic beings, if you like, but nothing follows from this about what forms of language are possible or ruled out. It cannot, for example, rule out an absolute commitment to certain values which therefore declines to contemplate changes of circumstances, external or internal, as reasons for changing those values. Such commitment is expressed in language, is made possible by language. It is not opposed to the nature of language, but rather one form which (religious and moral) language can take. As, of course, is the language of self-expression and experimentation. We have opposed forms of value here which are equally ungrounded: we recognize this ungroundedness precisely in resisting the idea that there is some intellectual way of resolving the opposition even by an appeal to 'ungroundedness'. What is needed is not a replacement for the inadequate metaphysical attempt at justification in the name of a return to human 'finitude' or 'historicality', but replacing 'justification' into the contexts where we can understand questions being raised and answered (and, of course, the very various forms these take).

Let us, for example, indicate, at least briefly, what this would involve in relation to the questions as to the 'human good'. This was part of Kierkegaard's concern in the writings by the pseudonymous Johannes Climacus. 'Let a doubting youth, but an existing doubter . . . venture to find in Hegelian positivity the truth, the truth for existence – he will write a dreadful epigram on Hegel . . . for an existing person pure thinking is a chimera when the truth is supposed to be the truth in which to exist.'[1] There is a misalignment between 'the truth in which to exist' and the philosophical inquiry which is meant to address it. The latter understands 'the truth' it aims at as claiming 'universal validity'. The inquiry requires, therefore, that the philosopher takes the object of research as the standard which he is to address imperson-ally. He must suspend his personal projects and desires to see what 'is really there' and so be able to claim his findings as valid for all who approach the matter in a similarly impersonal way. The determination of 'the truth' is one thing, relating to it another. In relation to 'truth' which matches this model, it is possible to accept the truth but deny any concern with it. One's relation to such a truth will derive from those projects and desires one suspends in order to see it, from the categories in terms of which one already lives. But the relation to 'the truth in which to exist' cannot be like this, since it offers us the categories in which to live themselves. Such a 'truth' is one for our lives and we cannot regard our own life 'disinterestedly' as an object of impersonal inquiry. To recognize such a 'truth', rather, is to adopt it, to rec-ognize it as the measure for one's life, whether through trying to form one's life in accordance with it, or in feeling guilt at being unable to do so. Hence, Climacus says that 'The inquiring, speculating, knowing subject accordingly asks about the truth but not about the subjective truth, the truth of appropriation.'[2] The sense of 'the truth in which to exist' is 'the truth of appropriation'. There is not first the determination of what that truth is, and then a relating to it: rather, its determination is the relating, is taking it as the measure of life. To think otherwise is precisely to avoid regarding the issue as the question of 'the truth in which to exist': 'wanting to understand it is a cunning evasion that wants to shirk its task',[3] the existential task of taking it as the truth of one's own life or rejecting it. The philosopher claims to raise the question of 'the truth in which to exist', and therefore treats it as an intellectual problem to be addressed with the disinterest such problems require. But this is to forget that the philosopher is himself a human being. If the philosopher has the general problem he claims, then he clearly must have a problem with his own life, and one which embraces that life in its totality since the issue is the 'significance of life'. But not only would such a problem then include his own intellectual pursuits and so his involvement with philosophy, but it would have the character, not of disinterest, but of total despair. For how else are individuals to raise the problem of the meaning of their own lives? Modern philosophy has, Climacus says,

> not a false presupposition but a comic presupposition, occasioned by its having forgotten in a kind of world-historical absentmindedness what it means to be a human being, not what it means to be a human being in general, for even speculators might be swayed to consider that sort of thing, but what it means that we, you and I and he, are human beings, each one on his own.[4]

What we need to be reminded of is that there can be no general issue of the significance of life which must be resolved in order to give the guidelines for the individual's life. To raise the question of life's significance is aways something done by an individual. There is no 'truth' here apart from its being lived by individuals: to say a certain view of life is 'true' is to adopt it, see one's life in its terms, whether to try to live it or feel guilt at one's failure to do so. It is to take it as the measure for one's life. This isn't 'relativism'. It does not commit me philosophically to saying 'These values are true for individual A', 'Those values are true for individual B'. Rather, it is not the role of the philosopher to determine what values are 'true' but to articulate the use of 'true' in these contexts, and that precludes my saying philosophically 'These values are true for individual A' just as much as it precludes me from saying 'This is the truth, valid for all'. And part of the articulation of the use of 'true' here would be to see in relation to what values appropriated by an individual it would make sense for her to say, of other values, that, although she didn't adhere to them herself, nevertheless they were the other's 'truth'. She must be able to see that they indeed constitute the value of the other's life, and she must be able to recognize, in terms of her own values, something in them, she must be able to respect them. In relation to some forms of life, the latter may be ruled out. Relativism just as much as absolutism assumes it is the role of the philosopher to determine the truth of values and thereby imports an alien conception of 'truth' (Kierkegaard would have called it an 'objective' notion) into this context.

For an individual the raising of the issue of 'the truth in which to exist' cannot be a matter of disinterested inquiry since it must involve herself: if we replace those words (what is the meaning of life?) back into their living context then they are an expression of despair. And this shows us the nature of the problem. When we speak of the 'meaning' or 'significance' of life, this is not something to be known or understood but refers rather to what we speak of when we ask what a relationship, activity and so forth means to individuals, where we are asking, for example, how committed they are to it, the nature of their involvement. And in that sense we can ask what doing philosophy means to someone, a question that is not to be resolved by philosophy: 'Even if a man his whole life through occupies himself exclusively with logic, he still does not become logic; he himself therefore exists in other categories.'[5] These are the categories in terms of which I can have 'problems' with my own life, engage in 'reflection' as to their character and cause, and arrive at certain 'resolutions' of them, for example. But none of these notions can be understood in terms of the disinterest and impersonality necessary for a 'cognitive inquiry'. The sense of 'problem' is not intellectual but one the individual has with her life, taking the form, for example, of despair, whose 'answer' lies in a recovering, redirection or intensification of passion, of one's involvement in one's life. The 'spheres of existence' which Climacus identifies, the aesthetic, ethical and the religious, represent, one might say, different degrees of passion with which individuals may live their lives and which determine the kinds of problem they can have with their lives. The philosophical construal of these notions involves confusing existential issues with cognitive ones,[6] whilst at the same time the thinker must be aware of the difference since he is an existing individual. Hence the treatment of the confusion is a matter of reminding us of what we already can't but know.

If the philosophical task now appears, then, to be a matter of such reminding as an antidote to our sceptical, metaphysical and post-metaphysical inclinations, how might we see its relation to literature? This issue is addressed in some of the writings of D. Z. Phillips which I will discuss in the next chapter, where I will consider too what may be made of the notion of God outside the 'universal problematic' of metaphysical and post-metaphysical thought. It might appear from what I have just said that I am dismissing Cavell's perfectionism or the conception of life found in Blanchot or Derrida as confused. Yet what they say may seem to address much of what we may recognize in our present situation, the difficulty of religious belief, the apparent breakdown in historically inherited conceptions of value and the search for new ways of living. What I am suggesting is confused in their treatment is, rather, its claim to validity, and the attendant implication that those who oppose what they suggest are making an intellectual mistake, failing, intellectually, to understand what our situation demands. It remains open that they are engaged in another form of activity, one which philosophers in the past too have embarked on, of articulating new forms of value and life in a way parallel to that we can recognize in certain forms of literature. I will take this up again in what follows.

10

D. Z. PHILLIPS
The mediation of sense

D. Z. Phillips has characterized his work in moral philosophy as 'interventions in ethics', and no doubt we could describe his work in the philosophy of religion in similar terms. Such interventions are needed 'because of our deep-rooted tendency to theorise in ethics'[1] and the philosophy of religion. These 'interventions' are directed at the theoretical ambitions of philosophy and take the form of 'reminders', either 'teaching differences' or 'elucidating philosophically neglected perspectives',[2] which show that the generalizing character of theoretical accounts is, when confronted by the actuality of moral and religious language use, obscuring and confusing in relation to the phenomena it is intended to illuminate. Such theorizing characteristically is related to the apparent possibility of raising fundamental questions about morality and religion, of whether moral concern or religious faith can be justified. The intellectual search then begins for an answer, whether affirmatively by reference to some foundation, metaphysical or in human nature, or negatively, proclaiming the absence of any such foundation and the necessity of a move to transform our language and life in new directions. Phillips's 'interventions' have often utilized detailed references to works of literature, whose point is not, as some critics have believed, to provide the data for further theorizing, but rather to intervene in the desire for theorizing at all.

From the point of view of theory, the use of literary examples appears dubious. Examples from literature can only provide data, either of our moral responses as readers or of the characters' responses to each other and their situations, which in either case await the formulation of the correct moral theory to determine their appropriateness. Non-literary examples would function just as well, indeed usually better. Our aim, after all, is to take our own intuitive moral responses, inquire as to their presuppositions, and then attempt to formulate an internal or external ground which would justify the greatest range of such responses or what appears the most central of them. The judgements we make about literary examples are not ones made to 'real' cases: they are second-rate evidence. And the judgements made by literary characters aren't ours in any case. Furthermore, we are often unsure how to describe in a determinate manner the situations presented in literature and even when this is not the case, we are sometimes unsure what judgement to make about them, thus indicating our need for, rather than possession of, an adequate ethical theory! All in all, we would do better sticking to moral judgements we feel sure about, relating to simple cases we can clearly describe.

Against this picture of the necessity for a justification for our moral values in philosophical theory set that provided by Edith Wharton of Undine Spragg in *The Condition of the Country*, on which Phillips comments:

> Her values at any time are essentially transient, serving the constant need for new pleasures, new conquests . . . With such an attitude she is condemned to perpetual rootlessness . . . It is precisely because Undine Spragg has reasons for her values which are externally related to those values that we see in her a fundamental rootlessness in which no form of decency can grow or flourish.[3]

What is the point of such a 'reminder'? The theoretician might say that he has no wish to embrace Undine Spragg's criterion of 'new pleasures, new conquests', and in any case whether he did or not would be determined by his intellectual (or intellectual and imaginative) inquiry. But the 'reminder' isn't given to suggest a possible answer to the theoretician's question. It is rather intended to get us to recognize that the character of theorizing, of looking for such justification, is at odds with its own claim to continuity with moral seriousness. To think our patterns of moral concern require a foundation or justification runs counter to that concern, or to what that concern may be. In terms of our moral understanding, which we show in being able to follow Wharton's novel, we can recognize that the individual who has reasons for the values she espouses is to be distinguished morally from the individual who rejects such reasons, whose reasons *are* her values. In recognizing this, we are returning the notion of 'reason' to moral life from the 'abstract reasonableness' of the theoretician, who must abstract the notion from our lived moral life since his inquiry is to stand in judgement on it. The theoretician's project could only produce an account of a life which is itself subject to moral criticism. In moral theories, language is 'on holiday': moral concepts are removed from the contexts where they have their use. They produce then a picture of a life which if lived would provide a context within which moral concepts could have only a deficient, parasitic role, of providing a moral veneer for other interests. The point of the reference to Undine Spragg is to return the notions of reason and justification to the moral context where they have their sense. This is not, of course, to deny that one can reflect on one's moral position. But what such 'reflection' amounts to has to be seen in terms of the use of the notion within moral cases. I may reflect on what counts as living in terms of certain values where this is unclear. Or I may reflect on the extent to which I can commit myself to certain values given my other commitments. Either way, the questioning proceeds in terms of values which provide the context for there being a 'question' and about which there isn't a problem – for the sense of 'problem' here is one with commitment. Or I may radically question moral values themselves. But such questioning proceeds itself from another perspective on life or is expressive of a loss of the sense of life, of despair. It does not constitute a privileged position from which moral values can themselves be judged.

Phillips contrasts the picture produced in terms of 'abstract reasonableness' with one formed in terms of 'moral reasons which are rooted in the ways people live and in their conceptions of what is important in life . . . The contrast depends on showing how much separates examples suggested by prevailing moral philosophies from other possibilities.'[4] When we return notions of reason and justification to moral life, we can see that the life of Undine Spragg is to be morally contrasted with the lives of those for whom their values are their reasons. And here Phillips refers to Countess Olenska in Wharton's *The Age of Innocence*. She flees from, and threatens to divorce, her husband. Newland Archer is sent by the influential families of New York to dissuade her from bringing scandal on herself and them. He is himself engaged to be married. Having put the case to the Countess, Archer finds himself in love with her and pleads for her to go away with him. But through his advocacy, Olenska has seen 'a moral reality in what to him was little more than decorum'.[5] She decides not to divorce and rejects Archer's proposal.

> Before Archer convinces her otherwise, the satisfaction of true love and her own happiness would have been of paramount importance to her. She would have described her elopement with Archer as a flight to freedom. But when she becomes aware of other values, values involving suffering, denial, endurance, discipline, she can no longer see things in that way. She says that her former way of looking at things is cheap by comparison. This judgement is not arrrived at by cashing the two attitudes into a common coinage by which one can be demonstrated to be cheaper than the other . . . On the contrary, her judgement about her former attitude is intelligible only in terms of the new moral perspective she comes to embrace.[6]

When we return the notion of 'reason' to the moral context where it has its moral sense, we see that Olenska does not have 'reason' for her change, but that the change is her coming to have new reasons, a new conception of what counts as a reason for her. Moral change is not 'progress' (or 'decline') in terms of some unitary standard or conception of practical truth: it is coming to a new perspective on one's life, coming to see the value of different things. Olenska moves from valuing satisfying genuine love, being frank and honest in one's relationships and the difficulties one may have with them, making up one's own mind and not paying too much attention to what one's parents or family have to say, on the one hand, to valuing family tradition, endurance, loyalty, faithfulness and subordinating one's own strongest desires, on the other. These perspectives on what is valuable in life are not subject to an impersonal standard or communally shared truth which can determine one as 'better' or 'truer' than the other. We see that 'truth' in its moral context is the truth of personal appropriation: to see certain values as 'true' is to take them as the measure for one's life. The novel shows us the heterogeneity of morals, that moral change involves a change of perspective on one's own life, and that these values can be themselves the individual's reasons. Through engaging with the novel we can be reminded of what we know already in so far as we can use moral concepts and so read it. We can be recalled to what we forget when we are tempted towards philosophical theorizing, the lived use of the notions of 'reason', 'truth', 'change', and so forth, in moral contexts. Philosophical theorizing abstracts these notions from those contexts since it aims to justify, or show to be unjustified, our moral practices. In producing such reminders, the philosopher is not, of course, endorsing or condemning his examples. In replacing the notions of 'reason' and 'truth' into their moral contexts, into the context of the significance individuals can see in their own life, we see that it can be no part of the philosopher's task to determine the 'truth' of such perspectives since 'truth' here is the truth of personal appropriation and not intellectual inquiry.

We can see why such 'reminders' should characteristically take a literary form. They are intended to bring the relevant notions back from the holiday of 'abstract reasonableness' to their use in moral life. Phillips's example of Olenska shows what it is to have reasons for one's 'moral values', it places the notion of 'reason' here within its lived context, and thereby shows the theoretical notion of having reason, justification, for our moral values to be an abstraction which has lost contact with the phenomena it claims to illuminate. What is needed to intervene in the theoretical ambition and its consequences is replacing the moral notions at issue within the context where they have their sense: in the significance which human beings find, or do not, in their lives. Phillips quotes Peter Winch: 'The seriousness of (moral) issues is not something we can add, or not, after the explanations of what these issues are, as a sort of emotional extra: it is something that "shows itself" . . . in the explanation of the issues.'[7] This seriousness is to be seen in an individual's life, in the way the issues are seen and in their ramifications for her other relationships, activities and so on. To show this seriousness, and so to illuminate the nature of the issues, rather than just state them, requires, then, something like a story, the revelation of an individual's life at a particular juncture in a specific situation. This showing of an individual's life in the significance it has for her must, to be such a showing, command our attention, prompt our contemplation and emotional involvement. It must convince. And it is naturally to works of fiction which involve us in these ways that we would look for such reminders. One way of 'combating utilitarianism', writes R. W. Beardsmore, would be to appeal to a work of literature like Faulkner's *Intruder in the Dust*. Faulkner's novel is not, of course, his greatest, and it is not always convincing, particularly in the later chapters, where he employs long polemical speeches by the lawyer Gavin Stevens to preach to the reader. What *is*, in my opinion, convincing (as in most of Faulkner's writing) is the portrayal of individual characters and their relationships. And it is such portrayals which can help break the hold on us of the abstract and mathematical account of human relationships embodied in the theory of utilitarianism . . . Unlike the relationship of a man's actions to the happiness of the greatest number (or some other variant), none of the relationships by which characters are impelled to act in Faulkner's novel, a man's relationship to his job, or to a particular human being (father, mother, friend), has any numerical or mathematical aspect.[8]

In recognizing this as a convincing portrayal of the lives of individuals and their relationships (if we do), we recognize the inadequacy of the categories of utilitarianism to account for them and that this inadequacy cannot show their irrationality as the claim of the utility principle to be the criterion of moral action would assert.

The recognition of the heterogeneity of morals which follows from replacing the notions of reason and truth into moral contexts doesn't mean, however, that we could understand anything whatever as the object of moral appraisal. In 'The Presumption of Theory', Phillips refers to Peter Winch's discussion of the notion of limiting conceptions in relation to human life. The very notion of human life is limited by the conceptions of birth, death and reproduction and it is to these that we look to gain a foothold in trying to understand the very various ways in which human beings find or fail to find sense in their lives. These limiting notions don't determine such perspectives, but rather 'their position as limits is shown by the role they play in that diversity'.[9] Thus in *From Fantasy to Faith*, he uses Hemingway's *The Old Man and the Sea* to remind his religiously inclined readers that non-religious moralities are possible. The Old Man has the values of a warrior, a hunter put to the test by the sea. The novel 'is a representation of life as a struggle against unconquerable natural forces in which a kind of victory is possible. It is an epic metaphor for life.'[10] The Old Man faces the forces of nature with awe, but this calls to him to become a hero, to triumph, temporarily, or be destroyed. We recognize this as a perspective within which human life can gain a sense: the Old Man has 'addressed life at certain of its limiting horizons'. He has referred life terminating in death to values whose point is not negated by death. He has turned 'from the temporal to the eternal'.[11] The value of pitting his strength, his endurance and courage against nature is independent of the outcome since it is recognized that in the end destruction is inevitable. As Phillips notes about the Cossacks in Babel's stories later in the same chapter, within such perspectives we are called on to live proud and free, 'not humbling ourselves before gods or men. But we are called on, not only to live like men but to die like men.'[12] Such perspectives involve a glorification of the self, of the human, but one which is preserved from vainglory in its encompassing of death and injury. We may find such perspectives profoundly unattractive, of course, but such a judgement is one inevitably proceeding from another perspective.

Changes in moral perspective both individually and culturally are not to be referred to some general standard. Old values die and are replaced by new ones, by different conceptions of what is important in life, without this constituting an 'objective' progress or decline. Yet such values, in order to give value to life, must relate to the limiting conceptions of the notion of human life. A way of life, in order to give reason to life, must not be valued for what is expected within life, within the temporal, but is rather that which gives the temporal its value. But this relation 'to the eternal' is itself historically contingent: it is possible for human life to cease to find significance in relation to such perspectives, to cease to be concerned in this sense with life as a whole. Then the picture painted by contemporary moral philosophy, of adherence to moral values depending on further reasons, would constitute a description of the culturally available possibilities in relation to what had been conceived as morality, whilst it could not, as it claimed to do, exhaust moral possibilities as such. Indeed, the dominance of such models in moral philosophy constitutes itself one of the forces in our culture working towards that end. If 'certain ways of regarding moral problems and difficulties are constantly ignored, misunderstood or misrepresented, those ways will sooner or later cease to be part of our conceptions of moral problems and difficulties'.[13] Since the notion of the 'essence' of morality is a chimera, what is meant by 'moral', indeed, if anything is meant, is a matter of the use of the term, the role it plays in human life. Phillips is able to refer to certain moral possibilities shown to us in literature because these works still speak to us, because we still recognize these perspectives as living possibilities or related to ones which are. Such references can show us the contrast with the picture of human life contained in contemporary moral philosophies. But these possibilities may cease to be so for us, or to stand in any meaningful relation to what we see as possible ways of life, precisely because the notion of the 'moral' has either radically altered or disappeared.

In both *Through a Darkening Glass* and *From Fantasy to Faith*, Phillips turns to Beckett's plays as 'an observation on a present state'[14] diagnosed as that in which such perspectives on life as a whole, in relation to the eternal, have been lost, but where the loss is still experienced, as absence. In *Waiting for Godot* this absence presents itself as a meaningless waiting. 'The objectless waiting that Beckett depicts gets its force by contrast with an absent meaning, an absence portrayed by memory of the past or inarticulate longing for the future.'[15] The absence of a relation to 'the eternal' in the sense of a perspective encompassing one's life as a whole has consequences for the conception of personal identity shown in the difficulties Beckett's characters have in recognizing and remembering each other. 'Moral considerations . . . enter into the determination of what does and does not constitute "the same" [person] and hence into what constitutes a justifiable claim on another. The characters in *Waiting for Godot* do not know any more what considerations should have weight in these matters.'[16] And in so far as this is no longer known, there are consequences for the language of emotions.

> What is it to commit oneself to someone divorced of all future implications? . . . One person would not recognize another as far as any claims are concerned from one day to the next. As Pozzo says, 'I don't remember having met anyone yesterday. But tomorrow I won't remember having met anybody today.' Such an isolation of relationships from a yesterday and a tomorrow attempts to reduce human relations to the status of sensations . . . But if this is what talk of love becomes – talk of a transient sensation? Could we not say that at least one concept of love has been forgotten?[17]

Beckett's play shows us life lived in the loss of a relation to the non-temporal, but where this absence is itself experienced, both in the pointless waiting and in the garbled memories of a religious and moral language which no longer makes sense to his characters. 'Beckett . . . is concerned with a particular time, our time, and with what he thinks has happened in it.'[18] That we find Beckett's plays comic in recognizing the character of the 'waiting' and the garbled memories as garbled shows we too have at least the memory of, and perhaps the desire for, other possibilities.

Moral philosophy and philosophizing about religion take place in a particular historical setting. We are situated in a time when, if we recognize Beckett's depiction, the possibility of moral values and religious belief has itself become a question. Because there is no essence of morality independent of how moral language is used, certain forms of such use that were once central, those concerned with making sense of one's life as a whole, may be forgotten. And since the human world within which we live is formed in terms of the concepts we use, that very world may come to preclude the application of terms in their previous meanings. What, for example, could it mean to commit oneself in love in circumstances where the relationships socially recognized are limited by temporal objectives, in a time, say, of 'serial monogamy'? Or what is it to see one's life in terms of vocation in a time of institutionalized 'labour flexibility' and the assessment of all occupations in terms of market outcomes?

If the occlusion of a relation to the non-temporal is transmuting what can be understood by our moral vocabulary, this cultural process is far advanced in relation to religion. In *From Fantasy to Faith*, Phillips quotes from Psalm

139 and remarks of the world of the psalmist that it is seen from the start as God's world. 'The movement of thought in the Old Testament is not from the world to God, but from God to the World.'[19] In such a world it would be senseless to ask for 'evidence for God'. But since the Renaissance this relation to the world and to human life has been under attack in terms of other, secular human values. It is in such a cultural setting that the need for 'evidence' is felt both by those hostile to, and those favourably disposed towards, religion. In such circumstances attacks on and justifications for religion come to form the nature of philosophical engagement with religion.

Just as philosophy has seen its role in relation to morality as providing foundations or the revelation of its true nature, so too in relation to religion. The religious life of worshipping God, thanking God, trying to do God's will, and so on, surely rests on the assumption that there is a God to worship, thank and to will. Philosophy must, therefore, consider whether there are good reasons for believing that God exists. But just as the philosophical construal of morality as requiring reasons distorts moral life, so too does its reading of religious life as resting on an 'existence claim' which needs to be justified. Such a conception of 'God' removes the term from the context where it has had its use. If 'God exists' makes a claim about 'the way things really are', it could be false. But a religious believer isn't prepared to say 'I believe in God but maybe God does not exist.' To say 'God exists but might not have done' is to use the language of things in the world. Such a 'thing' is one of a kind. But God isn't one of a kind, and not a unique object either, since a unique object is only contingently so. 'God' is not, then, the name of an object whose existence is claimed by the believer. To come 'to believe in God' is not to come to believe that what one thought was false ('there is a God') is true according to standards already accepted, but of coming to live in a new form of language, to come to have new standards of what can be said, new conceptions of reasons and justification. 'Coming to believe' is 'conversion'. 'Belief' here is not an 'epistemic' notion. To believe in God is to be affectively disposed, whether in love, revolt, guilt, or whatever. As Kierkegaard reminded his age, Christianity is an existence communication, the communication of a way of living, one within which the conception of one's life and the world as a gift plays a central role, so that one has nothing by right but is saved by 'grace' alone.

Yet it has to be recognized that, just as there is no 'essence' of morality over and beyond the use of moral language, so too with religion. In so far as religion is interpreted in a particular way both by opponents and defenders, so certain possible understandings become hidden. 'Philosophical observations have a feed back into the language which is misunderstood, so that philosophical confusions themselves become a substantive part of what is believed. This has happened again and again in the philosophy of religion.'[20] The language in which religion is understood, in which the inheritance of religion is mediated to a contemporary audience, overwhelmingly characterizes it in compensatory terms. 'Things may not seem to make much sense from the perspective we are locked into here on earth. But there is a higher perspective, one which will make everything all right in the end.'[21] Arguments then take place as to whether there is or is not reason for believing in that higher perspective. The dominance of this understanding makes it difficult for other voices to be heard. Many 'are genuinely at home in the shabby language they employ when discussing religion or when acting for or against it . . . Individual voices may break through, but the likelihood is that they will seem forced, extreme, distorted, or even absurd.'[22] Such voices are both literary and philosophical. The literary authors show possibilities of understanding religion, of mediating its sense in our world, which Phillips himself articulates in another way. *From Fantasy to Faith* passes from the compensatory understanding of religion to the possibilities shown by, for example, Flannery O'Connor and R. S. Thomas: 'The journey by which we have arrived at [these possibilities] has been both literary and philosophical. It is a journey, I believe, which must be undertaken by anyone seriously interested in the issues which confront philosophy and religion today.'[23] And in a reference to Flannery O'Connor in *Faith after Foundationalism* he compares the contemporary philosophical task of providing conceptual reminders to philosophy with that she faced as a Catholic writer, 'how to convey a religious perspective in literature in a pervasively secular American culture'.[24]

Phillips examines Thomas's project in his poetry at length in *R. S. Thomas: poet of the hidden god*.[25] His poetry places religious language within the context of its application in an individual's life and in relation to the social and natural context in which he finds himself. It is essential to this that the poetry shows a constant struggle to make sense of a religious language the poet, as priest, knows in a sense perfectly well, a struggle to apply that language to his life and his world, to see things in its terms.

Phillips speaks of a 'decisive drama' played out in the course of Thomas's poetry. 'It is the drama of concept formation in religion; the attempt to see whether or how religious belief can inform human life.'[26] The poet, as priest in a poor rural area of Wales, is challenged to make the religious language of Christianity speak to the Welsh peasant. In 'A Peasant', the poet refers to 'Something frightening in the vacancy of his mind', and yet he is 'your prototype' who nevertheless endures, and this very endurance represents a certain challenge to religion. As Thomas notes: 'the very fact that they endure at all – that they make a go of it at all – suggests that they have got some hard core within them. One has to face this as a priest, this sort of attack, as it were, from their side.'[27] The harshness of the peasants' lives and their endurance constitute a religious problem for the poet. How is religious praise to be related to the harshness and suffering of their lives? And relatedly, what religious response could be as adequate to the peasants' situation as their non-religious stoical endurance? Faced by the harshness and suffering of their lives, the poet's efforts to summon a religious sense of praise seem, Phillips remarks, either desperate and unearned[28] or ironic.[29] The situation of the peasant presents a challenge to the poet's faith in that he cannot make religious sense of what he sees. He has the religious vocabulary, the world is God's creation and God saw that it was good, but he cannot see how he could speak like that and be honest about what he confronts. The opposition to religion that is encountered with the peasant is itself experienced by the poet. How can he see this as good, as something to be praised, without being blind, insensitive to what is before him? How is human suffering to be seen so that the religious words are not hollow and dishonest? Phillips sees Thomas as moving towards a precariously maintained response to this. Quoting Simone Weil 'God decided to hide himself so that we might have an idea of what he is like', he comments 'I think R. S. Thomas, after a long journey in verse, comes to the meaning of these words . . . there is . . . this revelation in verse of the sense of waiting on a hidden God.'[30] What has provided the problem is the sense that human suffering of this kind cannot be justified and any attempt to do so is itself irreligious and immoral. The precariously held response involves trying to see this very impossibility as part of the sense of faith. The notion of the will of God comes in precisely where all attempts at understanding and justification cease. God's will is, in a sense, impartial, His rain falls on the just and the unjust alike. But this very impossibility makes it possible to see what comes as a gift.[31] The suffering of humanity too must be seen as the will of God. Phillips remarks: 'Due attention will have to be given to a necessary compassion in face of suffering with its imperative to remove it, but due attention too to the fact that some suffering is necessary, defying all efforts at elimination.'[32] But this in itself is not a religious perception and must be part of any view of life which is non-illusory. One may accept this as part of the human condition and so as to be endured as the peasant does. But Christianly, the necessary suffering of the world is not simply to be recognized and endured, but embraced. The 'poet shows us a religious faith which actually depends on embracing the mixed character of human life in a way which does not deny its character'.[33] We come to the sense of 'God' by seeing that to answer 'God' to the question 'who is responsible?' is nearer to answering 'no one' than it is to 'another person more powerful than ourselves'. The very silence in the face of our questions, that there are no answers, no justifications, is itself to be embraced.

> [The] reflections of God [are to be found] in embracing the absences our questions come up against. We come to God . . . by coming to see that the nature of his will is born . . . of a radical pointlessness in things . . . It is not by seeking explicit answers, but by seeing why such answers must be . . . died to, that the possibility of belief in a God who is present in all things emerges.[34]

The endurance of the peasant is here to be replaced by a religious patience sacrificial in character, which 'grows out of an embracing of the misfortune itself'.[35] By seeing grace in all things, by seeing all things as a gift, the 'giver' (Love) cannot be seen as alongside what is given: this God is present only as essentially absent.

Belief in a 'deus absconditus' has difficulties, not intellectual ones since it involves giving up the desire for understanding, but existential ones, 'the struggles which are involved in keeping hold of any deep faith'.[36] There is always here the question 'whether what [humans] are giving themselves to is an illusion or not', not an illusion in the sense of belief in the existence of what isn't really there, but rather in the sense of a self-deception that anyone could relate to suffering in these terms. Can one relate to one's own suffering in this way without it being a disguise for other motives, a self-hatred or a self-assertion over oneself, as Nietzsche thought? Can one really relate to the sufferings of others in these terms without it being a mask for indifference or motivations even worse? Isn't the peasants' moral endurance in the face of their hardship a human response with which one can join in human solidarity? Isn't the striving after a religious perspective a desire to break with humanity, and what desires might disguise themselves here? This sort of self-doubt is an ever-present possibility with religious faith. Phillips remarks that 'Religious belief can come in at the right place only if its essential precariousness is recognized, only if we see how a shift of aspect makes a world of difference.'[37]

This 'precariousness' would inhabit the possibility of religious belief under any circumstances because of what it demands of human beings. 'Wonder and awe come in at the right place not by the balancing of fortunes and misfortunes, but by an acceptance of the whole in which . . . all things are seen as a gift.'[38] But there are further forms of difficulty for religious belief now, in relation to the cultural and social setting in which it is to be lived.

Phillips remarks on a poem ('Inside'): 'The passages by which truth must be sought are narrower and narrower because the world which now awaits the mediation of religious sense is one which is increasingly resistant to it.'[39] This resistance takes several forms. The prestige of science has led to the supposition that religion needs defending and the production of justifications which are seen to be rationally inadequate and which betray the nature of religious life. The society in which religion tries to make itself heard is increasingly organized in terms of other values whose dominance drowns out its voice. But also, the very organization of society in terms of these other values makes it increasingly difficult to see what it is here and now to live in religious categories. We must be able to see what in these circumstances living in terms of God's grace and seeing the world as God's creation, as a gift of grace, can amount to. We cannot assume that because it was once clear what it was to live in these concepts it is now. 'We may not know what hope, love or faith amount to. We cannot take it for granted that we do.'[40] Could hills mined for the greed for gold 'declare the glory of God?'[41] 'It is hard in these circumstances to see how the very same hills could declare the glory of God, since the act of exploitation, the utilitarian attitude to the hills, would jar with regarding the hills as belonging to God.' Again, he asks, is it possible for the believer to thank God for the birth of a child

> if they have been trying to plan it to the day, if possible, to take advantage of tax benefits? Perhaps it *is* possible, but at least there is a tension, a question to be resolved, since the notion of planning and that of a gift seem to be in conflict here.[42]

As the transformation of the world in terms of other values increases, so too do the difficulties of applying religious concepts, of living in terms of them. What is it to see life as God's gift in a time of genetic engineering where we face the prospect of designer babies? What does it mean to see the world as God's creation in a time of multinational agribusiness and the genetic alteration of plants and animals? It is important too to stress, what Phillips I think rarely does, that changes in the world that take place in terms of other forms of value can stimulate religious change, can be the occasion for a reconsideration of the application of religious terms and a coming to a new understanding of what living in terms of them requires. New religious thinking on gender relations, gay sexuality, the environment and the position of animals have all been prompted by the development of social movements which originally had little to do with religion. But it remains the case that religious sense must be mediated: the religious language inherited from our tradition must be understood and it must be applied in our contemporary situation. 'If religion has redeeming sense, it will have to be expressed in a pattern of meaning which informs everyday life. Only in this way can a timeless truth be said again effectively.'[43] In a society increasingly formed in terms of non-religious values and in which the dominant interpretation of religion is in compensatory terms, there are particular difficulties which attend this mediation.

We live in a time when the possibility of moral and religious values has become problematic. They both involve a turning away from temporal goals towards the 'eternal'. But society is being transformed in terms of other values, re-creating social relations and the natural world in their image. In these circumstances, ethics and religion become interpreted even by their defenders in ways which produce a fundamental distortion, seeing them as justified in terms of non-moral or non-religious benefits. In so far as these interpretations pass into common currency, the resistance of religious and ethical values becomes increasingly invisible. At the same time, the social and natural setting makes it increasingly difficult to see what living in terms of these moral and religious values can concretely be. Phillips's 'reminders' seek to keep open a space within which an ethical and religious voice can be heard, just as the stories of Flannery O'Connor or the poems of R. S. Thomas do.

Literature attempting to convey a different understanding of what is involved in the religious life must take a disturbing form: the preconceptions about what is to be valued and about what religion is must be upset. Phillips quotes Flannery O'Connor writing about her own work:

> The novelist with Christian concerns will find in modern life distortions which are repugnant to him, and his problem will be to make these appear as distortions to an audience which is used to seeing them as natural; and he may well be forced to take ever more violent means to get his vision across to his hostile audience . . . you have to make your vision apparent by shock – to the hard of hearing you shout, and for the almost-blind you draw large and startling figures.[44]

The grotesquerie of which she was accused is rather a matter of using 'a certain distortion . . . to get at the truth'.[45]

The general difficulty of modernist forms of writing, of which Flannery O'Connor's shock-tactics are an example, is a mark of the faithfulness of their response to the situation they address. Phillips quotes T. S. Eliot on the necessity of difficulty in modern poetry: 'The poet must become more and more comprehensive, more allusive, more indirect, in order to force, to dislocate if necessary, language into his meaning.'[46] If we are indeed living in an age when the conception of moral value is itself under threat, when the notion of a relation to the non-temporal is becoming difficult to apprehend and live, and when religion is being forgotten or transmuted into compensatory belief, then this must be reflected in the character of the writer's work. What a work of literature says cannot be separated from how it is said. If a writer wishes to convey the possibility of a moral or religious perspective in such a situation, the necessity to disrupt the preconceptions of the reader and the difficulties of conveying that vision will make writing something other than it could be in a more morally or religiously confident age. Or if a writer wishes to communicate the nature of our situation, in which moral and religious values are losing their hold and life exists only with them as an uncertain memory, as Beckett does, then this would have to be conveyed in forms which question notions fundamental to the conceptions of selfhood which those moral and religious values made possible. Inherited literary forms, concerned with character development or decline, and so involving a narrative structure reflecting the intelligible patterns of individual histories, cannot address a situation where the very conceptions of character and individual history have themselves become questionable.

But this raises a possibility which Phillips does not discuss. Beckett's plays show us a time (and invite self-recognition on the part of the audience) when the very possibility of living in terms of our inherited moral and religious vocabularies has become problematic. Moral and religious traditions embody conceptions of the worthwhile life through which the individual can gain a sense of the significance of life as a whole and so a conception of the self, of her or his identity as an individual human being. In the context delineated in Beckett's plays, these fundamental concepts of the sense of life, of the self and personal identity are themselves destabilized. Such a situation may produce renewed efforts to articulate moral or religious perspectives. It may too result in a loss of a sense of the significance of life as a whole and a retreat into the pursuit of temporal objectives, a move Phillips sees reflected in the demands for the justification of moral and religious values we see in contemporary philosophy, where these justifications may become part of the transmutation of those vocabularies themselves. But equally it may produce an effort to articulate ways of living which are neither religious nor moral in the inherited sense of these terms, and which don't consist either simply in the pursuit of temporal goals. Morality and religion have given us a sense of the significance of life as a whole by offering us conceptions of the sort of person to be which are to be valued independently of contingent outcomes, patterns, as it were, of selfhood, of character which can encompass the entirety of a human life. It is in terms of the concrete unity of such a life that we can understand the lived sense of reference to 'the eternal'. But, as we have seen, morality and religion have been opposed at least since the writings of the early German Romantic Friedrich Schlegel, in the name of other ways of taking over the temporality of human life centred on an opposition to notions of finality in terms of unending 'becoming'. Living as constant becoming, as the maintaining of the possibility of the always new, disrupts the unity of the self: 'of this only a mind is capable that contains within itself simultaneously a plurality of minds and a whole system of persons'.[47] Perhaps Lawrence's conception that 'my soul is a dark forest' and that 'gods, strange gods, come forth from the forest into the clearing of my known self, and then go back . . . I must have the courage to let them come and go'[48] is analogous. Such values of creativity, the plurality of selves one may become, the passivity in responding to one's unknownness, and so forth, must still, presumably, appeal to a vestigial sense of self (who is going to hold these values) and sense of constancy (since there is at least to be the constancy of adherence to the values of becoming). But they stand in opposition to an absolute commitment to concrete conceptions of character and the relationships they involve to others and to ways of living within which ethical and religious understandings of the unity of a life can be formed. Rather, such relationships and inherited ways of living are to become the field for life as what Nietzsche called an experiment in living, for taking them over to make something constantly new. A reinterpretation of values central to ethical and religious conceptions of the unity of life is to take place in terms of becoming rather than 'the eternal'. Responsibility is to become responsiveness, a maintaining of a relationship to the unknown in oneself and others, integrity a remaining true to this unknown, commitment is to be to the open future rather than to particular others and ways of life, and courage the willingness to venture out into such a future. The lived sense of 'the eternal', and its attendant notions of character and of the unity of life, is to be replaced by 'becoming' and its conceptions of venturing into the existentially unknown and of the plurality of one's life, of its possibilities in relation to the essential openness of the future. It may be that we can understand certain forms of contemporary writing, both 'literary' and 'philosophical', as involved in the creation of new possibilities of life which involve new sorts of value which cannot be seen straightforwardly as ethical (concerned with character) or religious. Even if this is so, the attempt to justify them in a way which would show that adherence to ethical and religious values rested upon a failure of understanding (say, of the nature of our historical situation) would remain confused. The attraction of such forms of life and new values does not depend on dubious general theories as to the nature of language or history,[49] nor does opposition to them depend on an idea of being in possession of better arguments which would be binding on any disinterested inquirer, for in relation to this issue none of us are that. Whether such values are possible as a way of living needs showing in application, and this requires the detailed working out which literary forms can provide in showing the consequence of their adoption for individual and social living. Whether this is so or not, their suggestiveness should remind us that there may be possibilities of making sense of life beyond ethical and religious categories: there is no essence of human life which makes these the only possibilities.

To return for a moment to *R. S. Thomas: poet of the hidden god*. This is not a work of criticism. It neither attempts to situate Thomas in the context of Welsh or British poetry nor tries to show us the literary value of the poetry. The poetry's power as poetry is largely taken as read, or rather offered to us in quotation for our agreement in response. It is not an issue for the book. Rather, the book is an elucidation of a 'philosophically neglected perspective' through the presentation of that perspective in Thomas's poetry. The poet brings to language the experience of individuals trying to make religious sense of their own lives in particular historical and social circumstances. This involves finding what sense religious concepts can have in those circumstances (what application they can have) which is at the same time discovering what sense their lives can take, whether and how they can live religiously. In this way, the religious notions of the hidden God, grace and God's will are placed within the context of use where they have their sense, in the struggle of individuals to see and live the significance of their own lives. The philosopher in bringing out the nature of this lived context and the form which difficulties and resolutions can take there provides an articulation of a possibility of understanding religion which is forgotten by the dominant philosophical and popular voices of the age. In the Preface, Phillips comments on the parallel between his and Thomas's tasks. Thomas is engaged with 'the struggle with the possibility of a satisfactory religious syntax in verse today. That struggle, unsurprisingly, shares many features of the thrusts and counter thrusts which have characterized the discussion of religion in contemporary philosophy.'[50] The poet's mediation of religious sense is to bring to language in verse the individual's struggle to make religious sense of his life today. The philosopher's commentary brings out the nature of this sense, articulates the context within which the concepts have their use and so their sense there. The success of such an elucidation reminds us at the same time, when impressed by philosophical theorizing about the significance of life, that we turn to literature to encounter the possibilities of meaning in human life, to see what those possibilities have been and to be confronted by the question of what, if anything, can now be made of the moral and religious vocabularies we have inherited. To engage with literature in this way is to contemplate the possibilities and impossibilities of sense for us now (which involves, of course, our active, concerned reading), to contribute to the mediation, and perhaps abandonment, of these vocabularies in our own lives.

11

A CONCLUDING READING

Joseph Conrad's *Lord Jim*

Literature can explore the nature and possibilities of making sense of life in an appropriate form, in terms of narratives of individuals making or failing to make sense of their lives under specific social and historical circumstances. 'Truth' here is 'the truth of appropriation': to say a view of life is 'true' is to see one's own life in its terms, with all that that implies in terms of emotion and action. To ask about such truth is to be at a loss in one's own life, not to be confronted by an intellectual puzzle. There is, therefore, no general question which is that of life's significance. There is no significance of life which is not significance for someone. Literature can explore the nature of this making sense of one's life and the kinds of significance possible in specific historical circumstances.

Provided we abandon Murdoch's and Nussbaum's conception of literature as part of an inquiry into the truth as to the good of the human being, and see it rather as a historically situated exploration of the nature and possibilities of making sense of life, much of what they say holds good. Literature show us life as *seen*, in terms of some perspective, some conception of the nature and possibilities of its significance, even if the latter is of its meaninglessness. This perspective includes that of the 'implied author', the overall sense of life conveyed by the work, and those of the various characters whose lives the work concerns. The necessarily perspectival nature of literature constitutes itself, one might say, a rejection of the idea of the 'truth' in an 'objective' sense about life's significance. This form of presentation of life requires of the reader a certain kind of activity, but not one of following arguments. Any arguments we do follow have their sense in terms of the role they play in the development of character and the overall thematic structure of the work. Their validity or otherwise may be relevant to this but it is not the focus of our attention. Rather, we are involved in an exercise of the kinds of perception, thought and emotion which are involved in our making sense of our own lives. Literature shows us life lived by individuals, not the abstract 'agents' of much philosophizing, people who have a history which is irreversible and unique. As such, they can change, develop, deepen, and, of course, stagnate and ossify. The 'reasons' they find for what they do and don't do, feel and don't feel, proceed from their perspective on life, rather than claiming a universal validity. What reasons they find depends on how they see things, on the perspective provided by their values and the depth of their engagement with them. The individual does not stand as an abstract will before an impersonally specifiable situation, but rather must determine what the significant aspects of it are. Literature shows us individuals engaged in this active perception which is itself evaluative and from which action flows. 'Choice' in this is an exceptional moment and makes sense only where we can understand there being 'alternatives' in terms of the individual's perspective. We don't choose that there should be such alternatives. Further, our situations often have a uniqueness which can't be encompassed in generalities. What is significant then to those concerned is that it is just this individual with this history encountering now this other individual with his or her history. The narrative of individual histories alone can show us this. We respond to each other and our situations as the individuals we are and so in terms of what we value. Our response is both perceptive and emotional, or rather we see in terms of the way we care. What we feel is often as significant as what we do. The novel or play requires of the reader the exercise of this same capacity for making sense of our own and others' lives. It concerns the possibilities of making sense of life and so concerns us. We are emotionally involved with the characters, seeing things from their perspectives or from that of the implied author: we enter into ways of seeing life. And this involves our being actively engaged in following the thoughts and perceptions of the characters and in relating to the sense of the work as a whole. Since we are so actively engaged, reading literature can, to an extent, show us to ourselves. It reveals to us our emotional responses to characters and to the overall narrative in which they are involved and so can reveal, as Cavell points out, our own proclivities to misread in terms of stereotypes and generalities, as well as the fantasies about life which Murdoch comments on. As 'truth' in relation to life's significance is the truth of appropriation, it finds its contrast in the illusion of self-deception, where an adherence to certain values is claimed which is at odds with the way life is lived and felt. We shall see some forms this illusion can take in Conrad's *Lord Jim*. One may claim, for example, adherence to certain values when in reality this is motivated by a desire for social conformity or the approval of some group. As we shall see, Jim's 'romanticism' is love of a borrowed splendour which attaches to certain values through acclamation rather than a love of the values themselves. Underlying this is a desire for recognition by others, and even by the universe at large, a self-assertion which is the expression of an absence of meaning. At its extremes, as with Kurtz in *Heart of Darkness* or Gentleman Brown in *Lord Jim*, this may reveal itself in a wilful destruction of others, the naked will to power of an assertive nihilism. This relation to others, however, finds its more common parallel in the stereotypes of social conformity, where lacking a truth of one's own, one is unable to relate to others in their truth or its possibility. One makes of them a fiction which corresponds to that of one's own life.

At the same time, in reading, we are divorced from the active pursual of the sense of our own lives so that the very nature of making sense of life itself becomes the focus. Murdoch emphasizes the 'pointlessness' of such literature, that it cannot be understood in terms of some purpose which could then determine how it is to be read. Nevertheless, as an exploration of the nature of making sense of life and of the possibilities for individuals to make and fail to make sense of their lives at some historical juncture in some social setting, guidelines are set as to appropriate forms of response and interpretation. And in being read by individuals who must engage themselves in a perceptive and emotional relationship with the work, bringing with them their own understanding of what it is to make sense of life and their own sense of what matters in life, such readings cannot be delimited. The possibility of further readings is written into the claim such literature has on our reading it through our own sense of what is deep and what shallow, what is illusion and what reality, in relation to the significance of life, rather than being a product of a radical undecidability of language itself. Here conflict of readings is to be expected, as it is in relation to what is found in life. Some will see what one cannot see oneself, and some will find profound what one can only see as shallow. And literature may too be involved in the creation of new possibilities of making sense of life.

I would like to end by showing something of the exploration of the nature of making sense of life in Joseph Conrad's *Lord Jim* and the complexities of its literary strategies to remain true to its claim on us, to involve us in its examination. In particular, I shall try to show the following:

1   To read *Lord Jim* is to be confronted by the issues of the nature, and possibilities, of making sense of life. The central question raised by the novel is the nature of Jim's 'moral identity' and through this that of the distinction between reality and appearance in relation to such identity. We are shown a variety of perspectives on life and are invited to judge to what extent these are illusory in the sense that an individual may claim to live in terms of certain values and not do so. Indeed, the central issue of the book may be said to be whether we can say, either of ourselves or others, that, at a certain depth, life is lived in terms of the values espoused by an individual, whether the issue of reality and appearance may not be in certain cases (Jim's final act), undecidable.

2   This is something we have to determine for ourselves. To read the novel is to exercise our own capacities for moral assessment of situations and the people involved. The necessity for first-person judgement is emphasized by the contrast between the omniscient first narrator and Marlow's account which stays strictly within the parameters of the first-person perspective. Marlow presents us with evidence and conflicting assess-

ments which require our active consideration. The difficulty of doing this, and indeed perhaps the impossibility of arriving at a determinative assessment in certain cases, becomes evident in our own reading. The novel, that is, explores the distinction between 'reality' and 'appearance' in relation to the ethical in a way which involves, implicates, us, since this distinction is involved in our own understanding of our moral identity and there is no higher court of appeal to determine its nature than ourselves as speakers of the language.

3   Since we are not personally involved, the character of such consideration can, therefore, become manifest. We are, in our capacities for moral assessment, shown to ourselves.

4   But further, our own propensities to certain kinds of illusion are revealed by strategies which invite the reader to acquiesce in certain perspectives (that of the original narrator and Jim's romantic account of his adventures in Patusan) which other aspects of the text invite us to judge as illusory.

Joseph Conrad's *Lord Jim*[1]

In *Heart of Darkness*, the narrator contrasts Marlow's tales with those 'yarns of seamen' which have 'a direct simplicity',[2] where the point of the episodes lies in the ending which will show why they happened as they did, like the unravelling of the plot in a detective novel. The structure of *Lord Jim* would in itself prevent any attempt to read it in this fashion. Chapters 1–4 are provided by an unnamed narrator who then offers us in Chapters 5–35 a record of one of Marlow's after-dinner monologues, and then in Chapters 36–45 a written account by Marlow of the last events concerning Jim sent to a 'privileged man'. Furthermore, Marlow's oral narrative falls into two main parts. The first is concerned with Marlow's conversation with Jim after the Inquiry, the responses of other people to the *Patna* case, and the jobs Marlow manages to get for Jim after he loses his mate's certificate. The second part is concerned with Jim's career in Patusan, excluding its end. This part is itself framed by Chapters 21 and 35 which give certain indications how this account of Jim in Patusan is to be read and which prepare us for its difference from the written account beginning in Chapter 36. Any response to the novel has got to try to make sense of this complex literary strategy.

The narrator

The unnamed narrator occupies a position from which he knows not only the events of Jim's life before, during and immediately after the *Patna* incident, but also his thoughts, feelings and motivations. He occupies a transcendent, omniscient position in relation to Jim's life, into which, in reading, we enter unquestioningly. Jim, we are told, had entered the merchant marine when 'after a course of light holiday literature his vocation for the sea had declared itself'.[3] He dreams on the training ship of 'the sea-life of light literature' with its constant adventures in which he imagines himself playing a heroic part.[4] However, he fails to play his part in the collision which occurs near the training ship because he is rendered immobile by the *personal* attack of the elements: 'There was a fierce purpose in the gale, a furious earnestness in the screech of the wind, in the brutal tumult of earth and sky, that seemed directed at him, and made him hold his breath in awe. He stood still.'[5] But when the rescue has been accomplished by others, it and the elements which precipitated it appear poor things:

> The tumult and the menace of wind and sea now appeared very contemptible to Jim, increasing the regret of his awe at their inefficient menace. Now he knew what to think of it . . . He could affront greater perils. He would do so – better than anybody. Not a particle of fear was left.[6]

(This reference to 'fear' is new and presumably is not part of Jim's own self-understanding.) The telling of the tale of the rescue by those involved Jim thought 'a pitiful display of vanity. The gale had ministered to a heroism as spurious as its own pretence of terror.'[7] He is then *angry* with the elements 'for taking him unawares and checking unfairly a generous readiness for narrow escapes'.[8]

The narrator tells us that Jim then became chief mate of a fine ship 'without ever having been tested by those events of the sea that show in the light of day the inner worth of a man . . . that reveal the quality of his resistance and the secret truth of his pretences not only to others but also to himself'.[9] Jim, the narrator tells us, 'had to bear the criticism of men, the exactions of the sea, and the prosaic severity of the daily task that gives bread – but whose only reward is in the perfect love of the work. This reward eluded him.'[10] A man's inner worth is a matter of this 'perfect love' of the work, of his living in terms of the values of his vocation, and which gives him the 'resistance' to external dangers and temptations. This worth is directly revealed to us by a man's response to certain kinds of event, namely those which seem to intend 'to sweep the whole precious world utterly away from his sight by the simple and appalling act of taking his life'.[11] Where a man's life is put on the line, there is revealed whether he sees his life in terms of the values he espouses or the values in terms of this life. Jim's unsoundness is shown for the narrator by his staying in the East after an accident in which he is injured. He meets in the rest home other seamen who have not gone 'home': 'he found a fascination in the sight of those men, in their appearance of doing so well on such a small allowance of danger and toil'.[12]

Jim takes a job on the *Patna* which is transporting eight hundred Muslim pilgrims bound for Mecca. During his watches, the narrator tells us,

[Jim's] thoughts would be full of valorous deeds: he loved these dreams and the success of his imaginary achievements. They were the best parts of life, its secret truth, its hidden reality . . . they carried his soul away with them and made it drunk with the divine philtre of an unbounded confidence in itself. There was nothing he could not face.[13]

The narrator's account stays with Jim on the *Patna* to the point where the ship runs over a submerged object, and then, with 'A month or so afterwards', transports us to the Inquiry. His account now provides us with Jim's statements about going down into the hold and seeing the water in the forepeak and the rusty condition of the collision bulkhead,[14] and about the immediate reactions of the engineer and the captain: that the ship will sink and the engines must be stopped. But he doesn't tell us why the Inquiry is being held, or therefore what happened next, only that the facts the Inquiry is interested in 'had surged up all about [Jim] to cut him off from the rest of his kind'.[15] In these facts there is 'something invisible, a directing spirit of perdition that dwelt within, like a malevolent soul in a detestable body. He was anxious to make this clear.'[16]

The narrator's account then stops at the point where the issue for the reader is what Jim had done which had resulted in his appearance before the Inquiry. This issue will be taken up by Marlow's oral narrative. The difference between this and the narrator's account is marked. Marlow is one person addressing others. He will tell us what Jim said or said he thought or felt and if he goes beyond this, he will present it as a hypothesis about how things probably struck Jim. Where he makes some judgement as to Jim's motivations, it is his own, and the evidence upon which it is based will be given to us. Marlow's narrative, that is, accepts the conditions of a *first-person* account. It begins by an emphasis on the first-person pronoun: 'Oh yes. I attended the Inquiry.' The narrator, on the other hand, adopts a supra-personal standpoint from which Jim's actions, feelings, thoughts and motivations are open to view, and from which Jim can be judged. It is a narrative characterized by a confidence both in description and in judgement. In this, the narrator separates himself from Jim, as if he is in no way implicated in what Jim's case suggests. The move to Marlow's first-person account will then be one which puts in question the supposition of such a supra-personal position and its attendant conceptions of description and judgement, implying that it is itself an illusion, and just at the point where the issue will be Jim's reaction to exactly the sort of event which the narrator has claimed shows a man's 'inner worth'.

Marlow's narrative, first part (Chapters 5–20)

According to the narrator, Marlow 'many times . . . showed himself willing to remember Jim . . . at length, in detail and audibly'.[17] And Chapter 5 begins '"Oh yes. I attended the inquiry", he *would* say'[18] (my emphasis), as if we are about to get the narrator's account of the sort of thing Marlow used to say on such occasions. But this appearance of a general account is immediately undermined by the particularity of Marlow's mode of speech – he is recorded speaking on a particular occasion to particular people, with all the spontaneity of utterance and formulation this involves, the personal references ('Charley, my dear chap, your dinner was extremely good') and Marlow's own actions during the recitation ('Marlow paused to put new life into his expiring cheroot').[19] The oral narrative finishes with a report by the narrator of a particular event: 'with these words, Marlow had ended his narrative and his audience had broken up forthwith under his abstract pensive gaze'.[20] The conflict at its opening between the narrator's apparent generalizing stance and the particularity of Marlow's delivery makes us aware of the difference between the two voices and so brings to our attention the supra-personal stance of the narrator. That we had not noticed this before indicates our complicity in the narrator's position: we expected that, desired it. Marlow's first-person narrative reminds us that the supra-personal position, and its attendant forms of description and judgement, are illusory although conforming to a desire to simplify life to which we may succumb. If Marlow's narrative questions this narrative position, it will thereby question us too.

Marlow is recalling his own responses and conversations at that time, during and after the Inquiry. He begins by recalling how Jim appeared to him then, and this repeats (although now in the first person) views we have already encountered in the narrator's account. Jim looked the right sort. 'I liked his appearance; I knew his appearance; he came from the right place; he was one of us.'[21] This last phrase, 'he was one of us', will be repeated again and again during the narrative, changing its sense as the scope of 'us' is changed by the context. Here Marlow's explicit aim is to include Jim amongst those who have

> that inborn ability to look temptations straight in the face . . . an unthinking and blessed stiffness before the outward and inward terrors, before the might of nature and the seductive corruption of men – backed by a faith invulnerable to the strength of facts, to the contagion of example, to the solicitation of ideas. Hang ideas! They are tramps, vagabonds, knocking at the back door of your mind, each taking a little of your substance, each carrying away some crumb of that belief in a few simple notions you must cling to if you want to live decently and would like to die easy![22]

This passage at once seems to affirm the narrator's standpoint: perfect love of the work, adherence to duty, resistance to temptation and fear, these are the 'few simple notions' that characterize a man's inner worth, and Jim's appearance seems to be external evidence of their presence. And yet there is already a disturbance in the confidence of this assertion: for if one's inner worth renders one morally immune from external threat, how could ideas each 'take a little of your substance' and carry away the belief in the few simple notions? Perhaps *Lord Jim* is itself such an 'idea' and perhaps these are not such 'simple notions'.

Marlow's interest in the case he explains as looking for some way at that time of finding 'some merciful explanation, some convincing shadow of an excuse'[23] for how someone appearing as 'sound' as Jim could have done what he did: 'there was some infernal alloy in his metal'.[24] But this confident assurance that we can identify the 'alloy' and so re-affirm the true metal is now (that is, at the time of the recitation) seen by Marlow to be an illusion:

> I see well enough now that I hoped for the impossible – for the laying of what is the most obstinate ghost of man's creation, of the uneasy doubt uprising like a mist, secret and gnawing like a worm, and more chilling than the certitude of death – the doubt of the sovereign power enthroned in a fixed standard of conduct.[25]

For the narrator, a man's inner worth is to be seen where he faces the threat of destruction: there he shows what gives meaning to his life as what, if anything, is more valuable to him than life itself. There we may see the 'sovereign power enthroned in a fixed standard of conduct'. But what if this certainty of diagnosis is an illusion born of the supra-personal standpoint of the first narrator? Perhaps the nature of our relation to such values, at a certain depth, involves an opacity, a precariousness of recognition, in respect of our own case let alone that of others. Jim's case, perhaps, suggests something of general import, has a universal significance: 'he was one of us . . . the mystery of his attitude got hold of me as though he had been an individual in the forefront of his kind, as if the obscure truth involved were momentous enough to affect mankind's conception of itself'.[26] Here, Jim's being 'one of us' indicates his exemplary status for 'mankind' in relation to the nature of moral identity and the distinction between ethical reality and illusion.

Marlow's conversation with Jim, however, seems to bear out the narrator's confident reports. His jump from the *Patna* with the other white crew is attributed by him to their influence: 'I jumped! I told you I jumped; but I tell you they were too much for any man. It was their doing as plainly as if they had reached up with a boat hook and pulled me over.'[27] Jim had been taken unprepared: 'It is all in being ready. I wasn't; not – not then.'[28] His attitude towards what he has done sees it as a lost opportunity: 'Ah! what a chance missed',[29] he says, whereupon he again silently contemplates 'the impossible world of romantic achievements'. His attachment to his life at sea is determined by his aspiration to fame, to the 'heroism' he has read about, which marks an absence of adherence to those very values motivation by which is to be the object of the admiration of others. This dependency on the opinion of others is reflected now in his attribution of blame to the other white crew members for what he has done and in his attitude ('a chance missed') to his actions. Jim in his attendance at the Inquiry and his conversation with Marlow is 'struggling to save his idea of what his moral identity should be'.[30] In his dreams, he is the heroic saviour of ships and people in distress, acting out precisely what the narrator had looked for in those tests of a man's inner worth. That is what he really is, his life is truly given significance by the values of his calling, despite what has happened. But to believe in values has implications not merely in action but in feeling too. That one believes in certain values is not in itself disproved by a failure to act in accordance with them, but it requires a certain relation to such failure, feelings of guilt, remorse and so forth. Jim's relation, however, is one of declining responsibility and indeed of outrage at his treatment by events. His conception of himself on the *Patna* is of an essential passivity. Marlow says he feels bound to believe that 'he had preserved through it all a strange illusion of passiveness'.[31] '"I had jumped . . . It seems", he added . . . "I knew nothing about it till I looked up." '[32] This conception of his real moral identity leads him to see a gulf between himself and the other white crew members who had actively tried to abandon the ship and its eight hundred passengers. The degraded behaviour of the white crew in the lifeboat, with its 'filthy jargon' 'was sweet to hear . . . it kept me alive, I tell you. It has saved my life',[33] precisely by emphasizing his own superiority. And now, once again, he believes he is 'ready for anything'.[34] He faces the Inquiry rather than run away because he has to insist that his true moral identity has not been revealed by the action. He wants to show how this can be, by explaining how he has been 'tried', 'More than is fair'[35] by circumstances, by the crew, the elements and the ship. Having faced the Inquiry, he must then 'wait for another chance' where his moral identity and his conduct will be at one. It is characteristic of Jim (not to mention the other white crew members) that he was not even aware of the two Malay seamen who remained at their posts throughout the incident and were found in charge of the *Patna* by the rescuing French patrol boat.

Jim's conception of what he has done, that he was overwhelmed by circumstances in a way which was 'more than fair', his seeing, as the narrator rightly says, a 'directing spirit of perdition that dwelt within' the events, indicate to Marlow and to us something of Jim's true moral identity at this time. Marlow speaks of his 'sort of sublimated, idealised selfishness'. For Jim, the events on the *Patna* (in which the lives of eight hundred people were at risk) were 'a chance missed', the crew members were sent to be a vexation to him, and the elements to take him unawares. He has not been treated 'fairly'. The world of nature and humanity are there to serve his conception of himself: he has a claim on events and on the conduct of others because of who he is, where this identity is, of course, not provided by adherence to the values he claims as his own. He deserves his reward simply, as it were, for being who he is, and when it is not forthcoming, he is filled with anger, a sense of betrayal, of righteous indignation. In the lifeboat, he 'focussed on [the other crew members] his hatred of the whole thing: he would have liked to take a signal revenge for the abhorrent opportunity they had put in his way'.[36] Even the Inquiry itself is turned to play its role in relation to his sense of himself: ' "I feel as if nothing could ever touch me", he said in a tone of sombre conviction, "if this business couldn't knock me over, then there's no fear of there being not enough time to – climb out – and . . . " '.[37]

Jim's father is a clergyman and it later appears that Jim kept a letter from him which after Jim's death falls into Marlow's hands. 'The old chap goes on equably trusting Providence and the established order of the universe but alive to its small dangers and its small mercies',[38] whilst the narrator has told us that his father 'possessed such certain knowledge of the unknowable as made for the righteousness of people in cottages without disturbing the ease of mind of those whom an unerring Providence enables to live in mansions'.[39] All is part of the great plan which enables the clergyman and his parishioners to breathe 'equably the air of undisturbed rectitude'.[40] The son reveals the hidden egoism in this claim on the order of the universe where it appears nakedly in a personal form. His 'sublimated selfishness' expresses itself as a claim to recognition by others and indeed by the universe just for being Jim. But just in this way, it shows that he doesn't understand the significance of his life in terms of the values he claims as his own. Rather, his empty claim on the universe reveals a fundamental lack of a sense of the meaningfulness of his life. His egoism is the expression of a hollowness, an absence of value.

Marlow's discussion of Jim's case with a series of characters, which constitutes the remaining chapters before the Patusan episode, contributes to his feeling that Jim's case shows 'he had been an individual in the forefront of his kind', that his case suggests something of general significance in relation to the possibility of 'the sovereign power enthroned in a fixed standard of conduct'. Captain Brierly, one of the two nautical assessors in the Inquiry, is a supremely successful seaman. He had never made a mistake, had an accident or a mishap, or suffered any check in his steady rise to the top of his profession. His overt attitude to Jim is contemptuous disdain, as it is to others generally, including Marlow. He 'was acutely aware of his merits and of his rewards'.[41] 'His self-satisfaction presented to me and to the world a surface as hard as granite.' Yet, Marlow adds, 'He committed suicide very soon after.'[42] The Inquiry, Marlow surmises, must have been an occasion which prompted a 'silent inquiry into his own case. The verdict must have been of unmitigated guilt.' It had started 'into life some thought with which a man unused to such companionship finds it impossible to live':[43] the thought presumably of a community with Jim in his claim on others and the universe at large for recognition, of a hollowness in his claim to stand for the values of his calling. To find this revelation a reason for suicide, however, is to find life itself wanting, to revolt against it in a last, supreme assertion of one's own claim. Marlow remarks to Brierly's mate that whatever it was that had prompted his suicide, 'It wasn't anything that would have disturbed much either of us two', to which the mate replies 'Ay, ay! neither you nor I, sir, had ever thought so much of ourselves.'[44]

The French Lieutenant who had stayed on the *Patna* whilst it was brought into port sees Jim as acting simply through fear. Such fear is he says simply part of the human condition, 'Man is born a coward', but one 'puts up with it' through 'habit – necessity . . . the eye of others'.[45] Marlow thinks he is taking a lenient view of Jim's conduct, but is quickly corrected: 'the honour, monsieur . . . that is real, that is! And what life may be worth . . . when the honour is gone . . . I can offer no opinion . . . Because – monsieur – I know nothing of it.'[46] Marlow responds 'but couldn't it reduce itself to not being found out?', to which the Lieutenant says 'This, monsieur, is too fine for me – much above me – I don't think about it.'[47] Marlow's question raises that 'uneasy doubt' about the 'sovereign power' of the values the man of honour espouses, wondering if one can know, even in one's own case, whether it might not be a matter rather of 'not being found out'. He offers the Lieutenant the opportunity to accept this possibility and so his community with Jim's case. Perhaps his 'I don't think about it' indicates that, indeed, the thought has occurred to him, precipitating a disturbance which it is necessary to ignore if one's peace of mind is to be preserved.

The adventurer Chester who wants to employ Jim, after the Inquiry and his loss of his mate's certificate, to take charge of a guano island he has his eye on thinks Jim 'no good' for taking his loss to heart. 'What's all the to-do about? A bit of ass's skin.' Chester's values are explicitly ones of simple self-interest in terms of which he prides himself on seeing 'things exactly as they are . . . Look at me. I made it a practice never to take anything to heart.'[48] But Chester's plans are crazy. For him, 'it's the most splendid, sure chance' of a fortune, whilst he ignores what is actually the case with the island. 'Then there's the water supply. I'll have to fly around and get somebody to trust me for half-a-dozen second-hand iron tanks. Catch rain-water, hey?' to which Marlow points out 'There are whole years when not a drop of rain falls on Walpole.' 'Oh well, I will fix up something for them – or land a supply. Hang it all! That's not the question.'[49] Something will turn up, the world will conform to Chester's desires. It's no surprise that his vessel, when he finally gets one, is lost with all hands. Chester's assumption of a claim on the universe thus parallels Jim's sense of the 'malevolent' intention embodied in the elements and circumstances of the *Patna* incident: both reveal a lack of belief, in Chester's case even in his own self-centred values. He is shown living a life of illusion even in relation to his own self-interest.

Marlow's final conversation about Jim's case is with Stein, a rich merchant now turned naturalist who will arrange for Jim to manage his trading station in Patusan after Jim's abortive jobs at a rice-mill and as a water-clerk, which he left as soon as the *Patna* case was mentioned. Stein's judgement on Jim is that 'He is romantic.'[50] Jim's dreams of his future great exploits are of the externalities of adherence to the values he espouses and in terms of which such actions would acquire the praise he seeks. In this way, his relation to those values is revealed as external, not the belief in them which would be shown in action and feeling in reality, in the present (recall Jim's claim that at the time of the *Patna* incident he wasn't 'ready'). Stein sees this as part of the human condition: 'every time [man] shuts his eyes he sees himself as a very fine fellow – so fine as he can never be . . . In a dream.'[51] But for Stein, the way to live is to 'follow the dream, and again to follow the dream – and so – ewig – usque ad finem'.[52] And yet in uttering this thought 'the austere exaltation of a certitude seen in the dusk vanished from his face'.[53] For perhaps in articulating this thought, Stein becomes aware of the discrepancy between the external, specular relation to values of the dreamer and what would be required by an adherence to them in reality. Such romanticism is a form of escapism. He half recognizes, unlike Chester, this unreality, yet feels that without it his life would lack meaning. Stein's life-history shows a steady retreat from actualization, towards living in a dream. He had begun by following revolutionary political ideas in his native Bavaria, but forced to flee, and having joined forces with a Dutch naturalist, he had come east. He had remained, and worked with a Scottish trader, inherited his concern and grown wealthy. Now in his old age he devotes his time to his butterflies. When he looks at a butterfly, it is 'as though on the bronze sheen of these frail wings, in the white tracings, in the gorgeous markings, he could see other things, an image of something as perishable and defying destruction as these delicate and lifeless tissues displaying a splendour unmarred by death'.[54] The butterfly becomes an image of the dream and in that way both 'perishable', having its reality only in his imagination, and 'defying destruction' in being opposed to reality. In this his romanticism is Jim's. And it is *Stein's* idea to send Jim to Patusan.

Patusan 1 (Chapters 21–35)

Chapters 21 and 35 frame the story of Jim's triumphs in Patusan. Chapter 21 has certain significant peculiarities which should warn us that all is not as straightforward here as it might seem. In going to Patusan, we are told, Jim 'left his earthly failings behind him, and that sort of reputation he had, and there was a totally new set of conditions for his imaginative faculty to work upon'.[55] What he achieved in Patusan 'would have appeared as much beyond his control as the motions of the moon and the stars'.[56] Furthermore, 'It was inconceivable. That was the distinctive quality of the part into which Stein and I had tumbled him unwittingly.'[57] These are, I suggest, clear indications that what we are about to hear is precisely a *romantic* story, the sort of story which would satisfy (for the time of reading) romantic desires where one's claims to recognition by the world find fulfilment. It will be precisely such a story as Jim himself would love to read, of 'the impossible world of romantic achievements'.[58] Marlow immediately signals his alteration of key by presenting us with a (not so hidden) contradiction. He says, in the tone and with the sense of what has gone before in previous chapters, that 'the less I understood the more I was bound to him in the name of that doubt which is the inseparable part of our knowledge. I did not know so much about myself': that doubt as to the 'sovereign power of a fixed standard of conduct' and the question which arises as to the extent to which our lives generally share Jim's egoism. He does not see Jim 'distinctly', but, equally, he does not see himself so either.[59] But then Marlow, saying he was going home after seeing Jim in Patusan, launches into an extraordinary speech. Going home he says is like going to 'render an account' before 'the spirit that dwells within the land, under its sky, in its air, in its valleys, and on its rises, in its fields, in its waters and its trees – a mute friend, judge and inspirer'. And to face this 'one must return with a clear consciousness'.[60] It is, of course, just this 'clear consciousness' he has a page before denied he had about himself or Jim. And in the next sentence he remarks 'All this may seem to you sheer sentimentalism' but then continues in the same vein, 'The fact remains that you must touch your reward with clean hands, lest it turn to dead leaves, to thorns, in your grasp.'[61] It is because Jim 'felt confusedly but powerfully, the demand of some such truth or some such illusion – I don't care how you call it, there is so little difference, and the difference means so little. The thing is that in virtue of his feeling he mattered. He would never go home now.'[62] Not only does this cavalier indifference to the distinction between truth and illusion render pointless his previous insistence on 'clear consciousness' and 'clean hands', but this whole train of thought is here identified with one of *Jim's* illusions, the product of his romanticism which we are now being offered in Marlow's mouth for his audience's (and our) agreement. Marlow, however, doesn't stop there, but goes on, 'The spirit of the land, as becomes the ruler of great enterprises, is careless of innumerable lives. Woe to the stragglers! We exist only in so far as we hang together.'[63] We don't matter individually but only in so far as we express the power of the spirit of our native land. (We shall see that the 'privileged man' in Chapter 36 shares precisely these views which Marlow there objects to, emphasizing that Jim 'had no dealings but with himself' and had his significance in that.) Jim felt like this, but Jim, as befits a romantic, had 'imagination'.[64] But then Marlow immediately denies this of himself: 'As to me, I have no imagination (I would be more certain about him to-day, if I had).'[65] Marlow is inviting his audience, and us, in going with the flow of this romanticism without noticing, to reveal our own romantic desires, which will then find their (temporary) satisfaction in Jim's tale. For, Marlow says, 'He existed for me, and after all it is only through me that he exists for you.'[66] Will we not find that Jim is 'one of us' precisely in our desire that he achieve his dream, get another chance and triumph – don't we too desire a 'happy ending', feeling it is 'right'? 'I affirm he had achieved greatness',[67] Marlow says (he will refuse to affirm anything later): isn't that too what we desire for him, and perhaps for ourselves too?

Chapter 22 begins with an explicit statement of what we are about to get, the stuff of romantic fiction. 'The conquest of love, honour, men's confidence – the pride of it, the power of it, are fit materials for a heroic tale',[68] which locates the significance of the actions concerned (that 'conquer') in the opinions of others. Stein gives Jim a ring to present to Doramin, leader of one of the factions of Patusan life, as a token of his authority: '"It's like something you read of in books," he threw in appreciatively.'[69] And Jim's approach to Patusan up the river is described thus by Marlow:

> At the first bend he lost sight of the sea with its labouring waves for ever rising, sinking, and vanishing to rise again – the very image of struggling mankind – and faced the immovable forests rooted deep in the soil, soaring towards the sunshine, everlasting in the shadowy night of their traditions, like life itself.[70]

Here we have a familiar theme of adventure literature, of the West as a culture of change and progress, whilst the 'natives' live an unchanging life of tradition. We already know,[71] however, that Patusan has a long history, invaded by Dutch and English adventurers in search of pepper, in contact with the outside world through Arab and European merchants, and presently characterized by the conflict of antagonistic forces and by the presence of peoples from different parts of the Archipelago (country-born Malays, Bugis settlers from Celebes). When Marlow leaves Patusan, recounted in the other framing chapter of the first Patusan episode (Chapter 35), he likens it to 'a picture created by fancy on a canvas' which remains 'with its life arrested, in an unchanging light'.[72] He is returning to 'the world where events move, men change, light flickers' whilst in the world he is leaving 'I cannot imagine any alteration.'[73] Indeed, Marlow then lists the characters we have met in the tale giving them unchanging and essential characteristics: they are stereotypes. 'The immense and magnanimous Doramin and his little motherly witch of a wife ... Dain Waris, intelligent and brave, with his faith in Jim, the girl, absorbed in her frightened, suspicious adoration.'[74] This unchanging world is indeed the world of imperial romantic fiction, and Marlow explicitly tells us that these characters 'exist as if under an enchanter's wand'.[75] Earlier we get this description of Cornelius, the trader Jim is sent to displace:

his loathsomeness . . . was abject, so that a simply disgusting person would have appeared noble by his side. He has his place neither in the background nor in the foreground of the story; he is simply seen skulking on its outskirts, enigmatical and unclean, tainting the fragrance of its youth and of its naiveness.[76]

Not only is Cornelius, as with the other characters, summed up in a couple of characteristics without our being left to judge in the light of evidence (as contrasted with the earlier parts of Marlow's talk), but these characteristics are plainly intended to be ludicrous – here we see the blackest of villainy, a loathsomeness beyond the merely disgusting. Furthermore, Marlow says Cornelius's place in the story is on its outskirts, 'tainting the fragrance of its [that is, the story's] youth and of its naiveness'. And that story is one told, of course, by Jim to Marlow. It is a story characterized by its naivety, by its flight from the world 'where events move, men change, light flickers', from our world, which will shortly be shown to be the world of Patusan too.

The story itself contains all the ingredients of imperial romantic adventure. Jim is captured by the evil Rajah ('a dirty, little, used-up old man with evil eyes and a weak mouth' who is an opium addict to boot)[77] on his arrival in Patusan, but makes a daring, single-handed escape to the opposing faction, led by Doramin. There he takes control of a fearful populace to resist the oppression of the Rajah and the Arab trader Sherif Ali. He masterminds and fearlessly leads an attack on Ali's 'impregnable camp', driving the oppressors out. He then becomes the figure upon whom the population is absolutely dependent: 'His word decided everything.'[78] When Jim tells Marlow this story, he appears to Marlow as a figure who 'dominated the forest, the secular gloom, the old mankind. He was like a figure set up on a pedestal, to represent in his persistent youth the power, and perhaps the virtues, of races that never grow old, that have emerged from the gloom.'[79] In his firmness of purpose, courage and activity he stands for the West against the fearful passivity of races which have not emerged 'from the gloom'. His legend 'had gifted him with supernatural powers'.[80] And Marlow himself refers to Jim bursting 'into a Homeric peal of laughter',[81] a phrase it is difficult not to hear ironically.

The characters, the story, the setting, all are precisely what Marlow's listeners and readers would have expected (and wanted) and in assenting to the story they would reveal the romanticism, and what this involves, the stereotyping and the assumed superiority of the romantic's own position, they share with Jim. The framing chapters give explicit indication of the character of these chapters as I noted above. But there are within the story itself occasional hints of disruption of the fantasy (as with the description of Cornelius or the Homeric reference). Two of these occur when Marlow himself is personally involved with others rather than simply hearing about them from Jim. When Doramin is told by Marlow that Jim would never leave, as

Doramin has suggested all white men do, 'He was not very pleased, I fear, and evidently I had given him food for thought.'[82] (It later appears in the written account that Doramin has plans for his son to replace the Rajah and so 'magnanimous' Doramin may well regard Jim as a rival.) And when Jewel tells Marlow about her mother's death, keeping Cornelius out of the room, he is troubled by

> the passive, irremediable horror of the scene. It had the power to drive me out of my conception of existence, out of that shelter each of us makes for himself to creep under in moments of danger. For a moment I had a view of a world that seemed to wear a vast and dismal aspect of disorder, while, in truth, thanks to our universal efforts, it is as sunny an arrangement of small conveniences as the mind of man can conceive.[83]

Here the assumption of a world as conforming to our desires, as satisfying our claim on it, is seen for what it is, an illusion. This assumption will shortly be unmasked in events in Patusan too. And then the indigenous characters will appear with their own spontaneous lives and views of the world too outside of Jim's romantic tale.

Patusan 2 (Chapters 36–45)

Marlow provides a written account of the last events of Jim's life to a 'privileged man' who, having heard his oral narrative, had expressed an interest in his story. The privileged man holds views parallel to those expressed by Marlow in the first framing chapter of the first Patusan episode and which are implicit in the structure, characterization and imagery of the romantic story. Giving one's life to 'them (*them* meaning all of mankind with skins brown, yellow, or black in colour)' was 'like selling your soul to a brute'. It was only 'endurable and enduring when based on a firm conviction in the truth of ideas racially our own, in whose name are established the order, the morality of an ethical progress'.[84] We 'must fight in the ranks or our lives don't count'. This is part of Jim's own ostensible view and why he won't return home, intending in Patusan to 'keep in touch with . . . those whom, perhaps, I shall never see any more'[85] through his Homeric exploits. This is not, for the privileged man, however, sufficiently a matter of fighting in the ranks and he has prophesied a 'disaster' of 'weariness and disgust' with the 'self-appointed task' for Jim. Marlow, however, now sees Jim's separation from 'the ranks' as precisely what gives him his significance: 'The point . . . is that of all mankind Jim had no dealings but with himself, and the question is whether at the last he had not confessed to a faith mightier than the laws of order and progress.' But he adds 'I affirm nothing' (in contrast to his previous affirmation of Jim's 'greatness'). 'Perhaps you may pronounce – after you've read.'[86] The romance in its stereotypes and heroic action had spelt out its judgement to the listener or reader, but we are now to be left alone (as Jim has just been said to be). There 'shall be no message, unless such as each of us can interpret for himself from the language of facts that are so often more enigmatic than the craftiest arrangement of words',[87] although, of course, here that language is precisely such an arrangement.

This latter perception is contained in Marlow's description of the story he is about to tell, which he says 'is romantic beyond the wildest dreams of boyhood' in contrast to the previous romance characterized by its naivety and youth. It contains 'a sort of profound and terrifying logic in it . . . This astounding adventure, of which the most astounding part is that it is true, comes on as an unavoidable consequence. Something of the sort had to happen.'[88] The necessity at issue, the logic, is that of the true story as opposed to the romantic fiction. But what it is that is true is something we have ourselves to see: 'there is *to my mind* a sort of profound and terrifying logic in it' (my emphasis).

Into Jim's world of Patusan comes Gentleman Brown, an adventurer fleeing from the threat of imprisonment who arrives on a stolen schooner looking for food and plunder intending to make good his escape to Madagascar. Brown is characterized in terms which have an obvious relation to those through which the privileged man and the Marlow of Chapter 21 have differentiated the white races from the non-white. He exhibits 'an undisguised ruthlessness of purpose, a strange vengeful attitude towards his own past, and a blind belief in the righteousness of his will against all mankind'.[89] In Chapter 22 we had been introduced to Patusan's history (before it is glossed over by the rhetoric of the 'everlasting . . . night . . . of tradition')[90] and the intrusion of the European traders for pepper. These Dutch and English adventurers would 'cut each other's throats without hesitation and forswear their souls' to get pepper, and the 'bizarre obstinacy of that desire made them defy death in a thousand shapes'.[91] 'It made them great. By heavens! It made them heroic.' But this appearance of heroism is to us now, 'their less tried successors' to whom 'they appear magnified, not as agents of trade but as instruments of a recorded destiny, pushing out into the unknown in obedience to an inward voice, to an impulse beating in the blood, to a dream of the future. They were wonderful.'[92] The ruthless plundering of these adventurers appears great and heroic when incorporated into precisely that sort of myth of the 'spirit of the land' and its manifest destiny which Marlow had invited us to accept in Chapter 21. 'It seems impossible to believe that mere greed could hold men to such a steadfastness of purpose, to such a blind persistence in endeavour and sacrifice.'[93] The mere desire to possess could not motivate defying death: rather, their activities expressed a sense of their righteousness, their claim on the world. But Brown too defies death, that modern adventurer equally characterized by ruthlessness of purpose, indifference to the past, and a blind belief in his own righteousness, but who

172

can be examined without the obfuscations of later mythologizing. He exhibits a pure will to recognition against the world, an evil 'derived from intense egoism, inflamed by resistance'.[94] He robs 'a man as if only to demonstrate his poor opinion of the creature, and he would bring to the shooting or maiming of some quiet, unoffending stranger a savage and vengeful earnestness'.[95] The opposition of the inhabitants of Patusan breeds in him the desire 'to play havoc with that jungle town which had defied him, to see it strewn over with corpses and enveloped in flames'.[96] When he ambushes Dain Waris's party, 'It was not a vulgar and treacherous massacre; it was a lesson, a retaliation' but one which, Marlow says, demonstrates 'some obscure and awful attribute of our nature which, I am afraid, is not so very far under the surface as we like to think'.[97] It is that attribute which amongst much else (and precisely how much else is the question posed to us) had led Jim to complain that he had been unfairly treated by the elements and the conduct of the *Patna*'s white crew, that 'sublimated selfishness' which, in its bare self-assertion of a claim on others and the universe, marks its essential lack of meaning. The question posed to us by Jim's case (undecidably) is how general this is.

It is this commonality which is obscurely sensed by Jim in his conversation with Brown. Brown's talk indeed claims a more overt commonality with Jim since he is convinced that any European must be fleeing from something to live in Patusan and must be getting something out of the venture,[98] both suggestions which strike home with Jim. But underlying these and other references which have a meaning for Jim (when 'it comes to saving one's life in the dark, one didn't care who else went – 3, 30, 300 people'), 'there ran through the rough talk a vein of subtle reference to their common blood, an assumption of common experience, a sickening suggestion of common guilt, of secret knowledge that was like a bond of their minds and of their hearts'.[99] Jim responds to this sense of commonality by persuading the villagers to let Brown and his men go, saying that he would 'answer with his life for any harm that should come to' the people from this. Brown and his band then massacre Dain Waris (Doramin's son) and most of his men.

Jewel, Jim's Malay wife, pleads with him to fly: 'There is no escape'[100] he says; she urges him to fight for his life: 'I have no life.'[101] She tells him to defend himself: '"Nothing can touch me," he said in a last flicker of superb egoism.'[102] He intends to 'defy' the disaster, 'He was going to prove his power in another way and conquer the fatal destiny itself',[103] so he goes to Doramin and is shot dead. 'They say that the white man sent right and left at all those faces a proud and unflinching glance.'[104] Marlow says that perhaps in that glance he had seen his opportunity (previously veiled, like an 'Eastern bride') and so achieved the heroism he had so desired. But, on the other hand, we can see him 'tearing himself out of the arms of a jealous love at the sign, at the call of his exalted egoism. He goes away from a living woman to celebrate his pitiless wedding with a shadowy ideal of conduct.'[105] What is true? 'He is one of us' so 'we ought to know'. But 'who knows?'[106] The book, however, ends with Stein who has 'aged greatly of late' and says he is 'preparing to leave all this', gesturing at his butterflies. The butterflies, we remember, were 'an image' of 'a splendour unmarred by death',[107] of the dream. With the death of Jim perhaps such 'splendour' itself has died for him, has come to be fully acknowledged *as* dream, the illusion of an individual who has failed to live his values in reality, who could not do without their false splendour. With the death of Jim, of youth, of naivety, of the illusion of the 'glamour' of such illusions, Stein, the romantic, ages. We are left with the question of the nature of Jim's last act which requires us to engage in a reflection on the book as a whole, and to confront the nature of the illusion concerned, and to raise the question of our own complicity in it.

The strategy of **Lord Jim**

The narrator's account introduces the issue of 'the inner worth of a man', the 'secret truth of his pretences', of what it is to 'believe in' the values he espouses. It is against his conception of the transparency of this that he sees Jim's life as one of pretence. He is in the work because of his dreams of glory, in terms of recognition by others, which indicates his externality to his claimed values since it attributes to others a belief in them which he himself lacks. Yet the narrator's supra-personal position separates him from Jim in a radical way. It allows him to judge Jim because he assumes he is in no way implicated in Jim's case. From the narrator's point of view, he is not 'one of us'. Yet such a position is itself an illusion. Not only do we never, in relation to a certain depth of belief, have such a clarity of understanding of the motivations of others as he assumes, we do not have it of ourselves. This is, we might say, part of the 'grammar' of those values which can give sense to life and can provide notions of development and depth absent from the explicitly self-seeking values of a Chester, and to ignore it is to part company with them. Hence the narrator, precisely by separating himself from Jim, implicates himself in his illusion, and unknowingly at that, thereby showing the lack of self-understanding his supra-personal position implies. Our going along with this, finding unconsciously that it satisfies the kind of narrative we expect and desire, therefore, already implicates us in Jim's case. The strategy of the remainder of the novel is to bring this home to us. We desire a simplification of life which falsifies it. Marlow begins his narrative by repeating the narrator's views of Jim but in the first person, where the questions of evidence as to what others feel, think and what motivates them, on the one hand, and of the truth of one's own pretences, on the other, cannot be avoided. In providing the evidence, Marlow implicates us in the judgements he makes, which culminate in seeing Jim's romanticism as indeed a 'sort of sublimated idealised selfishness' in which he claims recognition from the world, and so shows his dependency on it for his sense of the significance of his life. At root, such 'selfishness' is a lack, a 'hollowness at the core', a failure to be motivated by the values he would claim as his own. Marlow then provides us with the evidence for concluding that Brierly and the French Lieutenant are further manifestations of this failure, being dependent on success or the opinion of others for their sense of the significance of their lives whilst claiming a motivation by the values of their calling alone. Chester too shows us a form of this illusion. His apparent values may simply be concerned with self-advancement, but, even so, his blind disregard for the contingencies of existence reveals a delusion in his self-understanding. Stein then shows us someone who, although to a certain extent recognizing the dream-like character of his view of life, cannot give it up without finding existence pointless. Yet as readers, we are still distanced from these judgements on others. The first Patusan episode, however, seeks to implicate us in the case at issue, Jim's. We are there given precisely such an apparent realization of Jim's dreams, a tale we are invited to desire, and so reveal our own romanticism, by accepting Marlow's myth of the 'spirit of the land', which is part of Jim's own illusion and which indicates its root in the desire to feel recognized by others ('the land'). In terms of this illusion, we make fictions of others, making of them something other than the dreamer himself: they become stereotypes, part players in the fantasy. This satisfaction of Jim's and our romanticism is then disrupted in the written narrative. There the character of Marlow's myth is revealed in the 'privileged man''s explicit formulation of the superiority of his race, before which he claims recognition, in terms of 'ethical progress', over the 'brutes'. And whereas the heroic judgement on Jim has been dictated to us, with our compliance, Marlow now explicitly puts the onus on us: 'Perhaps you may pronounce – after you've read.'[108] We are invited now to make the connection between the 'heroic' activities of the pepper traders and Brown, and through the commonality Jim senses with him, to connect this with Jim himself. Jim's death, heroic act or final act of a hollow egoism informed by 'a shadowy ideal of conduct' is presented to us as a question which rebounds on our previous satisfaction at Jim's success and its complicity with the stereotypes and their brutal suppression of the reality of others (something apparent on the *Patna* where Jim failed to even notice the conduct of the Malay crew). Stein senses in Jim's death a judgement on himself, as we are then invited to judge ourselves. We, like Stein, are left alone (and as readers we have been that all along), in the face of that 'doubt of the sovereign power enthroned in a fixed standard of conduct', whether in respect of our own case or that of others, faced by a certain impenetrability in relation to the central issue of life, what it is to live in terms of a conception of life's significance.

Lord Jim explores what it is to believe in the values one claims as determinative of the significance of one's own life. To believe in such values is to take them as one's 'truth', the truth of appropriation evinced in how one lives, in action and feeling. Such 'reality' is opposed to the 'illusion' of self-deception, of believing one adheres to certain vaues when one's life says otherwise. Jim's romantic dreams are one form in which such illusion manifests itself, for what he is in love with is the recognition by others for actions believed by them to have been motivated by the values at issue and not those values themselves. The absence of belief, and so the essential meaninglessness of Jim's life in so far as he remains a romantic, expresses itself in his 'egoism', in his resentment at events whose significance should, according to his own self-understanding, be given by the values themselves, as the field for action and appropriate emotion. This egoism, seen nakedly in Gentleman Brown, is the assertion of the will stripped of anything in which it can find significance. But although this distinction between 'reality' and 'appearance' may seem in these cases to be clearly drawn, *Lord Jim* shows us that self-understanding here is, at a certain depth, necessarily obscure and precarious, as D. Z. Phillips shows in relation to religious values in the case of R. S. Thomas's poetry. It does this in the only way it can be shown, by inviting a self-recognition through implicating us in Jim's case, forcing us to recognize him as 'one of us'. The novel's strategy invites our assent to what we must then recognize are illusions: the position of the omniscient judge of the first narrator and the romantic story Jim tells of his exploits. We are shown to ourselves as desiring to obscure a precariousness in our own self-understanding. In coming to see this, we are then put into a position where, at the crucial point where the 'inner worth' of Jim is at stake, we cannot judge, an undecidability which proceeds, not from the nature of language, but from what it is to be involved in the language of the significance of life, and so of what it is to be human, 'one of us'.

NOTES

ABBREVIATIONS USED IN NOTES

AF	Schlegel, *Athenaeum Fragments*
AL	Derrida, *Acts of Literature*
AM	Bataille, *The Absence of Myth*
BCF	Phillips, *Belief, Change and Forms of Life*
BGE	Nietzsche, *Beyond Good and Evil*
BP	Murdoch, *The Black Prince*
BR	Holland, *The Blanchot Reader*
CF	Schlegel, *Critical Fragments*
CHU	Cavell, *Conditions Handsome and Unhandsome*
CIS	Rorty, *Contingency, Irony, Solidarity*
CJ	Kant, *The Critique of Judgement*
CM	Derrida, *Given Time: 1. Counterfeit Money*
CP	Rorty, *Consequences of Pragmatism*
CR	Cavell, *The Claim of Reason*
CUP	Kierkegaard, *Concluding Unscientific Postscript*
DAP	Derrida, *Remarks on Deconstruction and Pragmatism*
DK	Cavell, *Disowning Knowledge*
DP	Schlegel, *Dialogue on Poetry*
E	Bataille, *Eroticism*
EH	Nietzsche, *Ecce Homo*
FAF	Phillips, *Faith after Foundationalism*
FG	Nussbaum, *The Fragility of Goodness*
FS	Murdoch, *The Fire and the Sun*
FTF	Phillips, *From Fantasy to Faith*
GD	Derrida, *The Gift of Death*
GO	Blanchot, *The Gaze of Orpheus*
GS	Nietzsche, *The Gay Science*
HO	Rorty, *Essays on Heidegger and Others*
I	Schlegel, 'Ideas'
IC	Blanchot, *The Infinite Conversation*
IE	Bataille, *Inner Experience*
IIE	Phillips, *Interventions in Ethics*
L	Schlegel, *Lucinde*
LE	Bataille, *Literature and Evil*
LJ	Conrad, *Lord Jim*
LK	Nussbaum, *Love's Knowledge*
MD	Blanchot, *The Madness of the Day*

ME	Bataille, *My Mother, Madame Edwarda*
MG	Murdoch, *Metaphysics as a Guide to Morals*
ON	Bataille, *On Nietzsche*
ORT	Rorty, *Objectivity, Relativism and Truth*
PCP	Phillips, *Philosophy's Cool Place*
PMN	Rorty, *Philosophy and the Mirror of Nature*
QO	Cavell, *Quest of the Ordinary*
RST	Phillips, *R. S. Thomas: Poet of the Hidden God*
SG	Murdoch, *The Sovereignty of Good*
SL	Blanchot, *The Space of Literature*
SS	Blanchot, *The Siren's Song*
TDG	Phillips, *Through a Darkening Glass*
TI	Nietzsche, *Twilight of the Idols*
TP	Rorty, *Truth and Progress*
TR	Bataille, *Theory of Religion*
TS	Cavell, *Themes out of School*
VE	Bataille, *Visions of Excess*
WD	Blanchot, *The Writing of the Disaster*
WP	Nietzsche, *The Will to Power*

INTRODUCTION

1 In the *Republic* at 607b.
2 *Phaedrus* 245a, trans. H. N. Fowler, London, 1977.
3 Aristophanes, *Frogs*, 1040 in D. A. Russell and M. Winterbottom (eds), *Ancient Literary Criticism*, Oxford, 1983.
4 *Ion* 536a, in *Ancient Literary Criticism*, p. 44.
5 R. Rorty, *Philosophy and the Mirror of Nature,* Oxford, 1980, p. 316.
6 R. Rorty, *Contingency, Irony, Solidarity*, Cambridge, 1989, p. 8.
7 F. Nietzsche, *Twilight of the Idols*, trans. R. Hollingdale, Harmondsworth, 1978, p. 40.
8 J. Derrida, *The Ear of the Other*, ed. C. McDonald, New York, 1985, p. 115.

1 LIFE AS ART: KANT, SCHLEGEL, NIETZSCHE

1 Immanuel Kant, *The Critique of Judgement*, trans. W. S. Pluher, Indianapolis, 1987, p. 14/German pagination 176. Hereafter CJ.
2 CJ p. 14/176.
3 CJ p. 18/179.
4 CJ p. 19/180.
5 CJ p. 19/180.
6 CJ p. 19/180.
7 CJ p. 27/187.
8 CJ p. 25/186.
9 CJ p. 29/189.
10 CJ p. 36–7/196.
11 CJ p. 91/240.
12 CJ p. 174/317.
13 CJ p. 196/326.
14 CJ p. 182/314.
15 CJ p. 182/314.
16 CJ p. 183/314.

17 CJ p. 217/344.
18 CJ p. 183/314.
19 CJ p. 182/314.
20 CJ p. 183/314.
21 F. Schlegel, *Athenaeum Fragments* 116 in *Lucinde and the Fragments*, trans.
    P. Firchow, Minneapolis, 1971. Hereafter AF.
22 Novalis, *Miscellaneous Writings*, section 105, in K. Wheeler (ed.), *The Romantic
    Ironists and Goethe*, Cambridge, 1984, p. 92.
23 AF 238.
24 F. Schlegel, *Critical Fragments* 115 in *Lucinde and the Fragments*, trans. P. Firchow,
    Minneapolis, 1971. Hereafter CF.
25 AF 238.
26 'On Incomprehensibility' in *Lucinde and the Fragments*, trans. P. Firchow,
    Minneapolis, 1971, p. 260.
27 AF 56.
28 CF 108.
29 CF 48.
30 'On Incomprehensibility', p. 268.
31 AF 267.
32 AF 164.
33 AF 53.
34 AF 116.
35 AF 116.
36 CF 20.
37 'On Incomprehensibility', p. 263.
38 F. Schlegel, *Dialogue on Poetry*, trans. E. Behler and R. Struc, Pennsylvania, 1968,
    p. 54. Hereafter DP.
39 DP p. 54.
40 AF 116.
41 DP p. 51.
42 'On Incomprehensibility', p. 268.
43 F. Schlegel, *Lucinde and the Fragments*, trans. P. Firchow, Minneapolis, 1971, p. 56.
    Hereafter L.
44 L p. 58.
45 L p. 132.
46 L p. 138.
47 CF 47.
48 'Ideas', 60 in *Lucinde*. Hereafter I.
49 L p. 65.
50 L p. 66.
51 L p. 98.
52 L p. 102.
53 L p. 102.
54 L p. 47.
55 AF 121.
56 I 92.
57 I 47.
58 AF 262.
59 L p. 45.
60 I 71.
61 L p. 58.
62 I 64.
63 I 129a.

64 AF 206.
65 AF 259.
66 CF 23.
67 I 69.
68 CF 112.
69 F. Nietzsche, *Twilight of the Idols*, trans. R. Hollingdale, Harmondsworth, 1978, p. 40. Hereafter TI.
70 TI p. 45.
71 TI p. 30.
72 TI pp. 45–6.
73 F. Nietzsche, *The Will to Power*, trans. W. Kaufmann and R. Hollingdale, New York, 1968, p. 318. Hereafter WP.
74 F. Nietzsche, *Beyond Good and Evil*, trans. R. Hollingdale, Harmondsworth, 1979, p. 64. Hereafter BGE.
75 F. Nietzsche, *The Gay Science*, trans. W. Kaufmann, New York, 1974, p. 265. Hereafter GS.
76 WP p. 500.
77 F. Nietzsche, *Ecce Homo*, trans. R. Hollingdale, Harmondsworth, 1979, p. 82. Hereafter EH.
78 WP p. 279.

2 GEORGES BATAILLE: THE IMPOSSIBLE

1 G. Bataille, 'Unknowing and Rebellion', *October*, 36, 1986, p. 86.
2 G. Bataille, *My Mother, Madame Edwarda, The Dead Man*, trans. A. Wainhouse, London, 1989, p. 218. Hereafter ME.
3 G. Bataille, *On Nietzsche*, trans. B. Boone, London, 1987, p. 100. Hereafter ON.
4 G. Bataille, *Inner Experience*, trans. L. A. Boldt, New York, 1988, p. 186. Hereafter IE.
5 G. Bataille, *Visions of Excess*, 'The Labyrinth', p. 173, trans. A. Stoekl, Minneapolis, 1985. Hereafter VE.
6 VE p. 173.
7 IE p. 9.
8 IE pp. 59–60.
9 IE p. 136.
10 G. Bataille, *Theory of Religion*, trans. R. Hurley, New York, 1992, p. 32. Hereafter TR.
11 IE pp. 136 and 208.
12 TR pp. 11, 12.
13 IE p. 89.
14 G. Bataille, *Eroticism*, trans. M. Dalwood, London, 1987, p. 12. Hereafter E.
15 E p. 12.
16 E p. 12.
17 E pp. 12–13.
18 IE p. 147.
19 E p. 86.
20 E p. 17.
21 E p. 258.
22 E p. 60.
23 E p. 18.
24 G. Bataille, *Literature and Evil*, trans. A. Hamilton, London, 1985, p. 139. Hereafter LE.

25 E p. 184.
26 E p. 41.
27 E p. 40.
28 E p. 39.
29 E p. 64.
30 E p. 59.
31 E p. 57.
32 E p. 13.
33 TR p. 56.
34 E p. 65.
35 E p. 67.
36 TR p. 44.
37 VE p. 96.
38 VE p. 81.
39 VE p. 97.
40 ON p. 17.
41 LE p. 165.
42 TR p. 52.
43 TR p. 50.
44 LE p. 26.
45 G. Bataille, *The Absence of Myth*, trans. M. Richardson, London, 1994, p. 67. Hereafter AM.
46 AM. p. 67.
47 IE p. 147.
48 G. Bataille, 'Unknowing: Laughter and Tears', *October*, 36, 1986, p. 99.
49 ON p. 28.
50 ON p. 38.
51 ON p. 45.
52 ON p. 146.
53 ON p. 149.
54 ON p. xxvii.
55 E p. 249.
56 E p. 249.
57 E p. 249.
58 E p. 251.
59 ON p. 32.
60 AM p. 170.
61 IE p. 12.
62 VE p. 97.
63 E p. 273.
64 E p. 275.
65 E p. 276.
66 AM p. 132.
67 LE p. 94.
68 E p. 264.
69 LE p. 25.
70 VE p. 119.
71 *October*, 36, 1986, p. 70.
72 E p. 192.
73 LE p. 21.
74 LE p. 22.
75 LE p. 25.
76 LE p. 25.

77 LE p. 146.
78 LE p. 142.
79 LE p. 144.
80 LE p. x.
81 IE p. 138.
82 IE p. 136.
83 LE p. 44.
84 LE p. 69.
85 AM p. 65.
86 AM p. 76.
87 AM p. 66.
88 AM p. 67.
89 AM p. 155.
90 AM p. 49.
91 AM p. 65.
92 AM p. 5.
93 ME p. 145.
94 ME p. 145.
95 ME pp. 140–1.
96 ME p. 150.
97 ME p. 150.
98 ME p. 155.
99 ME p. 151.
100 ME p. 152.
101 ME p. 153.
102 ME p. 156.
103 ME p. 158.
104 ME p. 158.
105 ME p. 159.
106 ME p. 159.
107 The following quotations are from Maurice Blanchot's *Infinite Conversation*,
     p. 210. Full references are given in the next chapter.

3 MAURICE BLANCHOT: LITERATURE'S SPACE

 1 M. Blanchot, *The Infinite Conversation*, trans. S. Hanson, Minneapolis, 1993,
    p. 119. Hereafter IC.
 2 IC p. 73.
 3 IC p. 405.
 4 IC p. 43.
 5 M. Blanchot, *The Space of Literature*, trans. A. Smock, Lincoln, Nebraska, 1982,
    p. 26. Hereafter SL.
 6 IC p. 12.
 7 SL p. 241.
 8 SL p. 167.
 9 SL p. 164.
10 SL p. 165.
11 SL p. 164.
12 IC p. 21.
13 IC p. 405.
14 IC p. 67.
15 IC p. 17.

16 IC p. 18.
17 IC p. 21.
18 IC p. 173.
19 IC p. 7.
20 SL p. 155.
21 SL p. 75.
22 IC p. 309.
23 SL p. 164.
24 SL p. 164.
25 SL p. 164.
26 IC p. 120.
27 SL p. 31.
28 IC p. 120.
29 IC p. 121.
30 IC p. 33.
31 IC p. 47.
32 SL p. 26.
33 SL p. 75.
34 SL p. 106.
35 M. Blanchot, *The Gaze of Orpheus*, trans. L. Davis, Station Hill, 1981, p. 49. Hereafter GO.
36 GO p. 46.
37 GO p. 47.
38 GO p. 48.
39 GO p. 48.
40 GO p. 50.
41 GO p. 61.
42 GO pp. 59–60.
43 GO pp. 59–60.
44 GO p. 62.
45 M. Holland, *The Blanchot Reader*, Oxford, 1997, p. 140. Hereafter BR.
46 BR p. 141.
47 BR p. 139.
48 IC p. 405.
49 IC p. 405.
50 SL p. 26.
51 SL p. 27.
52 BR p. 148.
53 SL p. 31.
54 SL p. 75.
55 IC p. 117.
56 BR p. 156.
57 IC p. 187.
58 M. Blanchot, *The Writing of the Disaster*, trans. A. Smock, Lincoln, Nebraska, 1986, p. 11. Hereafter WD.
59 WD p. 22.
60 SL p. 22.
61 SL p. 22.
62 SL p. 223.
63 SL p. 223.
64 IC p. 48.
65 IC p. 48.
66 IC p. 300.

67 IC p. 405.
68 SL p. 37.
69 M. Blanchot, *The Siren's Song*, trans. S. Rabinovich, Brighton, 1982, p. 65. Hereafter SS.
70 SL p. 12.
71 SL p. 32.
72 SL p. 234.
73 SL p. 234.
74 SL p. 232.
75 SL p. 232.
76 SL p. 26.
77 SL p. 27.
78 SL p. 234.
79 SL p. 183.
80 SL p. 33.
81 M. Blanchot, *The Madness of the Day*, trans. L. Davis, Station Hill, 1981. Hereafter MD.
82 MD p. 5.
83 MD p. 6.
84 GO p. 52.
85 MD pp. 7–8.
86 MD p. 7.
87 MD p. 8.
88 MD p. 8.
89 MD p. 10.
90 MD p. 11.
91 MD p. 12.
92 MD p. 13.
93 MD p. 14.
94 MD p. 14.
95 MD p. 14.
96 MD p. 15.
97 MD p. 17.
98 MD p. 18.

4 JACQUES DERRIDA: THE STAGING OF DECONSTRUCTION

1 J. Derrida, *Of Grammatology*, trans. G. Spivak, Baltimore, 1978, p. 143.
2 J. Derrida, *Acts of Literature*, ed. D. Attridge, London, 1994, p. 70. Hereafter AL.
3 Quoted in AL p. 16.
4 AL p. 41.
5 AL p. 47.
6 J. Derrida, *Given Time: 1. Counterfeit Money*, trans. P. Kamuf, Chicago, 1992, p. 80. Hereafter CM.
7 CM p. 80.
8 CM p. 14.
9 CM p. 14.
10 CM p. 27.
11 CM p. 14.
12 CM p. 30.
13 CM p. 122.

14 CM p. 93.
15 CM p. 86.
16 CM p. 100.
17 CM p. 152.
18 CM p. 152.
19 CM p. 153.
20 CM p. 170.
21 CM p. 122.
22 CM p. 125.
23 CM p. 124.
24 CM p. 169.
25 CM p. 164.
26 CM p. 169.
27 CM pp. 169–70.
28 J. Derrida, 'Structure, Sign and Play' in R. Macksey and E. Donato (eds), *The Structuralist Controversy*, London, 1972, p. 249.
29 'Psyche' in AL p. 211.
30 'Psyche' in AL p. 212.
31 'Psyche' in AL p. 184.
32 'Psyche' in AL p. 212.
33 AL pp. 311–43.
34 AL p. 326.
35 AL p. 325.
36 AL p. 326.
37 AL p. 328.
38 J. Derrrida, *The Gift of Death*, trans. D. Wills, Chicago, 1995, p. 63. Hereafter GD.
39 GD p. 61.
40 GD p. 71.
41 J. Derrida, 'Remarks on Deconstruction and Pragmatism' in C. Mouffe (ed.), *Deconstruction and Pragmatism*, London, 1996, p. 86. Hereafter DAP.
42 GD p. 86.
43 GD p. 86.
44 DAP p. 87.
45 DAP p. 67.
46 DAP p. 83.

5 IRIS MURDOCH: THE TRANSCENDENT GOOD

1 Iris Murdoch, *Metaphysics as a Guide to Morals*, Harmondsworth, 1992, p. 89. Hereafter MG.
2 Iris Murdoch, *The Sovereignty of Good*, London, 1970, p. 7. Hereafter SG.
3 SG pp. 7–8.
4 SG p. 10.
5 SG p. 13.
6 SG p. 16.
7 SG p. 16.
8 SG p. 87.
9 SG p. 71.
10 MG p. 24.
11 MG p. 25.
12 SG p. 66.
13 SG p. 67.

14 MG p. 14.
15 MG p. 25.
16 MG p. 26.
17 MG p. 26.
18 MG p. 29.
19 MG p. 28
20 MG p. 33.
21 MG p. 37.
22 MG p. 40.
23 MG p. 67.
24 MG p. 40.
25 MG p. 71.
26 MG p. 79.
27 MG p. 79.
28 MG p. 93.
29 MG p. 93.
30 MG p. 412.
31 MG p. 296.
32 SG p. 79.
33 Iris Murdoch, *The Fire and the Sun*, Oxford, 1977, p. 80. Hereafter FS.
34 SG p. 65.
35 SG p. 87.
36 MG p. 86.
37 MG p. 88.
38 SG p. 87.
39 SG p. 65.
40 SG p. 97.
41 FS p. 80.
42 SG p. 83.
43 SG p. 87.
44 MG p. 117.
45 MG pp. 104–5.
46 MG p. 106.
47 MG p. 123.
48 MG p. 123.
49 MG p. 322.
50 MG p. 90.
51 MG p. 507.
52 SG p. 75.
53 MG p. 55.
54 MG p. 56.
55 MG p. 507.
56 SG p. 44.
57 Iris Murdoch, *The Black Prince*, London, 1999, p. 391. All references (BP) are to the Vintage edition.
58 BP p. 390.
59 BP p. 9.
60 BP p. 66.
61 BP p. 85.
62 BP p. 185.
63 BP p. 187.
64 BP p. 74.
65 BP p. 202.

66 BP p. 201.
67 BP p. 272.
68 BP p. 199.
69 BP p. 392.
70 BP p. 391.
71 BP p. 232.
72 BP p. 210.
73 BP p. 389.
74 BP p. 348.
75 BP p. 392.
76 BP p. 392.
77 Martha Nussbaum, 'Love and Vision: Iris Murdoch on Eros and the Individual' in M. Antonaccio and W. Scheiker (eds), *Iris Murdoch and the Search for Human Goodness*, Chicago, 1996, p. 46.
78 Nussbaum, 'Love and Vision', p. 47.
79 FS p. 80.

6 MARTHA NUSSBAUM: MORAL FORTUNE

1 Martha Nussbaum, *Love's Knowledge*, Oxford, 1990, p. 26. Hereafter LK.
2 Martha Nussbaum, *The Fragility of Goodness*, Cambridge, 1986, p. 90. Hereafter FG.
3 LK p. 60.
4 FG p. 304.
5 FG p. 352.
6 Aristotle, *Nicomachean Ethics* 1097b7–11, quoted in FG p. 345.
7 FG p. 154.
8 LK p. 228.
9 LK p. 174.
10 LK p. 229.
11 J. Lear, *Aristotle: the desire to understand*, Cambridge, 1988, p. 7.
12 Aristotle, *Politics* 7.3.5.
13 LK p. 5.
14 LK p. 39.
15 LK p. 142.
16 LK p. 142.
17 LK p. 48.
18 LK p. 162.
19 LK p. 162.
20 FG p. 15.
21 Aristotle, *Poetics* 1449b, in D. A. Russell and M. Winterbottom, *Ancient Literary Criticism*, Oxford, 1972, p. 97.
22 FG p. 383.
23 FG p. 385.
24 FG p. 387.
25 FG p. 382.
26 'Tragedy and Self-sufficiency' in *Essays on Aristotle's Poetics*, ed. A. Rorty, Princeton, 1992, p. 263.
27 FG p. 43.
28 FG p. 35.
29 FG p. 50.
30 FG p. 57.

31 FG p. 58.
32 line 1258, quoted in FG p. 63.
33 FG p. 400.
34 FG p. 400.
35 FG p. 405.
36 FG p. 407.
37 FG p. 415.
38 Aristotle, *Poetics* 1452a38–b1.
39 'Tragedy and Self-sufficiency', p. 276.
40 'Tragedy and Self-sufficiency', p. 277.
41 'Tragedy and Self-sufficiency', p. 281.
42 FG p. 388.
43 FG p. 391.
44 LK p. 165.
45 FG p. 69.
46 FG p. 74.
47 FG p. 70.

7 RICHARD RORTY: PHILOSOPHY AS LITERATURE

1 R. Rorty, 'Pragmatism, Davidson and Truth' in *Objectivity, Relativism and Truth*, Cambridge, 1991, p. 127. Hereafter ORT.
2 R. Rorty, 'Pragmatism, Relativism, Irrationalism' in *Consequences of Pragmatism*, Brighton, 1982, p. 165. Hereafter CP.
3 R. Rorty, *Philosophy and the Mirror of Nature*, Oxford, 1980, p. 316. Hereafter PMN.
4 'Solidarity or Objectivity' in ORT p. 22.
5 R. Rorty, *Contingency, Irony, Solidarity*, Cambridge, 1989, p. 21. Hereafter CIS.
6 R. Rorty, 'John Searle on Realism and Relativism' in *Truth and Progress*, Cambridge, 1998, p. 78. Hereafter TP.
7 CIS p. 8.
8 CIS p. 125.
9 TP p. 42 footnote.
10 R. Rorty, 'A World without Essences or Substances' in *Philosophy and Social Hope*, London, 1999, p. 61.
11 'Robert Brandom on Social Practices' in TP p. 135.
12 'John Searle on Realism and Relativism' in TP p. 82.
13 'Solidarity or Objectivity?' in ORT p. 33.
14 PMN p. 361.
15 CIS p. 68.
16 'Inquiry as Recontextualization' in ORT p. 102.
17 'Inquiry as Recontextualization' in ORT p. 110.
18 'Introduction' in ORT p. 13.
19 'Solidarity or Objectivity?' in ORT p. 22.
20 'Inquiry as Recontextualization' in ORT p. 97.
21 'Inquiry as Recontextualization' in ORT p. 102.
22 See for example D.Z. Phillips, *Faith after Foundationalism*, Westview, 1988, p. 146. Hereafter FAF.
23 CIS p. 9.
24 'Robert Brandom on Social Practices' in ORT p. 132.
25 'Non-reductive Physicalism' in ORT p. 125.

26 'Idealism and Textualism' in CP p. 142.
27 'Pragmatism, Davidson and Truth' in ORT p. 127.
28 'De Man and the American Cultural Left' in *Essays on Heidegger and Others*, Cambridge, 1991, p. 132. Hereafter HO.
29 'John Searle on Realism and Relativism' in TP p. 83.
30 'John Searle on Realism and Relativism' in TP p. 64.
31 'De Man and the American Cultural Left' in HO p. 132.
32 'Introduction' in ORT p. 12.
33 'Introduction' in ORT p. 14.
34 CIS p. 60.
35 CIS p. 87.
36 CIS p. 74.
37 CIS p. 75.
38 D. Z. Phillips, *Philosophy's Cool Place*, Ithaca, NY, 1999, p. 74. Hereafter PCP.
39 PCP p. 74.
40 'Method, Social Science, Social Hope' in CP p. 203.
41 CIS p. 80.
42 CIS p. 80.
43 CIS p. 141.
44 CIS p. 35.
45 HO p. 154.
46 CIS p. 102.
47 CIS p. 100.
48 CIS p. 103.
49 CIS p. 107.
50 CIS p. 119.
51 CIS p. 125.
52 CIS p. 125.
53 CIS p. 137.
54 'Heidegger, Kundera and Dickens' in HO p. 74.
55 'Postmodernist Bourgeois Liberalism' in ORT p. 200.
56 L. Wittgenstein, 'Cause and Effect', trans. P. Winch, *Philosophia*, 6 (3–4), 1976, p. 411.

8 STANLEY CAVELL: LANGUAGE, THERAPY AND PERFECTIONISM

1 S. Cavell, 'The Uncanniness of the Ordinary' in *In Quest of the Ordinary*, Chicago, 1988, p. 174. Hereafter QO.
2 S. Cavell, *The Claim of Reason*, Oxford, 1979, p. 175. Hereafter CR.
3 CR p. 207.
4 CR p. 209.
5 CR p. 216.
6 CR p. 217.
7 CR p. 144.
8 CR p. 218.
9 CR p. 216.
10 CR p. 236.
11 CR p. 224.
12 CR p. 239.
13 CR p. 14.
14 CR p. 16.

15 CR p. 76.
16 CR p. 94.
17 CR p. 179.
18 CR p. 179.
19 CR p. 115.
20 CR p. 33.
21 CR p. 115.
22 CR p. 241.
23 S. Cavell, *Disowning Knowledge*, Cambridge, 1988, p. 95. Hereafter DK.
24 DK p. 104.
25 L. Wittgenstein, 'Cause and Effect', pp. 410–11.
26 L. Wittgenstein, *Zettel*, trans. G. Anscombe, Oxford, 1967, section 541.
27 *Zettel*, sect. 545.
28 L. Wittgenstein, *Philosophical Investigations*, trans. G. Anscombe, Oxford, 1953, II, sect. 4.
29 DK p. 95.
30 CR p. 454.
31 CR pp. 46–7.
32 CR p. 20.
33 QO p. 48.
34 CR p. 369.
35 QO p. 119.
36 QO p. 118.
37 QO p. 137.
38 QO p. 144.
39 DK p. 109.
40 QO p. 113.
41 CR. p. 448.
42 CR p. 448.
43 CR p. 453.
44 S. Cavell, *Conditions Handsome and Unhandsome*, La Salle, 1990, p. xxxvi. Hereafter CHU.
45 CHU p. 12.
46 CHU p. 58.
47 CHU pp. 117–18.
48 CHU p. 125.
49 CHU p. 43.
50 CHU p. 46.
51 CHU p. 57.
52 CHU p. 59.
53 DK p. 218.
54 DK p. 21.
55 DK p. 19.
56 DK p. 17.
57 DK p. 29.
58 S. Cavell, *Themes out of School*, Chicago, 1998, p. 193. Hereafter TS.
59 DK p. 62.
60 DK p. 40.
61 DK p. 137.
62 DK p. 211.
63 DK p. 125.
64 DK p. 13.
65 DK p. 149.

66 DK p. 144.
67 DK p. 185.
68 DK p. 13.
69 DK p. 187.
70 DK p. 187.
71 DK p. 168.
72 DK p. 29.
73 DK p. 54.
74 DK p. 85.
75 DK p. 89.
76 DK p. 109.
77 DK p. 105.

9 A KIERKEGAARDIAN INTERVENTION

1 S. Kierkegaard, *Concluding Unscientific Postscript*, vol. 1, trans. H. V. Hong and E. H. Hong, Princeton, 1992, p. 310. Hereafter CUP.
2 CUP p. 17.
3 CUP p. 371 footnote.
4 CUP p. 120.
5 CUP p. 93.
6 I have discussed this at greater length in *Kierkegaard and Modern Continental Philosophy*, London, 1994.

10 D. Z. PHILLIPS: THE MEDIATION OF SENSE

1 D. Z. Phillips, *Interventions in Ethics*, Basingstoke, 1992, p. viii. Hereafter IIE.
2 IIE p. xv.
3 D. Z. Phillips, *Through a Darkening Glass*, Oxford, 1982, pp. 23–4. Hereafter TDG.
4 TDG p. 10.
5 TDG p. 19.
6 TDG pp. 22–3.
7 IIE p. 62.
8 R. W. Beardsmore, 'Literary Examples and Philosophical Confusion' in A. Phillips Griffiths (ed.), *Philosophy and Literature*, Cambridge, 1984, pp. 70–1.
9 IIE p. 65.
10 D. Z. Phillips, *From Fantasy to Faith*, Basingstoke, 1991, p. 140. Hereafter FTF.
11 FTF p. 140.
12 FTF p. 154.
13 IIE p. 47.
14 TDG p. 119.
15 TDG p. 121.
16 TDG p. 126.
17 TDG p. 125.
18 TDG p. 127.
19 FTF p. 1.
20 D. Z. Phillips, *Belief, Change and Forms of Life*, Basingstoke, 1986, pp. 50–1. Hereafter BCF.
21 FTF p. 47.
22 FTF p. 124.
23 FTF pp. 220–1.
24 D. Z. Phillips, *Faith after Foundationalism*, Boulder, 1995, p. 311. Hereafter FAF.

25 Basingstoke, 1986. Hereafter RST.
26 RST p. 20.
27 Quoted in FTF p. 204.
28 Referring to 'The Cry', quoted in RST p. 41.
29 Referring to 'Because', quoted in RST p. 53.
30 RST p. 207.
31 Quoting 'The Moor', RST p. 61.
32 RST p. 62.
33 RST p. 77.
34 RST p. 82.
35 RST p. 87.
36 RST p. 153.
37 RST p. ix.
38 RST p. 104.
39 RST p. 169.
40 FTF p. 6.
41 BCF p. 90.
42 BCF p. 89.
43 FTF p. 9.
44 FAF p. 317.
45 FAF p. 317.
46 FTF p. 3.
47 L p. 92.
48 D. H. Lawrence, *Studies in Classic American Literature*, Harmondsworth, 1971, p. 22.
49 For a critique of the conception of language involved in Derrida's work, see Chapter 5 of my *Kierkegaard and Modern Continental Philosophy*, London, 1994.
50 RST p. xiii.

11 A CONCLUDING READING: JOSEPH CONRAD'S *LORD JIM*

1 All references are to The World's Classics edition, edited by J. Batchelor, Oxford, 1983. Hereafter LJ.
2 J. Conrad, *Heart of Darkness*, ed. P. O'Prey, Harmondsworth, 1989, p. 30.
3 LJ p. 5.
4 LJ p. 6.
5 LJ p. 7.
6 LJ p. 8.
7 LJ p. 9.
8 LJ p. 9.
9 LJ p. 10.
10 LJ p. 10.
11 LJ p. 11.
12 LJ p. 13.
13 LJ p. 20.
14 LJ pp. 29–30.
15 LJ p. 31.
16 LJ p. 31.
17 LJ p. 33.
18 LJ p. 34.
19 LJ p. 94.

20 LJ p. 337.
21 LJ p. 43.
22 LJ p. 43.
23 LJ p. 50.
24 LJ p. 46.
25 LJ p. 50.
26 LJ p. 93.
27 LJ p. 123.
28 LJ p. 81.
29 LJ p. 83.
30 LJ p. 81.
31 LJ p. 108.
32 LJ p. 111.
33 LJ p. 118.
34 LJ p. 120.
35 LJ p. 124.
36 LJ p. 121.
37 LJ p. 179.
38 LJ p. 341.
39 LJ p. 5.
40 LJ p. 342.
41 LJ p. 57.
42 LJ p. 58.
43 LJ p. 59.
44 LJ p. 65.
45 LJ p. 147.
46 LJ p. 148.
47 LJ p. 149.
48 LJ p. 162.
49 LJ p. 167.
50 LJ p. 212.
51 LJ p. 213.
52 LJ pp. 214–15.
53 LJ p. 214.
54 LJ p. 207.
55 LJ p. 218.
56 LJ p. 221.
57 LJ p. 221.
58 LJ p. 83.
59 LJ p. 221.
60 LJ p. 222.
61 LJ p. 222.
62 LJ p. 223.
63 LJ p. 223.
64 LJ p. 223.
65 LJ p. 223.
66 LJ p. 224.
67 LJ p. 225.
68 LJ p. 226.
69 LJ pp. 233–4.
70 LJ p. 243.
71 LJ pp. 226–8.
72 LJ p. 330.

73   LJ p. 330.
74   LJ p. 330.
75   LJ p. 330.
76   LJ p. 286.
77   LJ p. 228.
78   LJ p. 269.
79   LJ p. 265.
80   LJ p. 266.
81   LJ p. 267.
82   LJ p. 275.
83   LJ p. 313.
84   LJ p. 339.
85   LJ p. 334.
86   LJ p. 339.
87   LJ p. 340.
88   LJ p. 343.
89   LJ p. 370.
90   LJ p. 243.
91   LJ p. 226.
92   LJ p. 227.
93   LJ p. 227.
94   LJ p. 344.
95   LJ p. 353.
96   LJ p. 370.
97   LJ p. 404.
98   LJ p. 383.
99   LJ p. 387.
100 LJ p. 412.
101 LJ p. 409.
102 LJ p. 413.
103 LJ p. 410.
104 LJ p. 416.
105 LJ p. 416.
106 LJ p. 416.
107 LJ p. 207.
108 LJ p. 339.

BIBLIOGRAPHY

Bataille, G., *The Absence of Myth*, trans. M. Richardson, London, 1994.

Bataille, G., *Eroticism*, trans. M. Dalwood, London, 1987.

Bataille, G., *Inner Experience*, trans. L. A. Boldt, New York, 1988.

Bataille, G., *Literature and Evil*, trans. A. Hamilton, London, 1985.

Bataille, G., *My Mother, Madame Edwarda, The Dead Man*, trans. A. Wainhouse, London, 1989.

Bataille, G., *On Nietzsche*, trans. B. Boone, London, 1987.

Bataille, G., 'Unknowing and Rebellion', *October*, 36, 1986.

Bataille, G., 'Unknowing: Laughter and Tears', *October*, 36, 1986.

Bataille, G., *Visions of Excess*, trans. A. Stoekl, Minneapolis, 1985.

Beardsmore, R.W., 'Literary Examples and Philosophical Confusion' in A. Phillips Griffiths (ed.), *Philosophy and Literature*, Cambridge, 1984.

Blanchot, M., *The Gaze of Orpheus*, trans. L. Davis, Station Hill, 1981.

Blanchot, M., *The Infinite Conversation*, trans. S. Hanson, Minneapolis, 1993.

Blanchot, M., *The Madness of the Day*, trans. L. Davis, Station Hill, 1981.

Blanchot, M., *The Siren's Song*, trans. S. Rabinovich, Brighton, 1982.

Blanchot, M., *The Space of Literature*, trans. A. Smock, Lincoln, Nebraska, 1982.

Blanchot, M., *The Writing of the Disaster*, trans. A. Smock, Lincoln, Nebraska, 1986.

Cavell, S., *The Claim of Reason*, Oxford, 1979.

Cavell, S., *Conditions Handsome and Unhandsome*, La Salle, 1990.

Cavell, S., *Disowning Knowledge*, Cambridge, 1988.

Cavell, S., *In Quest of the Ordinary*, Chicago, 1988.

Cavell, S., *Themes out of School*, Chicago, 1988.

Conrad, J., *Heart of Darkness*, ed. P. O'Prey, Harmondsworth, 1989.

Conrad, J., *Lord Jim*, ed. J. Batchelor, Oxford, 1983.

Derrida, J., *Acts of Literature*, trans. D. Attridge, London, 1994.

Derrida, J., *The Ear of the Other*, ed. C. McDonald, New York, 1985.

Derrida, J., *The Gift of Death*, trans. D. Wills, Chicago, 1995.

Derrida, J., *Given Time: 1. Counterfeit Money*, trans. P. Kamuf, Chicago, 1992.

Derrida, J., *Of Grammatology*, trans. G. Spivak, Baltimore, 1978.

Derrida, J., 'Remarks on Deconstruction and Pragmatism', in C. Mouffe (ed.), *Deconstruction and Pragmatism*, London, 1996.

Derrida, J., 'Structure, Sign and Play', in R. Macksey and E. Donato (eds), *The Structuralist Controversy*, London, 1972.

Holland, M., *The Blanchot Reader*, Oxford, 1997.

Kant, I., *The Critique of Judgement*, trans. W. S. Pluher, Indianapolis, 1987.

Kierkegaard, S., *Concluding Unscientific Postscript*, trans. H. V. Hong and E. H. Hong, Princeton, 1992.

Lawrence, D. H., *Studies in Classic American Literature*, Harmondsworth, 1971.

Lear, J., *Aristotle: the Desire to Understand*, Cambridge, 1988.

Murdoch, I., *The Black Prince*, London, 1999.

Murdoch, I., *The Fire and the Sun*, Oxford, 1977.

Murdoch, I., *Metaphysics as a Guide to Morals*, Harmondsworth, 1992.

Murdoch, I., *The Sovereignty of Good*, London, 1970.

Nietzsche, F., *Beyond Good and Evil*, trans. R. Hollingdale, Harmondsworth, 1979.

Nietzsche, F., *Ecce Homo*, trans. R. Hollingdale, Harmondsworth, 1979.

Nietzsche, F., *The Gay Science*, trans. W. Kaufmann, New York, 1974.

Nietzsche, F., *Twilight of the Idols*, trans. R. Hollingdale, Harmondsworth, 1978.

Nietzsche, F., *The Will to Power*, trans. W. Kaufmann and R. Hollingdale, New York, 1968.

Nussbaum, M., *The Fragility of Goodness*, Cambridge, 1986.

Nussbaum, M., 'Love and Vision: Iris Murdoch on Eros and the Individual' in M. Antonaccio and W. Scheiker (eds), *Iris Murdoch and the Search for Human Goodness*, Chicago, 1996.

Nussbaum, M., *Love's Knowledge*, Oxford, 1990.

Nussbaum, M., 'Tragedy and Self-sufficiency' in A. Rorty (ed.), *Essays on Aristotle's Poetics*, Princeton, 1992.

Phillips, D. Z., *Belief, Change and Forms of Life*, Basingstoke, 1986.

Phillips, D. Z., *Faith after Foundationalism*, Boulder, 1988.

Phillips, D. Z., *From Fantasy to Faith*, Basingstoke, 1991.

Phillips, D. Z., *Interventions in Ethics*, Basingstoke, 1992.

Phillips, D. Z., *Philosophy's Cool Place*, Ithaca, NY, 1999.

Phillips, D. Z., *R. S. Thomas: poet of the hidden god*, Basingstoke, 1986.

Phillips, D. Z., *Through a Darkening Glass*, Oxford, 1982.

Plato, *Phaedrus*, trans. H.N. Fowler, London, 1977.

Plato, *Republic*, trans. P Shorey, London, 1979.

Rorty, R., *Consequences of Pragmatism*, Brighton, 1982.

Rorty, R., *Contingency, Irony and Solidarity*, Cambridge, 1989.

Rorty, R., *Essays on Heidegger and Others*, Cambridge, 1991.

Rorty, R., *Objectivity, Relativism and Truth*, Cambridge, 1991.

Rorty, R., *Philosophy and Social Hope*, London, 1999.

Rorty, R., *Philosophy and the Mirror of Nature*, Oxford, 1980.

Rorty, R., *Truth and Progress*, Cambridge, 1998.

Russell, D. A., and M. Winterbottom, *Ancient Literary Criticism*, Oxford 1983.

Schlegel, F., *Dialogue on Poetry*, trans. E. Behler and R. Struc, Pennsylvania, 1968.

Schlegel, F., *Lucinde and the Fragments*, trans. P. Firchow, Minneapolis, 1971.

Weston, M., *Kierkegaard and Modern Continental Philosophy*, London, 1994.

Wheeler, K. (ed.), *The Romantic Ironists and Goethe*, Cambridge, 1984.

Wittgenstein, L., 'Cause and Effect', trans. P. Winch, *Philosophia*, 6, 1976.

Wittgenstein, L., *Philosophical Investigations*, trans. G. Anscombe, Oxford, 1953.

Wittgenstein, L., *Zettel*, trans. G. Anscombe, Oxford, 1967.

INDEX